Lazarus Spengler

BY HAROLD J. GRIMM

Lazarus Spengler

a lay leader of the reformation

OHIO STATE UNIVERSITY PRESS : COLUMBUS

Library of Congress Cataloguing in Publication Data
Grimm, Harold John, 1901–
    Lazarus Spengler: a lay leader of the Reformation.

    Bibliography: p. 211
    Includes index.
    1. Spengler, Lazarus, 1479-1534. 2. Reformation—
German, West—Nuremberg-Biography. 3. Nuremberg—
Biography.
BR350.S67G74   270.6'092'4   78-13508
ISBN 0-8142-0290-X

To My Students

Contents

Preface   xi

1 Spengler's Family and His City   3

2 Broadening Interests and Concerns   17

3 From Christian Humanist to Lutheran   31

4 Early Religious Changes   45

5 The Road to Reformation   57

6 The Break with Rome   73

7 Social and Religious Ferment   93

8 New Structures   109

9 Nuremberg and the Diets of Speyer, 1526-1529   121

10 The Question of a Protestant Alliance   137

11 Diplomacy of Nuremberg, 1530-1534   157

12 Spengler's Last Years   169

Notes   183

Bibliography   211

Index   229

Illustrations

1 Nuremberg at the end of the fifteenth century.
Sketch based on Michel Wolgemut's woodcut
for Hartmann Schedel's *Liber cronicarum*
of 1493 and produced in color in 1526 for
the so-called *Hallerbuch* of 1533. Courtesy
of the Staatsarchiv Nurnberg. 15

2 The territory of Nuremberg in the sixteenth
century. Courtesy of Fritz Gries, producer of
the map, and C. H. Beck'sche Verlagsbuch-
handlung, Munich. 55

3 Dürer's facetious drawing for Spengler (1511)
of a smithy, a printer, and a baker (probably
Hieronymus Holzschuher [left], Lazarus
Spengler [center], and Kaspar Nützel [right])
preparing diplomatic reports for the city
council. Reproduced with the permission of
the Musée Bonat, Bayonne, France. 91

4 Spengler's home, "Zum Einhorn" and "Zum
Rosenbusch," in the Zisselgasse, today
Albrecht-Dürer Strasse 19, as seen from the
north in 1909, reproduced with the permis-
sion of Erich Mulzer, who published it in
"Das Jamnitzerhaus in Nürnberg und der
Goldschmid Wenzel Jamnitzer" (*MVGN* 61
[1974]), and the Stadtarchiv Nürnberg. 167

Preface

Historians have given considerable attention in recent years to the importance of cities in the spread of the Reformation and its influence on the development of urban institutions. Whereas numerous studies have opened new vistas in our look at the movement, much more research must be devoted to individual urban leaders before scholars can make valid generalizations concerning it.

The career of Lazarus Spengler of Nuremberg, secretary of its city council, not only illustrates the complexity of the spread of the Reformation but also provides an excellent example of what an intelligent layman in an urban society in Germany considered the movement to be. Busy with the manifold responsibilities of his office that involved religious and cultural as well as political, economic, and social issues, he played an important role in the development of his community as a whole, associating with all its leaders. He was familiar with their chief concerns, made them his own, and helped embody them in appropriate institutions. Fully aware of the needs and interests of all the citizens, he did his best to meet them according to his conception of the responsibility of his government to serve the general welfare of the entire community.

Already a mature, man, thirty-nine years of age, when he first met Martin Luther, he appropriated the fundamental doctrines of the Reformation in a surprisingly short period of time, made them basic to his decisions with respect to secular matters, and applied them in his relationship with others. An examination of his role as a lay leader of the Reformation gives us new insights into the many aspects of the movement, for one learns about it not only from the literature of the reformers and the sermons of the preachers but also from the deliberations of the city council, the memorandums of its jurisconsults, and its vast correspondence. Present at its meetings and instrumental in preserving its records, Spengler had the knowledge as well as the diplomatic ability to influence persons in authority both at home and abroad.

It is a pleasant task to acknowledge my indebtedness to the many persons who helped me produce this book. Work in the archives in Nuremberg was facilitated by the kindness of the officials shown my numerous graduate students and me far beyond the line of duty. I am particularly grateful to Fritz Schnelbögl, Otto Puchner, and Günther Schuhmann of the Staatsarchiv Nürnberg; Werner Schultheiss and Gerhard Hirschmann of the Stadtarchiv Nürnberg; Ludwig Veit of the Germanisches Nationalmuseum Nürnberg; and Georg Luhr and Helene Burger of the Landeskirchliches Archiv Nürnberg.

The following members of the faculty of the University of Erlangen-Nürnberg have given me much friendly advice and assistance: Hans Liermann, Wilhelm Maurer, Gerhard Pfeiffer, Irmgard Höss, Gerhard Müller, and Gottfried Seebass. Gerhard Pfeiffer read the entire manuscript and gave me his acute comments and suggestions. The imperfections and errors that persist are my own.

I have had considerable help from the officials at the Widener Library at Harvard, the Ohio State University Library, the Center for Reformation Research, and especially from Stanley J. Kahrl of the Center for Medieval and Renaissance Studies at the Ohio State University. I also am grateful to those of my former students who assisted me in my research, especially Phillip N. Bebb, Lawrence P. Buck, and Jonathan W. Zophy. Gratitude also is due Miss Margarete von Schubert and Mrs. Erika Dingler for making available to the Stadtarchiv Nürnberg materials relating to Spengler formerly in the possession of their father, Hans von Schubert. My thanks likewise are due Weldon A. Kefauver and Robert S. Demorest of the Ohio State University Press for guiding the process of publishing the book to a successful conclusion. I owe a heavy debt to my wife for her patience and help.

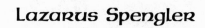

Lazarus Spengler

chapter one

SPENGLER'S FAMILY AND HIS CITY

One can study the complexities of the Reformation in Germany to great advantage by examining the vicissitudes of the imperial city of Nuremberg during the decade and a half following the first appearance of Luther's doctrines within its walls.[1] Foremost leader of the Reformation there was Lazarus Spengler (1479-1534), *Ratsschreiber*,[2] or secretary, of the city council, who helped steer Nuremberg through the turbulent waters of his day between the Scylla of Lutheranism and the Charybdis of loyalty to the empire to a political solution that persisted in its main features to the end of the city's existence as a free imperial city in 1806 and to a religious settlement that, in its main features, has continued to our own day.

FAMILY BACKGROUND

Spengler was able to play a significant role in the Reformation because of his broad cultural background, legal education and training, knowledge of business affairs, diplomatic experience and skill, understanding of human nature, and strong Protestant commitment. He had an opportunity to assert his leadership because of the unique nature of his position in the city government. As council secretary he supervised the secretarial work of that body; took part in its secret sessions and kept its records; carried on its official correspondence; was its chief legal, political, and financial adviser; and served in a diplomatic capacity, often attending imperial diets, diets of cities, and meetings of princes in addition to corresponding with the city's diplomats on mission.

Serving in such capacities and having a good salary and perquisites that enabled him to devote all his time to his profession, Spengler could have a complete grasp of the city's politics, both internal and foreign. Although the patricians could rely upon the advice of their official jurisconsults in secular matters and on the city clergy in spiritual matters, neither of whom were permitted to attend meetings of the council, they ultimately looked to Spengler for advice to the extent that their critical decisions during the first decade of the Reformation bear the stamp of his character and leadership.

Lazarus Spengler was born in 1479 in a house called "Zum Einhorn," next to the Ulmer family home "Zum Rosenbusch" in the Zisselgasse, today called Albrecht-Dürer-Strasse. The house is number 19.[3] He was the ninth of twenty-one children (two were stillborn) of the council secretary Georg Spengler (1424-96) and Agnes Ulmer Spengler. The father came from a merchant family of Donauwörth that had received a coat of arms from the emperor in addition to the title *ehrbar*, or "honorable," given to prominent families of the empire. He studied at a university, probably Ingolstadt, and became territorial secretary (*Landschreiber*) for Margrave Albert of Brandenburg at Ansbach. He later accepted the invitation of the Nuremberg City Council to become its chancellery secretary (*Kanzleischreiber*) and in 1475 was made council secretary (*Ratsschreiber*). He served the city until his death in 1496, that is, about thirty years, concerning himself largely with internal affairs. Among the duties that he apparently enjoyed the most was serving as custodian of the City Council Library, one of the first of its kind in Germany. Founded in the 1370s, it had approximately four hundred volumes by 1500, including books on theological, legal, scientific, and humanist subjects.[4]

Agnes, whom he married in 1468 when she was fourteen years of age, was the only daughter of Daniel Ulmer, a native of Ulm with whom Georg had served as secretary of the margrave of Brandenburg. After Georg's death in 1496, Agnes lived with Lazarus and his family until her death in 1505. Despite having a large family to care for, Lazarus's parents added to their considerable inheritance and passed this on to their children. This demonstration of family pride and loyalty Georg recorded in his account of the family's history (*Geschlechtsbuch*), to which Lazarus later added his account in which he explained why he had been unable to increase the family wealth, the symbol of success and public service in sixteenth-century Nuremberg. The death of his father while Lazarus was still a young man, he explained, placed upon him the responsibility of providing for his brothers and sisters, mother, and mother-in-law.[5]

Among Lazarus's brothers and sisters who lived to maturity were Martha (1476-1538) and Magdalena (1482-1536), who entered convents in 1492, Martha as a Dominican at Bamberg who later became a Lutheran, and Magdalena as a Cistercian near Nördlingen who remained a Catholic; Georg (1480-1529), who became a prominent merchant, active at the Fondaco dei Tedeschi, or German Merchant House, in Venice; Paulus (1490-1527), who lived in Nuremberg; Felicitas (1472-1523) and Ursula (b. 1489), who were married to citizens of Nuremberg; and Margaretha, who in 1503 was married to a nobleman, Georg von Hirnkofen, called Rennwart, son of a humanistically inclined citizen of Nuremberg and for a while a member of the city council. This marriage provided Lazarus with important contacts with the Franconian nobility. Felicitas's second marriage was with Sebald Buhler, who owned a manorial estate in the margravate of Brandenburg and who served the margrave as secretary. Georg's marriage to Juliana Tucher brought the Spenglers into relation with one of the most influential patrician families of Nuremberg. At the time of this marriage in 1516, the council admitted both Georg and Lazarus to the great council, the members of which were given the honorary designation of *Genannte*, or "Designated Men."

CULTURAL ENVIRONMENT AND EDUCATION

An ambitious and studious young Nuremberg lad like Lazarus Spengler might well have been inspired by such illustrious men as Hartmann Schedel (1440-1514), a city doctor and humanist who was the author of the popular *World Chronicle* and widely used *Book of Songs*; Conrad Celtis (1459-1508), who helped arouse an interest in classical literature and philosophy in Nuremberg and was crowned poet laureate by the emperor in the city; and Martin Behaim (1459-1507), who went to Portugal as a merchant, took part in a voyage of discovery with Admiral Cam in 1484, was knighted by the king of Portugal, came to Nuremberg in 1491 where he completed his famous globe, and returned to Lisbon where he died in 1507. Persons with a sense of beauty admired and patronized the works of such artists as Adam Kraft (d. 1507), Michael Wolgemut (1434-1519), Veit Stoss (ca. 1447-1533), and Peter Vischer (1460-1529).

Like Philip Melanchthon and other intelligent boys of his day, Lazarus began his professional studies at an early age. He went to the University of Leipzig to study jurisprudence when he was only fifteen. When his father died in 1496, Lazarus returned to Nuremberg to help support the family. The next year he entered the service of the secretary of the municipal court as an apprentice. In this position he became acquainted with leading members of the city council, for the court secretary served in both the civil court, comprising eight members of the great council, two judges, and three or four doctors of law; and the criminal court, which was in the council and consisted of thirteen jurors. Both of these courts met in the city hall and were presided over by the city judge.

In January 1501, Lazarus, now twenty-one, married sixteen-year-old Ursula, the only child of the deceased Hans Sulmeister. When Lazarus's mother died, four years later, the young couple moved into the family home. They took with them Ursula's mother, Margaretha, who caused Lazarus some problems and considerable expense, for he states in his testament that she "was unable to help with the housework and for many years was weak and bedfast." Lazarus and Ursula had nine children, four of whom died in infancy and only four of whom, all boys, were living when Lazarus made his first will and testament in 1529. He provided them with a tutor and sent them to good schools. He sent the third son, Lazarus, to two universities, one of which was Wittenberg. None of the boys, however, was inclined to study. His namesake, on whom he had placed his greatest hopes, became a businessman and died in Latin America.

Ursula died soon after the birth of Sebald in 1516. With no daughters to take care of the children, Lazarus leaned heavily on his sister-in-law Juliana Tucher Spengler. He willed a considerable part of his inheritance to her in gratitude for her assistance.

In 1501, the year of Lazarus's marriage, the city council gave him the important position of secretary in the chancellery (*Regierungskanzlei*), where he previously had been in charge of the council's books (*Ratsbücher*), in which summaries of important council action were kept as a permanent record and carefully indexed for quick reference. In this position, Spengler became familiar with most of the council's business, both past and present. He now was given supervision of hundreds of other council books, among them the council minutes (*Ratsverlässe*); correspondence (*Briefbücher*); memorandums (*Gutachten*), prepared by the council's jurisconsults and city preachers (*Ratschlagbücher*); a book of statutes (*Satzungsbuch*) containing new laws; and many boxes of other kinds of official documents. These sources delight historians today because of the efficient way in which they were, and still are, kept and the detailed information they contain.[6]

On Easter Day 1507, Lazarus Spengler and Kaspar Schmutterherr were sworn in as council secretaries with equal salaries and responsibilities and with six educated secretaries under them. It was in this important position in the city hall, which Lazarus held for life and which he and his father together held for more than half a century, that he attained a position of leadership at home and abroad.

Nuremberg was an imperial city of an estimated 40,000 inhabitants within its walls and about 25,000 in its territory.[7] It owed allegiance only to the emperor. It never was an episcopal city, for its bishop resided at Bamberg, a considerable distance away, so it was relatively easy for the city council to appropriate numerous functions usually reserved to the bishop, such as supervision of parishes and monasteries, election of clergymen, control of education, care of the poor, and regulation of morals.

The city, which had grown up at the foot of the steep sandstone hill on which the emperor had built an imperial castle cared for by his burgrave, or castellan, was given its Great Charter by Emperor Frederick II in 1219. It was at first governed by a royal executive and city judge (Schultheiss) appointed by the emperor, and a city council. By 1313, when Emperor Henry VII issued the Great Privilege, the role of the royal executive had become subordinate to that of the city council of wealthy citizens. The council usually joined the emperor in curbing the power of the burgrave, whose authority in Nuremberg now was restricted to his castle and to representing the emperor as administrator of the imperial lands near the city. Emperor Sigismund, in 1422, gave the imperial part of the castle complex to the city to administer in the absence of the king and made Burgrave Frederick VI of Hohenzollern, the family that had held the burgravate since 1192, the first margrave and elector of Brandenburg. Because he also had the margravate in Franconia, Bayreuth, Kulmbach, Schwabach, Ansbach, and Erlangen, his successors began to play the role of territorial princes who, having Nuremberg in a vise as it were, for many years attempted to regain some of the rights given the city. In 1427 the city bought from Elector Frederick the burgrave's part of the castle with all rights, incomes, and perquisites in the city and the monasteries and villages surrounding it, and also acquired the imperial forest northeast of the city with its wood, charcoal furnaces, honey, and sandstone quarries.

The emperor in 1424 showed his confidence in the strength and loyalty of Nuremberg by placing the imperial regalia, consisting of the imperial crown, the sword and ring of Charles the Great, thorns from the crown of Christ, a chip from the cross of Christ, the spear that had pierced Christ's side, and other relics, in the city for safekeeping. Thereafter it became customary to choose the emperor at Frankfort am Main, crown him king at Aachen, and hold his first diet in Nuremberg.[8]

In many ways, Nuremberg played a significant role as a territorial state by the beginning of the sixteenth century.[9] The city council began to develop its authority outside the city walls with the acquisition of the imperial forest, originally under the jurisdiction of the burgrave. It appointed one of its citizens the chief forester; supervised the various courts, offices, and benefices there, and acquired castles by purchase or conquest; established its authority over the churches and monasteries; and treated the inhabitants of the territory as subjects rather than feudal vassals. It added greatly to its territory by joining Bavaria-Munich in the Bavarian War of Succession (1503-7), also called Landshut War of Succession, after the death of Duke George of Bavaria-Landshut late in 1503. George had willed his duchy to his daughter Elizabeth, who was married to Rupert, a son of the elector of the Palatinate. This was contrary to contracts made among members of the Wittelsbach family with respect to Bavarian lands and deprived George's cousins, Dukes Albert and Wolfgang of Bavaria-Munich, of their rightful inheritance. Emperor Maximilian, who as feudal overlord supported Albert and Wolfgang, assured Nuremberg that it could keep all the conquests it made in the war. In this way, the city acquired the towns of Lauf, Altdorf, Gräfenberg, Hersbruck, and Velden, the castles Reicheneck and Stierberg, and other less-important possessions. With imperial support, it consolidated its control of the entire territory in 1513 by creating a centralized, bureaucratic administrative system with all the important positions occupied by citizens of Nuremberg. The territory was divided into thirteen superintendencies (*Pflegeämter*) and administered by superintendents (*Pfleger*). It placed at the head of these officers a territorial superintendency comprising four members of the council with both administrative and judicial powers. Although the development of the largest territorial state acquired by an imperial city provided Nuremberg with a relatively good *cordon sanitaire*, conflicts with the feudal nobility, the landgrave of Hesse, the margraves of Brandenburg, and various lawless elements that plundered the city's merchants continued throughout much of the sixteenth century. Lazarus Spengler played an important part in obtaining and maintaining this expanded territory by participating in diplomatic missions to imperial diets, diets of the Swabian League, and meetings of city representatives.

The city council, which Spengler served to the end of his life, took its peculiar form from the character and abilities of its citizens, its responses to the various problems it faced during its long history, and its imitation of the governments of other cities, notably that of Venice. As in the past, the aristocratic patricians remained firmly in control, despite the fact that the city artisans, like those in many other European cities, rebelled against them in 1348-49, demanding recognition of their corporate groups as guilds and a share of the government of the city. With the support of Emperor Charles IV, the patricians suppressed the rebellion and emerged stronger than ever. Conscious of the importance of the artisans in the city's economy, however, the patricians furthered their economic and social interests and gave eight of the crafts—butchers, bakers, leather workers, smiths, tailors, furriers, clothiers, and brewers—representation in the council.

Because of their success over the years in serving the common welfare of all the city's inhabitants, the thirty-four patrician families of Spengler's time were accepted as the appropriate, though not divine-right, leaders of the entire community with respect to all its interests, spiritual and secular. This community was held together by oath, a *coniuratio*, in which each individual freely recognized his obligations to the entire group, a society based on voluntary consent. This oath was repeated annually as a reminder of the mutual interdependence of the citizens and of their responsibilities as well as their rights.

Set apart by their role of governing yet mingling with all other social groups in their city, the patricians made their contributions by means of governmental institutions well described by Christoph Scheurl (1481-1542), a doctor of civil and canon law who served his native city as jurisconsult but who, as a university-trained man, could not be a member of the city council.[10] In a letter to Staupitz, he explains that the sovereign authority of the city rested in the council, really the small council, consisting of forty-two men, thirty-four of whom were patricians, and eight commoners, or representatives of the eight major crafts who seldom attended. Of the thirty-four patricians, eight were called designated elders (*Alte Genannte*) and twenty-six burgomasters (*Bürgermeister*). Thirteen of the latter were also called jurors (*Schöffen*). In the course of time, thirteen were called senior burgomasters and thirteen junior burgomasters, one senior and one junior burgomaster serving as a governing team for a period of twenty-eight days. Of the thirteen senior burgomasters, seven were called elders (*Ältere Heeren* or *septemviri*) and met in secret daily to discuss the most important business at hand and submitted it to the rest of the council for action. These seven elders consitituted the heart of the government. Three of them were appointed captains-general (*oberste Haupt-*

männer) with custody of the keys to the city gates, the imperial regalia, and the city's seals. Two of these three were named the chief treasurers (*Losunger*). The senior treasurer was looked upon as the most important official in the government.

In Spengler's time, the great council consisted of approximately two hundred distinguished citizens, honored for life with this title by the small council. About a third of these were patricians, of whom eight were taken into the small council as distinguished elders. The great council ratified such matters as those pertaining to taxation, diplomacy, and war for which the small council wished broad popular support. The *Genannte* could serve as official notaries for private persons. All of them had access to the official inn (*Herrentrinkstube*) together with the families of patricians, big merchants, and noble guests, and all participated in a complicated system of electing members to the small council each year at Easter.[11] They selected as electors one burgomaster and one juror who served with three senior distinguished elders chosen by the small council. These five electors voted for the members of the small council and chose the governing burgomasters and the thirteen jurors. The small council at its first session named the distinguished elders, appointed the city officials, and assigned the pairs of governing burgomasters to their respective periods of service.

Legal matters were decided in the last instance by the small council. Penal cases were heard by the seven elders, who were at the same time jurors; and cases involving capital punishment were tried by the thirteen jurors, whose verdicts invariably followed the vote of the council in full session. There was a special "Court of Five" (*Fünfergericht*), which applied the sumptuary laws and heard cases of slander and personal injury. Three council members, designated guardians of widows and orphans, divided legacies, executed testaments, and assigned guardians. A bailiff (*Pfänder*), selected from the great council, decided cases between domestic servants and employees, made certain that the streets were kept clean and that victuals were sold at just prices, and presided over a court including four councilmen, called *Rugsherren*, to try cases involving the crafts and even appointed the masters of the crafts.

The city's civil court was separated from the council in 1497. It was composed of eight distinguished citizens elected by the council, two councilmen as assessors, and three or four doctors of the law to advise the court. It interrogated persons, interpreted the law, and passed judgment on matters involving fewer than thirty-two gulden. Important judgments could be appealed to the council and those involving six hundred or more gulden to the Imperial Chamber Court (*Reichskammergericht*). The municipal judge executed the verdicts, was present during the torture of a person, and presided over cases involving capital punishment. The peasants court consisted of young members of the great council and younger sons of councilmen who were appointed to the court to gain legal experience, the number varying from time to time. It tried cases between citizens of Nuremberg and peasants in the city's territory.

Six or seven jurisconsults, or "learned men," as they were also called, were full-time employees of the council whose duty it was to advise it on legal matters. So important were the consultants to the smooth running of the government that people considered them the social equals of the seven elders and the nobility, regardless of family or birth.[12] Because most of them were doctors of canon law as well as of Roman law, their legal opinions, or memorandums (*Ratschläge*), were particularly significant in matters related to the Reformation.

It was this government by conservative patricians that Lazarus Spengler served loyally and that his fellow citizens almost uniformly accepted as the divine arrangement by means of which order could be maintained in a society faced by great changes and growing restlessness. Because order was of utmost importance in late medieval urban society, the city council regulated every aspect of public and private life whether important or insignificant, whether such matters as peace and war or means for keeping dogs out of the churches or punishing boys for breaking windows in their schools, whether appointing pastors or regulating the dress of Nuremberg's citizens.[13] Daily contacts of people of all social groups with the patricians tended to imbue them with those municipal ideals and virtues that played a part in the formulation of attitudes toward the Reformation. Because the faithful service of the patricians was appreciated, the annual election of the council was to a large degree a mere formality with virtually no adding or dropping of councilmen.

Uppermost in the minds of those who inhabited imperial cities like Nuremberg was the conception of the community best expressed by the term *corpus Christianum*. This was a society in which every citizen lived for the group and the group for the citizen. In the microcosm of the city, the ideals of the macrocosm of Western Christendom as a whole prevailed. The governing body was in a real sense the representative of the community that was divinely instituted to serve both its temporal and spiritual needs. Men skilled in the practical affairs of the city provided the leadership, while men trained in law advised them in temporal matters and men trained in theology were their advisers in spiritual matters. This concern for the general welfare was an inheritance from antiquity expressed by the phrase, *salus publica suprema lex*. It was revived in Western Europe in Carolingian times, embodied in feudal chivalry as the *communis utilitas*, and appropriated by the emerging cities.[14] Although Luther, like most of his contemporaries, expressed his high regard for the common welfare, his emphasis upon the importance of the individual's justification by faith alone did much to cause a conflict in the political thinking of those who embraced his theology.

The current conception of the *corpus Christianum* was in part responsible for the attitude of many townsmen toward the clergy. Many of them were foreigners appointed by ecclesiastical authorities outside the cities. They did not pay taxes, help provide for defense, or man the city's walls, yet they enjoyed all the advantages of the citizens and in addition had privileges and exemptions that help explain the growing feeling of resentment against them, especially when neglect of spiritual functions and, in many cases, immorality became notorious. As a consequence, Nuremberg's city council early in the fifteenth century began to demand reforms in monasteries and parishes within its territory, improvement of morals, a share in, if not outright control over, the selection of regular and secular clergy, administration of ecclesiastical properties and endowments, care of the poor, and supervision of education.

That the citizens of Nuremberg were conscious of their right to control all their affairs for the general welfare as a right derived from the Holy Roman Empire is evinced in their attitude toward their city as imperial. This attitude, increasingly strong as the empire declined, was furthered in Nuremberg by the sight of the imperial castle within its own city walls, the frequent visits of the emperors, often accompanied by great pomp and ceremony, and the presence of the imperial regalia in the Church of the Hospital of the Holy Spirit in their midst. This attitude explains to a great degree the continued loyalty of Spengler and the city council to Emperor Charles V after the adoption of Lutheranism in 1525.

Municipal ethics, which stressed those virtues without which the community could not exist harmoniously and which gave the citizens of Nuremberg a sense of security, coincided with Protestant ethics at numerous important points.[15] The doctrine of the universal priesthood of believers minimized the sharp medieval distinction between clergy and laity and justified the strong emphasis upon a cooperative society. This was further strengthened by Luther's emphasis on the freedom of a Christian who because of God's love was compelled to serve his neighbor in love, and by his ennobling every calling as a divine service to the entire community.

Spengler and his fellow citizens also were strongly influenced by the inner spirituality of Christian mysticism, especially as it was preached by Johann Staupitz, general vicar of the Augustinian Eremites, and Wenzeslas Linck, his successor, to large audiences in Nuremberg from time to time. Their espousal of a simple, practical, strongly ethical Christianity appealed to the townsmen much more than the highly rational sermons of the scholastic preachers or the incredulous tales of saints often recounted for their edification.

Popular among the educated citizens of Nuremberg and part of the cultural background of Spengler was Christian humanism. Many merchants and councilmen had come into contact with the movement while studying in Italian or German universities, serving in the courts of princes, or engaging in commercial activities in such cities as Venice, Milan, Basel, and Antwerp, to mention only a few cultural centers. The Christian humanists, like the mystics, stressed inner spirituality, encouraged the study of the Bible and the church fathers, and emphasized classical as well as Christian ethics.

The great trading centers of Europe always have been great centers for the exchange of ideas and the encouragement of culture. During the first half of the sixteenth century, Nuremberg was first among the South German cities in the amount and extent of its trade. Its economic influence was apparent in the fact that approximately 230 of its merchants were doing business in Venice through the Fondaco dei Tedeschi, as compared with sixty-two from Augsburg and five from Strassburg.[16] Twelve main highways reached out from Nuremberg like spokes from the hub of a wheel to all the major trading centers of Europe. There were Nuremberg merchants in trading posts from Amsterdam, Hamburg, and Lübeck in the north to Venice, Milan, and Genoa in the south, from Lisbon, Seville, and Lyons in the west to Cracow, Prague, and Buda in the east. Moreover, merchants from other cities and countries were given many privileges to attract them to Nuremberg. The exchange of ideas as well as of goods fostered a lively book trade and encouraged learning, particularly of a practical, scientific nature.

Whereas the patricians and designated citizens and other wealthy citizens comprised approximately 6 to 8 percent of the entire population of Nuremberg, the craftsmen, middle-class merchants, and shopkeepers comprised the great majority, approximately 60 percent.[17] Because industry was diversified, this middle class was more stable than that of Augsburg, for example, with its predominance of textile production. The craftsmen were generally satisfied with their nominal participation in the government of the city. Many of them possessed the rudiments of education, so they could read the many books and pamphlets coming from the presses and participate in discussions of the major issues of their day.

Nuremberg also had its share of poor people who were unattached to land or guilds and were dependent for their living on occasional work, municipal charity, or begging. Among these were the gardeners and small farmers, who had at one time made respectable livings; inhabitants of the suburbs, who were in most respects a kind of second-class citizenry; mercenary foot soldiers and free laborers, who comprised a colorful floating population; journeymen unable to become masters in their guilds; professional beggars and officially licensed poor people; and, at the bottom, the outcasts, members of the proscribed professions such as prostitutes and gravediggers. It is estimated that these propertyless people constituted about a third of the population of Nuremberg. By comparison, the poor of Augsburg at the same time comprised about half of its population.[18]

Whereas there had been considerable mobility between social groups in Nuremberg in the fourteenth and fifteenth centuries, entrance into the patrician class was closed by the beginning of the sixteenth, as evinced in the Dance Statute of 1521, which listed the names of families permitted to dance in the City Hall. The families of Lazarus Spengler and Albrecht Dürer, for example, were not permitted to attend, and only one family was permitted to join the patrician class after this time. Movement between the middle and lower classes was almost exclusively downward. All classes still had a conception of their responsibilities for the common welfare, but the increasing gaps between the social groups and growing number of the lowest classes led to increasing conflicts of interest.

FIG. 2. The territory of Nuremberg in the sixteenth century.

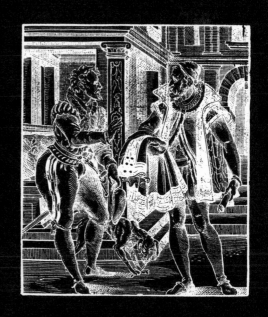

chapter two

BROADENING INTERESTS AND CONCERNS

Lazarus Spengler gained his position of leadership in Nuremberg not only by keeping the city council's books and associating with the councilmen but also by engaging in diplomatic missions, being active in the local intellectual and religious circles, and writing pamphlets. At an early age, he extended his interests beyond those of his father to include the broader currents of thought and action that were transforming the world in which Nuremberg was playing an important role.

DIPLOMATIC EXPERIENCE

Having become familiar with the city council's objectives, activities, and methods of governing, he prepared himself to play a part in charting its course for the future. Even before entering the chancellery, he had been sent to represent Nuremberg at meetings of the Swabian League, which the city had rejoined in 1500.[1] Emperor Maximilian's ambitious foreign policy in Italy during his conflict with France tended to disrupt the trade upon which cities like Nuremberg flourished and at the same time weakened royal authority in Germany to the extent that the cities were compelled to provide their own security. For Nuremberg, this meant cooperation with other members of the Swabian League, either individually or as members of this body. Her main objectives were to protect her merchants on the highways and rivers, prevent absorption by the territorial princes surrounding her, work out legal and administrative problems not made definite at the time that she acquired the lands outside her walls, and retain the support of the emperor, whose aims and ambitions often ran counter to her own.

As early as 1505, Spengler attended a meeting of the Swabian League at Würzburg with Willibald Pirckheimer, Georg Holzschuher, Anton Tetzel, Dr. Ulrich Nadler, and Kaspar Nützel, Nuremberg's official representative to the league. The purpose of the delegation was to make good Nuremberg's claims to the lands of the Upper Palatinate that the emperor had assured her would be hers because of her participation in the Bavarian War of Succession. After lengthy negotiations at various meetings, the city council gave Spengler the task of writing the official account of the war and the diplomatic negotiations involved, to be used in subsequent negotiations with the elector of the Palatinate.[2] He performed his task so well that the council gave him an honorarium of two hundred florins for his efforts. Characteristic of his desire to use whenever possible peaceful methods to obtain objectives is the conclusion that he draws after having estimated the total cost of the war at more than 360,000 florins. He states that the council could have obtained the lands by purchase at a much lower cost and makes the interesting observations that it is easy to start a war but hard to stop it, for stopping it requires the consent of the enemy; and that before beginning such an undertaking, one should carefully and exactly weigh the costs.[3] He and the council must have realized, however, that the broader question of territorial expansion was involved, for the elector would not have sold these lands to Nuremberg.

Much more complicated were the relations of Nuremberg with the margrave of Brandenburg. While, in 1502, Elector Frederick of Brandenburg was trying to work out differences with the city, his son Casimir began his expansionist program with an attack on it. The attack was replused by the armed citizens of Nuremberg under their supreme commander, Ulman Stromer, with Willibald Pirckheimer leading the reserves. In 1507, Spengler prepared a document for the city council explaining Nuremberg's position with respect to the margrave's complaints concerning her fortifications, conflicting legal jurisdiction, and other points of conflict.[4] These matters were discussed by the city's representatives at numerous diets and meetings, with Spengler usually in attendance. To prevent absorption of Nuremberg into the margrave's territorial state, the council found it necessary to appeal to both the Swabian League and the emperor. Although the diet of the league that met in Augsburg in 1507 supported the margrave and Maximilian was inclined to do likewise, Nuremberg profited by the emperor's military difficulties in Italy, which led him to appeal to the city for money.

When Spengler attended the diet of the Swabian League at Augsburg in 1511 with Kaspar Nützel and Hieronymus Ebner, these two men permitted him to compose the delegation's reports to the city council over their signatures. The attempts made by these three men to obtain the protection of the league against the expansionist policy of the margrave proved sufficiently promising, with the result that Nuremburg decided to rejoin it in 1512, at the close of its twelve-year period of membership. Spengler joined Anton Tucher, Anton Tetzel, Hieronymus Ebner, and Kaspar Nützel in a meeting with the representatives of the margrave in Nuremberg early in 1512, and was sent with Ebner and Nützel to Würzburg to meet with both the margrave and the emperor. They had only partial success.

Difficulties with the margrave were complicated by the depredations of the Franconian knights, who sought to further their interests by fighting both princes and cities. Despite this, the princes did not cooperate to establish order, and the emperor could do little more than ask the belligerents to cease fighting. Spengler repeatedly wrote statements summarizing for the council and its representatives at the diets of the Swabian League the complicated circumstances involved in the various feuds.[5] At Augsburg in 1512, Pirckheimer, Nützel, Groland and Spengler again met with the emperor and did their best to get from him a firm commitment to suppress the feuds and the robbery of Nuremberg merchants. Their failure was well expressed in their reports to Treasurers Tucher and Ebner, in which they stated that one could expect little at a court where "there is neither confidence nor faith, only [an interest in] money."[6]

In all these negotiations, Spengler became well acquainted with politics, the characters of the negotiators, and the great amount of wire-pulling going on in the negotiations. But he also established lifelong friendships with such able men as Hans von Schwarzenberg, chief steward of the bishop of Bamberg's court, and Georg Vogler, secretary of the margrave's court, men with whom he subsequently engaged in many weighty matters, especially of a religious nature. He also was drawn closer to the leading patricians of Nuremberg's city council, Hieronymus Ebner and Kaspar Nützel, and to Willibald Pirckheimer. Even though the emperor seemed inclined to favor the princes, the representatives of Nuremberg compelled him to consider their needs and demands. When Margrave Casimir (1515-27) took the reins from his father in 1515, relations with Brandenburg-Ansbach had improved to such an extent that Nuremberg could turn its attention to new problems confronting her. In these, Spengler's experiences and contacts, especially his friendship with Georg Vogler, proved valuable.

Although he henceforth was sent on few diplomatic missions, his experiences as one of the city's representatives at important meetings and diets during his first decade of service prepared him for a leading role in the critical years ahead.

Highly significant for Spengler's future development as a statesman was his participation in the imperial Diet of Augsburg in 1518, on which occasion Emperor Maximilian, a year before his death, attempted to have the seven electors of the empire agree to make his grandson Charles his successor, to gain support for a holy war against the Turks, and to wrestle with the many grievances (*gravamina*) of the estates that were aimed particularly at the papacy's legal and financial power and immorality among the clergy. It was Frederick the Wise, elector of Saxony and Luther's prince, who took the lead in refusing a tax for a crusade in which the pope would assume a leading role.

Spengler made this trip to Augsburg with Kaspar Nützel, Leonhard Groland, and Albrecht Dürer, "and many a merry day did the three friends [Nützel, Dürer and Spengler] enjoy together." He participated in the deliberations and prepared and signed the expense account submitted to the city council, giving such details as the overnight stops on the way, the length of the stay at Augsburg (twenty-one days), and the cost of staying with "our innkeeper," which was three hundred gulden, or the equivalent of a high city official's annual salary.[7] Because this diet was concerned primarily with problems that ultimately led to the Reformation, Spengler became familiar with imperial and papal policies with respect to the general dissatisfaction present among the Germans that served as a background for Luther's break with Rome. Luther, who was called to Augsburg to recant certain of his religious views before Cardinal Cajetan, representative of the papal curia at the Diet of Augsburg, passed through Nuremberg on his way to and from Augsburg and was enthusiastically received by the intellectual circle to which Spengler belonged.

That members of the city council were pleased with Spengler's work both at home and on diplomatic missions is evinced in a letter written to him by Kaspar Nützel on 16 June 1518. In it he refers to a report that Spengler had prepared for the council and expresses his appreciation for his "diligently prepared information" and his "industry."[8]

INTELLECTUAL CIRCLE

If Spengler did not become interested in current intellectual and religious movements by the inspiration of his teachers in Nuremberg, by perusal of books in the municipal library supervised by his father, or by his contacts with students and teachers at the University of Leipzig, there is no doubt that he was greatly stimulated along these lines on his diplomatic missions with Willibald Pirckheimer, his senior by nine years. The friendship between these two men begun on these missions continued for many years.

The cultural life of Nuremberg naturally mirrored the practical interests of her citizens and was not influenced by a court patronized by a ruler or by a wealthy citizen who devoted his time and money to cultural pursuits.[9] It is for this reason, among others, that humanism was not a force that greatly altered the lives of her citizens, although it was much appreciated by members of the intellectual circle.[10] The city council indirectly encouraged humanist studies by giving honoraria to humanists like Conrad Celtis, furthering Latin education in its schools, and paying its jurisconsults good enough salaries to attract men who had studied law and humanism in Italy. But the citizens were more interested in such matters as historical chronicles, which stressed continuity with the past; works in mathematics, which aided them in their calculations and production of technical instruments; books on astronomy, which were necessary for developing tables used by seamen and, incidently, prognostications for the future; geographical treatises, maps, and globes of value to merchants everywhere; and in furthering the art of printing.

One can measure Nuremberg's cultural interest and importance to a large degree by the number of printers and kinds of books they published.[11] One of the most popular universal histories produced in Germany at the end of the fifteenth century was Hartmann Schedel's *Book of Chronicles* with its 1809 illustrations, mostly of German cities, made from woodcuts by Michael Wolgemut (1434-1519) and Wilhelm Pleydenwurff (d. 1494) and published by Anton Koberger (1445-1513) in 1493. Johann Schöner (1477-1547), one of Germany's best-known mathematicians and astronomers, published his first important work on cosmography and geography in 1515, in which he referred to the New World as "America" and which was followed by his many widely used maps and globes. One of his globes, made in 1523, traced Magellan's circumnavigation of the world. Copernicus's *Revolution of Heavenly Bodies* was published by Johann Petrejus (d. 1551) in 1543. Andreas Osiander, a leading preacher and reformer in Nuremberg, who was interested in astronomy, provided the preface for the book, in which he made it appear that Copernicus had written it to present a mere hypothesis. In 1484 the city council published its book on the city's legal "Reformation," a widely read and influential legal compilation, one of the first of its kind. As early as 1483 Koberger published his beautifully illustrated German Bible in two volumes. In addition to Koberger, who at one time operated twenty-four presses, there were well-known printers such as Friedrich Creuszner, who published the *Travels* of Marco Polo in 1477; Peter Wagner, who published Brant's *Ship of Fools* in 1494; and Friedrich Peypus, who published numerous books by humanists and the first Nuremberg edition of Luther's New Testament in 1522. Among the booklovers who came to Nuremberg to buy books was Fernando Colón, son of Christopher Columbus, who was in the city in December 1521 and January 1522, when he added about three hundred volumes to his library.

Because of the interest of its citizens in business and travel, Nuremberg became one of the best centers in Germany for the production of maps. In 1492 Erhard Etzlaub's map of Nuremberg's environment appeared, the oldest German political map, indicating definite political boundaries. Jörg Nöttelein (d. 1567), musician and cartographer, produced numerous outstanding maps of Nuremberg and its territory for the city council, using exact measuring devices. He and other scholars also produced missals, chorales, and hymns for churches and schools as well as manuals on musical theory and on the construction of musical instruments.

The city council encouraged the visual arts, not only for use in illustrating books and maps, although it and the citizens of Nuremberg continued to look upon most artists as mere artisans.[12] Paintings, sculpture, woodcuts, copper engravings, and architecture flourished at the beginning of the sixteenth century to such an extent that one can speak of this period as Nuremberg's golden age of art. Her products were bought and appreciated by princes, churchmen, and cities throughout Europe. One need only mention Veit Stoss (ca. 1447-1533), the sculptor whose *Angelic Greeting* still adorns the interior of the church of Saint Lorenz in Nuremberg; Adam Kraft (ca. 1450-ca. 1509), whose immense stone tabernacle stands in the same parish church and whose large stone relief *Christ's Burial*, made for the Schreyer family, is on the outside wall of Saint Sebald's east choir; Peter Vischer (ca. 1460-1529), whose monumental bronze shrine housing the remains of the city's patron saint, Sebald, is in the parish church bearing his name, and whose bronze sculpture, including the famous *King Arthur*, made for Maximilian's tomb, is in Innsbruck; Mathes Gebel (d. 1574), a medalist who provided medals for the great and the wealthy throughout Europe; and Albrecht Dürer (1471-1528), one of the few creative German painters who emerged from the status of artisans to that of artists at this time.

Like his Nuremberg contemporaries, Dürer portrayed his environment naturally, a skill he had learned from his well-known teacher, Michael Wolgemuth. But he went beyond this to wrestle with wide-ranging interests that he discussed with Pirckheimer, Spengler, and other members of his circle, especially after his highly significant visits to Bologna and Venice, where he associated with great Italian painters and became interested not only in technical skill but in the nature of the world about him, beauty, and the artist as a creator. He discussed technical skill in his *Instructions in Measuring with the Compass and the Ruler*, based to a large extent on his studies of classical geometry, perspective, and architecture and published in German in 1525. His newly acquired understanding of perspective he presented in his *Four Books on Human Proportion*,[13] based on his knowledge of classical and Italian art and his own observations. But he rose above all rules, his own and others, to produce such masterpieces as his *St. Jerome* and *Knight, Death, and Devil*, engravings produced in 1513, and such paintings as *The Four Evangelists*, made in 1526 for the ceremonial hall in the *Rathaus* of Nuremberg, all works that show his deep religious concerns.

Although Hans Sachs (1494-1576), cobbler-poet and meistersinger of Nuremberg, was not a member of the patrician circle, he gained a considerable reputation for himself and his brotherhood of poets and musicians. As a strong supporter of Luther, more than forty of whose works he had in his personal library, he also played an important part in spreading the Reformation, particulary among the common people.[14] He was the first person to versify biblical drama as a teaching vehicle instead of a form of entertainment. In Nuremberg, as in other cities in southern and western Germany, meistersingers performed about three times a year in public, but much more frequently in secret "schools," developing their art according to many stultifying rules, admitting as meistersingers only those who had developed new "tones," or musical modes, according to these rules, and giving prizes to those who sang before the members and their judges with the fewest number of mistakes. There were about two hundred meistersingers in the "guild" in Spengler's day. Hans Sachs managed to show considerable originality within this strait jacket and to address himself to an astonishing number of subjects, which he seems to have gathered from a wide reading in the Bible, legends, chronicles, fables, and the classics. It is this that gave him great popularity among the common people. He was best, however, when he forsook the rules of the brotherhood and wrote freely in epic and didactic poems, dramas, carnival songs, dialogues, and hymns. But he soon was forgotten. It was not until the time of Goethe and Wagner that his earthy folk literature came to be widely appreciated.

A relatively small group of citizens of Nuremberg showed an interest in classical literature and humanist concerns still flourishing in Italy. The city council, however, recognized the importance of the knowledge of Latin and promoted its study in the four Latin schools connected with the churches of Saint Sebald, Saint Lorenz, Saint Egidien (Saint Giles), and Hospital of the Holy Spirit. In them were taught the grammar, rhetoric, and logic of the *trivium*, for which reason they were called *Trivialschulen*. Within that curriculum, young boys learned both German and Latin and became familiar with some of the classical and modern Latin writers. But at the turn of the century, a number of citizens, eager to introduce features of humanist education, induced the city council to create a new primary school with the expectation that the gifted German humanist, Conrad Celtis (1459-1508), who had received the crown of poet laureate from Emperor Frederick III in Nuremberg in 1487 and who had numerous friends in the city, would become head of the school. When he declined the offer, the council selected Heinrich Grieninger as rector. Despite his efforts and the active support of Willibald Pirckheimer and others, this "Poets' School," as it was called, was disbanded, and Pirckheimer and his friends turned their attention to the improvement of the Latin schools. For a number of years, Johannes Cochlaeus (1479-1552), who as a boy had attended the Poets' School, was rector of the school of Saint Lorenz, encouraging young boys to study the classics and music by teaching and writing good textbooks; but he did not stay long. Later he gained fame as one of Luther's most bitter opponents.[15]

Although Conrad Celtis did not stay in Nuremberg for any length of time, he returned frequently, and he aroused a real interest in humanism in a number of prominent people such as Hartmann Schedel, Georg Alt, Sixtus Tucher, Johann Pirckheimer, Dietrich Ulsenius, Peter Danhauser, and Sebald Schreyer, canon of Saint Sebald whose home became the center of humanists and always stood open to Celtis. The circle came to be known as the *Sodalitas celtica*. Among the better-known works of Celtis were the *Amores*, a collection of Latin poems; the *Odes*, descriptions of learning, life, and love; the *Oratio*, containing his ideas on educational reform; a collection of six dramas by Roswitha, a German nun of the tenth century; and the *Norimberga*, intended to be a part of his projected *Germania illustrata*, and translated into German by Georg Alt. The city council gave Celtis an honorarium of twenty gulden for this laudatory work. Dürer and his assistants caught the spirit of Celtis's humanist philosophy in the woodcut of "Philosophia," made for the *Amores*. Celtis would solve the problems of his day by this kind of a philosophy, poetical and rhetorical rather than metaphysical or theological, and showed little interest in Christianity other than by criticizing its institutions and the clergy. Yet the two great Swiss reformers, Zwingli and Vadian, were among his followers.

Lazarus Spengler was influenced by Celtis indirectly through Willibald Pirckheimer (1470-1530).[16] Willibald came from a wealthy family of Nuremberg that for a long time had had cultural as well as business ties with Italy. His father, Dr. Johann Pirckheimer (1440-1501), who had received his doctor's degree in law in Padua, became counselor of the bishop of Eichstätt, where Willibald was born, then of Duke Albert IV of Bavaria, and later of Archduke Sigismund of Tyrol. Meanwhile he served as jurisconsult for the city council in Nuremberg, where he helped prepare the revision of the municipal laws known as "the Nuremberg Reformation."

Willibald, the only boy among eight children, spent much of his boyhood in Munich and on diplomatic missions with his father, who taught him the classics and other subjects, even on their many travels. When he was sixteen years of age, his father sent him to the court of the bishop of Eichstätt, where be became proficient in diplomacy, the chivalric graces of that day, and military affairs, which he, as a large and vigorous young man, enjoyed to the fullest. His father then sent him to Padua and Pavia to study law, but he devoted much of his time there to the study of Greek and to contacts with humanists. After seven years in Italy, he returned to Nuremberg, but without the doctor's degree, so that he could follow his father's wish that he become a councilman. He served in that capacity until 1523.

Pirckheimer's attractive home on the west side of the Market Square, near the *Schöner Brunnen*, or Beautiful Fountain, became a hospitable center for cultured people from both home and abroad, and his library, one of the best private collections in Germany, was used by Willibald, his well-educated sisters and daughters—he had no sons—and friends. Among the Nuremberg citizens who most appreciated his exceptional qualities and abilities were the Treasurers Hieronymus Ebner and Anton Tucher, the brothers Endres and Martin Tucher, Kaspar Nützel, Christoph and Sigmund Fürer, Christoph Scheurl, Jakob Welser, Hieronymus Holzschuher, Albrecht Dürer, and Lazarus Spengler. These men constituted a humanist sodality of intellectuals similar to the *Sodalitas celtica*.[17]

The wide range of Pirckheimer's interests was demonstrated by his participation in, and writing about, military affairs; the translation of

Lucian's *The Writing of History*, Ptolemy's *Cosmography*, and other works from Greek into Latin and some from Greek and Latin into German; the publication of his *Germany Explicated*, revealing his patriotism and interest in Germany's geography; and his *Praise of the Gout*, the affliction that made him miserable much of his life.

Unlike Celtis, Pirckheimer had a great appreciation for Christianity, especially as interpreted by the Platonic Academy of Florence, which stressed morality and ethics at the expense of theology. Like Erasmus, he became interested in the Greek church fathers and published his *Six Orations of Gregory Nazianzen* as evidence of his interest. Like Luther, he stressed the importance of Scripture and faith in the promises of the Gospel, severely criticizing the scholastics for obfuscating Christian theology with their Aristotelianism. As might be expected, he was on Reuchlin's side in the latter's conflict with the Dominicans of Cologne and published an apology in his defense. But when his support of Luther and attacks on Eck led to his inclusion with Lazarus Spengler, Luther, and four other theologians in the papal bull *Exsurge Domine* of 15 June 1520 that threatened excommunication, and in the bull *Decet pontificem romanum* of 2 January 1521 that carried out the threat, he detached himself from the Reformation. Especially after his encounters with Oecolampadius and other Zwinglians and left-wing reformers, he attempted the difficult task of retaining Luther's basic evangelical doctrines while supporting the institutions of the Catholic Church, especially monasticism, to which his sisters had dedicated their lives. That he, like Erasmus, died without the sacrament of extreme unction, does not mean that he was indifferent to the Catholic Church, which he never had left. He died, as he had lived, a Christian humanist who sought in the classics as well as in Christianity that which might assist him and his generation in establishing a practical, ethical system and reform of the church.

Spengler was impressed by Pirckheimer's religious earnestness and suffered with him the consequences of having been condemned in two papal bulls aimed primarily at Luther, yet the two parted company after Spengler had assumed active leadership in making Nuremberg's break with Rome official in 1525 and attacked monasticism in the city and its territory. Despite his interests in humanism, Spengler found his salvation in Luther's evangelical doctrines.

Christoph Scheurl (1481-1542) was, like Pirckheimer, profoundly interested in law and humanism and was professionally associated with Spengler throughout much of the latter's career. He was the son of an emigrant from Swabia, Christoph I Scheurl, who became a successful and wealthy businessman, and of the beautiful and intelligent Helena Tucher, sister of First Treasurer Anton Tucher and of Martin Tucher, provost of Saint Lorenz. He studied at Heidelberg for a while and in 1498 went to Bologna, where he studied law and was honored by being made a syndic for two years, a position in which he represented the university in foreign courts. He received the degree of doctor of both laws there in 1506. The next year he was called to the new University of Wittenberg, where he distinguished himself as a professor of law, as rector of the university, and as a counselor and diplomat for Elector Frederick the Wise. Following the wishes of his parents, he returned to Nuremberg as chief jurisconsult for the city council, a position that he retained for the rest of his life.

In his capacities as legal expert, diplomat, and humanist, Scheurl became known as "the glory of Nuremberg." He produced no important humanist works but carried on an exceptionally wide correspondence with rulers, statesmen, and scholars, receiving as many as 673 letters in one year. He wrote in Latin for his friend Johann Staupitz *The Polity and Government of Nuremberg*[18] in the form of a letter, the work on which scholars have based much of their knowledge of the government of the city. He was an enthusiastic collector, primarily of historical data concerning Germany, Nuremberg, and genealogical items, especially of the Tucher family.

Like Erasmus and Pirckheimer, Scheurl preferred to remain aloof from the struggles growing out of the Reformation. He even tried for a while to reconcile Luther and Eck. Despite his early enthusiasm for Luther, he never embraced his evangelical doctrines and retained his friendship for Eck. He remained Catholic to his death. Spengler, with his early and strong commitment to Lutheranism, disliked Scheurl's humanist approach to religion and his vacillating character. Pirckheimer also disliked him but did not break openly with him until 1528. In his early years in Nuremberg, however, Scheurl played a leading role in the city's intellectual circle and contributed much toward bringing Nuremberg and Wittenberg together. Spengler was pleased when Scheurl dedicated the German translation of his *Forty Letters Translated from the Latin into the German* to him.[19]

Among other well-educated persons with whom Spengler came into close contact were Anton Tucher (1457-1524), first treasurer from 1507 to 1524, a close friend of Elector Frederick the Wise and an early supporter of Luther, and Hieronymus Ebner (1477-1532), a mild and irenical person who followed Anton Tucher as first treasurer in 1524. Ebner had studied law at Ingolstadt, where he also had become interested in humanism. He had become familiar with diplomacy on a broad scale while serving for a time in the court of Emperor Maximilian.

CHRISTIAN HUMANIST

Spengler's contacts with Christian humanists and men of learning with various interests added to his store of knowledge and influenced his approach to the problems of the day. In the spirit of his time, he and his friend Albrecht Dürer wrote little poems in jest as early as 1509, efforts which Pirckheimer mildly ridiculed and sometimes corrected. On one occasion, Dürer turned in fun to Spengler for help against the hilarious criticisms of their common friend. Spengler responded by writing for him a poem about "Apelles and the Shoemaker," in which he advised Dürer "to stick to his last." Dürer answered with verses comparing Spengler to a dull and confused notary.[20]

When Hieronymus Holzschuher and Kaspar Nützel turned over to Spengler the writing of reports to the city council while they were on diplomatic missions in 1511, Dürer presented his "dear Lazarus Spengler" with a facetious drawing (see page 91) portraying these three men as smithy, printer and baker who were preparing such official reports. The printer, apparently Spengler, uses a book press to affix with vigor his seal on the documents.[21] That the friendship between Dürer and Spengler continued is indicated by the fact that Dürer made a portrait of his friend, which since has been lost. There also is reason to believe that Durer was helpful in creating the Spengler seal used by him in a legal action of 1518.[22]

Illustrative of Spengler's concern for Christian, classical, and burgher ethics was his *Admonition and Instruction for a Virtuous Life*,[23] written in rhyme for, and dedicated to, Dürer, his "special, intimate, and brotherly friend." Using classical quotations, Bible passages, and folklore, he presents his collection of virtues and vices in clear, sincere rhymes. He suggests that one should control reason, the master of all human life, "as a rider reins his untamed horse," drink deeply from ancient books on philosophy and morals, and rely on God's grace:

> Initium Sapientiae, Timor Domini.
> Vor allen dingen lieb und forcht Got
> Als das höchst und best gut.

The central purpose of his life is to serve the public welfare of his city. The virtues required to do this effectively are fear of God, reasonableness, equanimity in suffering, friendliness, loyalty, humility, discretion, restraint, trustworthiness, compassion, and love of peace. The chief vices he lists are pride, desire for revenge, pleasure in seeing others suffer, flattery, gossip, contentiousness, and love of praise.

Like many of his contemporary Christian humanists, Spengler was interested in the church fathers. The favorite among the citizens of Nuremberg was Saint Jerome (Hieronymus), as evinced in the large number of children given that Christian name at birth. This church father, a learned, sincere, Christian translator, Bible commentator, and theologian, embodied the ideals of Spengler's contemporaries. Dürer, for example, portrayed the saint ten times in his art. In 1514, Spengler published his translation from Latin into German of the pseudo-Eusebius biography *The Life and Death of St. Jerome.*[24] Dürer showed his interest in this work by giving Spengler his woodcut of "Jerome in the Grotto" to include in it.[25] Spengler dedicated the work to his "honorable master and friend," Hieronymus Ebner.[26] Its main theme had to do with a virtuous life prompted by the love of Christ and leading to salvation. The translation pleased the members of the intellectual circle, above all Scheurl, who encouraged Spengler to translate other items, including Saint Augustine's *Psalm of Lamentation*, written during the siege of Hippo Regius and also some of the Tucher correspondence being collected by Scheurl.

Spengler's preoccupation with the church fathers during his early contacts with the intellectual circle of Nuremberg was indicative of the concerns that soon led him to devote much of his thought and time to the important religious currents culminating in the Reformation. In this he was followed by a number of his friends and acquaintances such as Albrecht Dürer, Hieronymus Ebner, Kaspar Nützel, and Sigmund and Christopher Fürer.

chapter three

FROM CHRISTIAN HUMANIST TO LUTHERAN

The religious thought of Lazarus Spengler and his friends in Nuremberg's intellectual circle underwent a gradual but fundamental change toward the end of the second decade of the sixteenth century. Christian humanists, with their opposition to the theological and philosophical speculations of the scholastics and their own emphasis on a synthesis of classical, Christian, and urban ethics, did not seem able to solve the problems raised by a rapidly increasing religious dissatisfaction among all classes. Their detached intellectual and cultural approach did much to stimulate discussions of religious issues, criticism of weaknesses in the religious establishment, and encouragement of inner spirituality, but it did not fire their followers with the kind of religious devotion and conviction needed to change inherited customs and institutions and again make Christianity a dynamic force.

RELIGIOUS PROBLEMS IN NUREMBERG

As *Ratsschreiber*, Spengler became thoroughly familiar with the religious problems facing the city council, a body conscious of its responsibility to serve the spiritual as well as secular welfare of the people and eager to gain complete control over the entire ecclesiastical structure of the city.[1] He learned of disturbing problems related to indulgences, endowments for relics, and life among the secular and regular clergy.

One of the most shocking cases of immorality among the regular clergy, which greatly disturbed Spengler and the city council, involved

Johannes Hänlein, prior of the local Dominican monastery, and Barbara Schleiffer, a nun in the cloister at Engelthal that had fallen to Nuremberg as a consequence of the Bavarian War of Succession.[2] Hänlein, who had flattered himself into the good graces of a number of patricians, including Treasurer Anton Tetzel, and especially of women, was suspected of irregularities when Tetzel fled to the Dominican monastery after his downfall. Tetzel had been deprived of all his offices and honors and eventually put into the Luginsland Tower for having disclosed confidential council matters and having sold his influence for money. In 1515, letters between Hänlein and Barbara Schleiffer were intercepted that disclosed a passionate love affair between the two. Spengler, who had been instrumental in uncovering this romantic episode, was made a member of the committee selected to look into the matter. It included Anton Tucher, Hieronymus Ebner, and Kaspar Nützel. After a thorough investigation, the committee recommended that Hänlein be dismissed and the nun expelled from Engelthal. It is not surprising that the members of this committee were among the first to demand the dissolution of monasteries.

It also is no mere coincidence that a positive solution for religious problems emanated from the Augustinian monastery in Nuremberg. It had been reformed as early as 1437 with strong support from the city council. By 1500, it was a model of piety and propriety. Its priors insisted upon strict observance of the monastic rule and also furthered education and preaching of an inner spirituality based on the theology of Saint Augustine. The intellectual circle of Nuremberg appreciated the fact that the Augustinians did not condemn humanism as the Dominicans and some other monasteries did but put it to Christian uses. The city council also supported Johann Staupitz (ca. 1470-1524), who was made vicar general of the order in 1503; Nikolaus Besler, Staupitz' friend and the local prior; and Besler's successor, Wolfgang Volprecht, a learned person who later became active in the Reformation of the city.

THE PREACHING OF STAUPITZ AND LINCK

Staupitz frequently visited Nuremberg and preached in the Augustinian church, where he drew large crowds of people because of his Augustinian and Pauline emphases, practical application of Christianity to human relations, and his firm belief in God's love for man and the importance of man's love in furthering the welfare of his neighbor. All this explains his opposition to workrighteousness and especially to abuses associated with the selling of indulgences. It is no wonder that he appealed to many people and that Spengler and others took copious notes from his sermons for later reflection and use.

We have frequent references to the impact of the preaching of Staupitz from Christoph Scheurl, who had become acquainted with him in Bologna and later in Wittenberg, where the Augustinians had a chair of theology and where Scheurl had taught. The two became good friends after Scheurl's return to Nuremberg.

Staupitz, whom Scheurl called "the tongue of the Apostles," was particularly effective in delivering his Advent and Christmas sermons of 1516 and his Lenten and Easter sermons of 1517, in which he dealt with such topics as the fall of man and the promise of divine grace. Among the intellectuals and patricians who regularly attended these sermons and who were table companions of Staupitz in the refectory of the Augustinian monastery or in their homes were Scheurl, Anton Tucher, Hieronymus Ebner, Kaspar Nützel, Hieronymus Holzschuher, Endres and Martin Tucher, Sigmund and Christoph Fürer, Jacob Welser, provosts Georg Beheim and Georg Pesler, Albrecht Dürer, and Lazarus and Georg Spengler. Lazarus copied about thirty of these table talks (*sermones*), which today are in the Scheurl family archive.[3] These conversations were delightful, entertaining, occasionally witty, but always expressive of a practical religious concern. It is not surprising that Scheurl now referred to the Nuremberg intellectual circle as the *Sodalitas staupitziana*. Staupitz's sermons, however, were heard also by the masses, who took them to heart and played a much-overlooked role in the events that sped the city on to embracing the evangelical theology emanating from Wittenberg.

When, in 1517, business of the Augustinian Order compelled Staupitz to absent himself from Nuremberg, except for short stopovers, he sent Wenceslas Linck (1483-1547) to the city as his substitute.[4] This brilliant preacher, the life-long friend of Martin Luther and Lazarus Spengler and a leading reformer in Nuremberg, appealed to the members of the city council and the intellectual circle in many ways. The son of a prosperous city councilman of Kolditz in Saxony, he had become interested in humanism as a student at Leipzig and Wittenberg, had entered the Augustinian monastery, and had received the degree of doctor of theology at the University of Wittenberg in 1512, becoming dean of its faculty that same year. Already, in 1511, he had been made prior of the Augustinian monastery in Wittenberg, with Martin Luther a subprior under him a year later. He left Nuremberg in 1521 to become a preacher in Altenburg, but he returned three years later as custodian and preacher at the Hospital of the Holy Spirit, where he served until his death.

From the outset, Linck drew large audiences to hear his strongly ethical and practical sermons. His thirty Advent sermons on the Beatitudes in 1518 reflected Luther's reliance on God's Word. Scheurl praised his eloquence, piety, love of learning, and zeal in behalf of the Gospel, yet he and Linck never became close friends. Wolfgang Volprecht (d. 1528), prior of the Augustinians in Nuremberg, supported Linck in every way, even as the latter followed Luther step by step to become a reformer and to change the Staupitz sodality into a circle of "Martinians," or followers of Luther. As this change took place, Ebner, Nützel, and Spengler replaced Scheurl and Pirckheimer as the leaders. Luther showed his respect for Ebner by dedicating to him his first *Commentary on Psalm 100* (1518), for which Spalatin wrote the introduction.[5]

As early as 3 November 1517, Luther's *Ninety-five Theses* were in the hands of the members of the Nuremberg circle, despite the fact that Luther had not wanted them to circulate. Kaspar Nützel prepared a German translation of them, and Albrecht Dürer gave Luther a gift, probably woodcuts, in recognition of his work. Wolfgang Volprecht arranged for a printing of Luther's *Sermon on Indulgences*. Scheurl sent copies of the *Ninety-five Theses* to friends at Augsburg, Eichstätt, and Ingolstadt. Johann Eck (1486-1543), professor of theology at the University of Ingolstadt, sent a list of his objections to the work to Bernhard Adelmann (1457-1523) in Augsburg, who in turn sent a copy to Linck. Through Linck, these objections reached Luther, who, in March, 1518, published his answer in a work called *Asterisks (Asterici)*,[6] dedicated to Linck. Linck explained the *Ninety-five Theses* in a Palm Sunday sermon printed by Jobst Gutknecht in Nuremberg the next year.

Excitement over Luther's cause increased when, in April 1518, Linck and a companion, probably Volprecht, attended a meeting of the Augustinians at Heidelberg where they became aware of mounting opposition to the *Ninety-five Theses* and heard Luther present his doctrines concerning sin, free will, and grace in the Heidelberg Disputation. When the meeting broke up, Luther rode with Linck in the Nuremberg wagon as far as Würzburg, where they parted.

The same year, in August, Philip Melanchthon (1497-1560) stopped in Nuremberg on his way from Tübingen to Wittenberg, where he had been appointed to a professorship. He was a guest in the home of Pirckheimer, where he personally became acquainted with Spengler, Linck, and other members of the Martinian circle with whom he continued to maintain close relations.

ACQUAINTANCE WITH LUTHER

Spengler met Luther for the first time in 1518, when the Reformer was on his way to and from his hearings with Cardinal Cajetan in Augsburg. He arrived in Nuremberg 5 October in a despondent mood, for he was expecting to be burned as a heretic and a number of his friends had warned him not to meet with Cajetan. Linck and other members of the Martinian sodality, however, met with him during his short visit and encouraged him in his determination to give an account of his religious convictions. Linck presented him with a new cowl, made the business arrangements for the last leg of the trip, and accompanied him to Augsburg.

In Augsburg, Linck and Staupitz stayed with Luther at the Carmelite monastery, whose prior, Johann Frosch, had received his degree of licentiate in theology from Luther at Wittenberg. Linck and Staupitz saw to it that Luther met Konrad Peutinger. Bernhard Adelmann, and other members of Augsburg's intellectual circle, who offered him their friendship and hospitality during his trying and disappointing experiences with Cajetan. It was here in Augsburg that Staupitz absolved Luther of his monastic vows. Linck provided the money necessary for his precipitate flight from the city.

Luther stopped at Nuremberg again on his way home, about 23 October, this time as a guest in Pirckheimer's home. It was here that he received from Georg Spalatin, his friend and the chaplain and secretary of Elector Frederick the Wise,[7] a copy of the papal breve of 23 August addressed to Cajetan, ordering him to arrest Luther and excommunicate him and his supporters. This condemnation of Luther before he had had a hearing served to make him a special hero among his Nuremberg friends, among them Lazarus Spengler, the only person to give a written account of this visit, contained in his first pamphlet published in defense of Luther. Luther's sermon in the church of Saint Egidien Monastery, the "Schottenkloster," further strengthened the loyalities of the Martinians to him. After his return to Wittenberg, Luther sent a copy of his *Augustana*, or account of the proceedings at Augsburg, to his friends in Nuremberg. When he prepared to flee Wittenberg to avoid implicating his prince, Frederick the Wise, in this matter, the Martinians feared a great setback to the cause of the evangelical movement.

Another disturbing event was Johann Eck's visit to Nuremberg on the occasion of Scheurl's wedding on 29 August 1519. Having compelled Luther to draw some of the conclusions of his evangelical theology with respect to the papacy and church councils at the Leipzig

Debate 27 June to 16 July 1519, Eck now boasted of his victory, thereby intensifying the antipathy of the Martinians against him and his cause. Spengler increased his activities in behalf of religious change to the extent that a canon of the cathedral chapter of Bamberg complained to Pirckheimer that the secretary was neglecting council duties by spending too much time with religious matters.[8]

The city council's disgust with the papacy was aggravated by the citation, in 1519, of the patrician Hieronymus Holzschuher and his wife to the papal curia in a secular matter involving the will and testament of another citizen of Nuremberg. The plaintiff had argued in support of his action that he could not have obtained a fair hearing in Nuremberg or the Imperial Chamber Court because of Holzschuher's importance. Whereas Scheurl as jurisconsult counseled giving in to the papacy, the city council was determined to maintain its legal rights. Although the case eventually was settled to the satisaction of the council, it accentuated the conflict between church and state over legal jurisdiction.[9]

Spengler was directly involved in another incident that influenced his attitude toward the religious establishment, the transfer of his sister Martha from one monastery to another. In this lengthy conflict, the Saxon superior of the order, Dr. Hermann Rab, an enemy of Luther, was victorious. Spengler, however, had one more occasion to become disgusted with the monastic system, for the superior clearly had ignored the reasonable wishes of the Spengler family.[10]

Spengler's strong spiritual concerns and his friendship for Luther led him to write for his friends and acquaintances one of the first widely read apologies for Luther, his *Defense and Christian Reply of an Honorable Lover of the Divine Truth of Holy Scripture Against Several Opponents with Reasons Why Doctor Martin Luther's Teaching Should Not be Rejected But on the Contrary be Considered Christian.*[11] Although he wrote it in 1518, it did not appear in print until the next year, when it was published against his wishes and anonymously by Silvan Ottmar in Augsburg. In 1520, Adam Petri published a new edition in Basel and M. Lotther one in Wittenberg. Numerous printings were made elsewhere. After a short introduction, in which Spengler states that the church should consider Luther a champion of the faith and a preacher of evangelical doctrines, he lists six points that he develops in a simple, direct prose with examples taken from both the Bible and folklore.

First, Luther's doctrines are Christian, Spengler maintains, because they are based on the Gospel, the holy prophets, and Saint Paul. Because Thomas Aquinas, Bonaventura, Scotus, and others whom his opponents cite against Luther erred as human beings, it is reasonable to believe that God might appoint a contemporary person through whom he could reform the church.

Second, Luther's doctrines point the right way to freedom, for they conform to human reason. "I know without a doubt," says Spengler, "that I, who do not consider myself especially brilliant or clever, have never found teachings or sermons so reasonable as those of Luther and his followers." Then follow sharp attacks on preachers of "fairy tales"; of outward ceremonies in place of Christ, faith, and love; of law instead of Gospel; of flesh rather than spirit; of confession and indulgences instead of contrition. He asks, "Is not the man who eats meat on Friday considered more evil that the one who commits adultery or blasphemes God?" Luther's attacks on such abuses, he adds, make sense.

Third, Luther's actions are justified because they are ethical. Unlike the indulgence preachers, he seeks Christ rather than his own selfish advancement. Spengler here states that Luther, on his second stop in Nuremberg in 1518, told him personally that "if his teachings are of God and from God, he has no doubt that God will further and protect them; but if they are only human, they will in time and without any opposition crash in ruins."

Fourth, Luther frees from conscientious scruples those people who recognize the truth in his sermons and those of his followers. Spengler opposes those who maintain that Luther should have submitted his own religious problems to learned people for discussion and advice before making them known to others.

Fifth, Luther's teachings grew out of a practical situation. When he became aware of the abominable preaching by Tetzel in support of the sale of indulgences, he was compelled to speak out against it, for he was, first, a monk, second, a preacher, and third, a doctor of theology. Thus by profession he did not dare to remain silent as most people in high places did but had to protest, even if this would lead to persecution and death. Spengler is certain "that God Almighty has awakened a Daniel among the people against this stupid and damnable error for the purpose of opening their eyes, blinded for so long a time by the misleading teachings of our theologians, and to dispel the fog and darkness of such indecency."

Finally, Luther based his teachings squarely on the Gospel and acted according to his conscience. He promised both in writing and orally that he would cease presenting these doctrines if the pope and the church or scholars in French or German universities would prove them in error. But Christ, "the master fencing teacher," has "taught Luther well so that he has honorably defeated his enemies who have fought him with childish arguments. These are my reasons for considering Luther and his teachings unconquered and undestroyed. . . . Praise God."

The *Defense*, which appealed to all classes but especially to the common man, marked the beginning of the Reformation in Nuremberg. But its influence was also felt elsewhere. It appeared in Augsburg about the same time as the direct attack on Eck, the *Unlearned Canons* (*Canonicis indoctis*), written by Johann Oecolampadius (1482-1531), preacher at the main church in Augsburg, who had been urged to do so by Bernhard Adelmann von Adelmanns-felden (1457-1523), one of Luther's admirers. This satire soon was translated into German and circulated widely.[12] Eck considered himself personally attacked by both the *Defense* and the *Unlearned Canons*.

At the end of February 1520, there was published anonymously a third work against him and scholastic theology, the brilliant satire *The Corner [Ecke] Planed Smooth* (*Eccius dedolatus*), which Eck, Luther, Scheurl, and others immediately attributed to Pirckheimer, who denied having written it.[13] Although Pirckheimer probably helped spread the work, his authorship has not been proven. Eck erroneously believed that Spengler had assisted Pirckheimer in writing it and had translated it into German. The Ingolstadt professor soon had an opportunity to strike back. Late in March, he went to Rome to press the case against Luther. With Cajetan and others, he drafted the papal bull *Exsurge Domine*, made official 15 June 1520, demanding that Luther retract the forty-one articles listed in it as heretical within sixty days or be excommunicated. Furthermore, Eck was given the right to cite others in the bull. The six whom he named were Spengler, Pirckheimer, Adelmann, the Zwickau pastor Silvanus Egranus, and Luther's Wittenberg colleagues Carlstadt and Feldkirchen, thus striking at both theologians and laymen who had impugned his reputation. The bull demanded that they, as well as Luther, should seek absolution from Eck within sixty days.

Eck was given the task of publishing the bull in Germany. He began by taking it to the Fondaco dei Tedeschi in Venice and then posted it publicly in Meissen on 21 September, in Merseburg on 25 September, and in Brandenburg on 29 September. He gave it to Karl von Miltitz, a papal chamberlain, to present to Frederick the Wise and the University of Wittenberg. He did not send a copy of it to Nuremberg until 15 October or to the Bishop of Bamberg until 19 October. Whereas the court of Electoral Saxony could play off Eck's mission with that of Miltitz, which soon followed, and could marshal the sentiments of numerous ecclesiastics against Eck, Nuremberg was in a difficult position to defend Spengler and Pirckheimer, for the city council still was negotiating with the elector of the Palatinate and the margrave of Brandenburg over jurisdiction in its territorial possessions and in this needed the support of the Bavarian court, where Eck had considerable influence.

Spengler and Pirckheimer were drawn together closer than ever by the papal bull. Spengler assured Pirckheimer that "we will, God willing, stand together in these and other matters like the Swiss—no one will separate us."[14] Because of a severe plague in Nuremberg, Pirckheimer fled to the estate of his brother-in-law Martin Geuder in Neunhof and did not return to the city until January 1521. In addition to carrying out his many professional duties, Spengler worked on a dialogue, "Counterattack and Resolution," an enlargement of his *Defense,* which he dedicated to Adelmann but which he did not have printed in deference to the wishes of the city council. In it he shows how much he had become preoccupied with the study of the Bible and with working out a personal confesson of faith.[15] Leaning heavily on Luther's *Sermon on Good Works* and *Commentary on Galatians,* he stresses his conviction that salvation depends upon faith alone, not on works.

Eck enclosed with the copy of the bull *Exsurge domine* that he sent to the city council of Nuremberg a letter in which he assured the council of his good will toward Nuremberg and stated that he had for a long time "resisted the papal order to publish and execute the bull."[16] He stated that Spengler and Pirckheimer had been included in the threat of excommunication because they had "praised, furthered, and exaggerated Luther's erroneous and misleading doctrines more than was proper." To please the council, he promised to absolve them if they would make the proper kind of confession to him as papal plenipotentiary. But he also demanded that the council forbid the publication and sale of Luther's books and have all available copies burned.

Although the city council at first feared that Spengler and Pirckheimer had aroused Eck's anger in some way not known to it, it did not permit Eck to drive a wedge between it and its two illustrious citizens as he had hoped. It considered his move an attack upon the city's rights as well as upon Spengler and Pirckheimer and reasoned that if Eck could attack anyone whom he disliked, all prominent people would be threatened. Consequently,it decided that the cause of

Spengler and Pirckheimer was its own cause and therefore defended them courageously while at the same time acting with diplomatic wisdom.

Spengler and Pirckheimer naturally wished to avoid excommunication and the humiliation of appealing to Eck for absolution. The city council, therefore, readily induced them to appeal to the well-educated bishop of Bamberg, George III of Limburg. In doing so, they stressed the illegality of Eck's first publishing their names in other bishoprics and petitioned the bishop to inform Eck of their profession of Christian obedience. They also requested him kindly to consider their profession a sufficient response to the bull and to free them from its threat. They added that they would be willing to answer for their actions not only to the bishop, their proper judge, but to all impartial spiritual and temporal authorities in the empire. The council sent this profession with a covering letter to the bishop, having been assured that he was sympathetic toward Luther and thoroughly disliked Eck, who on one occasion had appeared in Bamberg "drunk as a sow."[17] The bishop's answer of 2 November 1520, however, was disappointing, for he stated that he had no authority over Eck, a papal nuncio. He added, however, that to show his good will toward the council he would forward the petition and letter to Eck. At the request of the council, Spengler wrote to the bishop, expressing his and Pirckheimer's surprise that he had sent the profession to Eck, thereby recognizing Eck's authority over him in this matter.

That Spengler and Pirckheimer could expect no help from the bishop of Bamberg became clear to them when they learned that he had been induced by the bishop of Würzburg, an outright opponent of Luther, to give up his support of the Reformer and his followers. Furthermore, Eck had written him on 12 November that the two were guilty of heresy, that they had not done enough to merit absolution, that they had not denounced Luther's doctrines, and that the time was too short for them to appeal to the pope. He added that he had absolved Adelmann because of the intercession of Duke William of Bavaria, Eck's prince. This letter amounted to an outright refusal.

Meanwhile, on 30 October, the council had appealed to Duke William, who had not yet taken a definite stand with respect to Luther's doctrines, to speak to Eck in behalf of Spengler and Pirckheimer,[18] calling attention to the bad effect Eck's actions would have on conditions in Germany as a whole if he were not restrained. The duke answered that he would have to obtain from Eck details concerning the matter before he could act. Eck assured the duke that he held Nuremberg and its Council in high regard and would gladly carry out its wishes. Because of the pope's command, however, he was compelled to uphold the Christian faith against Luther's supporters, Spengler and Pirckheimer. Wanting to humiliate the two thoroughly, he added with tongue in cheek that he did not have the authority to accede to the wishes of Nuremberg. Even though he was aware that the time was too short, he stated that the two, whom he admitted having named in the bull of his own accord, should follow the instructions of the bull and send a confession of their faith to the pope. The duke sent this answer to the council on 23 November, stating that he had tried in vain to get Eck to absolve the two.

Meanwhile, Spengler wrote Luther for advice. Luther answered on 17 November, stating that he was greatly pleased with Spengler's "great courage in this matter concerning Christian truth." He added that he himself had arranged for a second printing of his appeal in Latin and in German, even though he did not consider this necessary, for the bull was "so shameless in condemning him in an unchristian manner." He stated that he did not believe that the bull had been presented legally and that the bishops would execute it.[19]

When Spengler learned that Adelmann had appealed directly to the pope before approaching Eck and obtained a copy of Adelmann's appeal, he and Pirckheimer agreed to do likewise and approached the council for its advice. The council commissioned Spengler and Nützel, with the assistance of the municipal jurisconsults, to prepare an appropriate appeal. On 1 December, the two burgomasters published the formal, notarized appeal of Spengler and Pirckheimer. Spengler sent a copy of it to the bishop of Bamberg with an enclosure criticizing Eck's procedure point by point.[20]

The city council then sent Jakob Muffel, its able and highly respected councilman and ambassador, to Duke William. Spengler prepared for him "the stately instruction" in which he urged him to impress upon the duke the fact that if Eck's plans would be carried out and left unchallenged, the secular authority not only of Nuremberg but of the entire empire would be imperiled, that Nuremberg's cause was that of all the German estates, and that therefore Spengler and Pirckheimer should not be excommunicated.[21] Eck, however, refused to absolve the two, stating that they should have approached him rather than the bishop of Bamberg and the pope, and that their general statements had ignored the forty-one articles of Luther that had been declared heretical in the bull. Furthermore, he declared, they had appealed to a general church council, which the bull had forbidden. Yet he expressed his willingness to treat them leniently in deference to the city council, even though the sixty days of grace had expired, provided that they humbled themselves before him. Seeing that the duke could not induce Eck to give in, the council advised the two men to approach Eck through a plenipotentiary, even though they detested humiliating themselves in this way.

Having convinced the two that this was the only course that had a chance of success, the city council sent its jurisconsult, Dr. Jakob Rorer, to Eck on 4 January 1521, with instructions prepared by Pirckheimer making it clear that he was acting for the entire council, not only for the two,[22] and asking him to inquire of Eck what he still would demand of them. During Rorer's discussion with Eck, who called in three witnesses and a university professor as notary, he was asked whether he had the power of attorney to swear an oath in behalf of Spengler and Pirckheimer and the Nuremberg City Council. Rorer, taken by surprise by this question, answered in the negative, for Spengler and Pirckheimer had not known that Adelmann had given such an oath through such a legal representative or that Eck had bound Adelmann not to disclose to anyone what he had done to gain Eck's absolution.[23]

Eck's maneuvers to postpone granting the absolution greatly increased Spengler's dislike of the man, whom he called "our monster." But he and Pirckheimer and the council now knew what Adelmann had done and decided to follow his example. Accordingly, they employed a notary of Ingolstadt, a Dr. Heinrich Voyt, who had offered his services and to whom they gave the power of attorney to act for them. Like Adelmann, the two chose to ask for absolution in the event that they were considered to have done anything detrimental to the church and worthy of excommunication by being influenced too much by Luther and his teachings.

Once more the triumphant Eck postponed matters when Dr. Voyt was compelled by a brief illness of Pirckheimer to postpone for a few days the meeting arranged with Eck. When they met, on 1 February 1521, Eck would not permit Spengler and Pirckheimer to make use of the mild form of absolution (*ad cautelam*), in which they could ask for absolution provided that they had been influenced by Luther to the extent that they had done something worthy of excommunication and swore that they would henceforth avoid all heresy. Although Eck had written the bishop of Bamberg the previous November that he would permit this form of absolution, he now demanded the severe form (*absolutio simplex*), in which they were compelled to state that they had not adhered to Luther and had not approved his doctrines. Thereby Eck succeeded in thoroughly humiliating the two men before finally absolving them during the month of February, as it was reported. The two men would not have submitted to this humiliation unless compelled to do so by their city council. Whether or not Eck absolved them, he did not report this to the papal curia in time to prevent their excommunication along with Luther and Ulrich von Hutten in the papal bull *Decet pontificem romanum*, which Aleander, the papal nuncio, received at Worms on 10 February.[24] When Spengler, who was at the Diet of Worms at this time, learned about the bull, he protested strongly and sent a written appeal to Emperor Charles V, as did Pirckheimer, stating that he always had been obedient to the papacy and had already been absolved by Eck. The emperor referred the matter to Aleander, who obtained from the pope a breve empowering him to absolve the two men. This he did in the latter part of the summer.

An important consequence of Pirckheimer's absence from Nuremberg during much of the negotiation concerning the bull *Exsurge domine* is the correspondence carried on between him and Spengler, who remained in the city and carried the much greater share of the burden of obtaining absolution from the threat of the bull. Throughout the negotiations, Spengler remained loyal to Pirckheimer, as this correspondence shows, even when Scheurl tried to drive a wedge between the two men.[25]

Even though Spengler had to humiliate himself before Eck and later before Aleander by swearing to oppose all heresy, he never denied the contents of his *Defense* and continued to be a driving force in the religious changes taking place in Nuremberg. He consistently maintained that what he believed was not Luther's doctrine but his own, based on the Gospel, the prophets, and Saint Paul, and he promised to obey the church and the pope as vicar of Christ. Pirckheimer found it much easier to abjure all heresy and readily turned against Luther, whom he had once greatly admired, and even against Spengler for continuing to support Luther.[26]

chapter four

EARLY RELIGIOUS CHANGES

Lazarus Spengler, thoroughly shaken by the realization that he, with Luther, Pirckheimer, and others, had been excommunicated unjustly and without a hearing, became even more disgusted with the papacy and the entire ecclesiastical hierarchy of the church while at the Diet of Worms and returned to Nuremberg an avowed proponent of Luther and his doctrines. That his conflict with Eck had not adversely affected the high regard of the City Council of Nuremberg for him is demonstrated by the fact that it included him as a delegate to the diet together with Kaspar Nützel and Leonhard Groland. Other influential citizens of Nuremberg were present from time to time.

POLITICAL INVOLVEMENTS

In addition to devoting considerable time and effort to obtaining absolution from the papal bull by negotiating with Aleander and Charles V, Spengler was involved in political problems of great importance to Nuremberg as well as to the empire. The emperor's first diet was to meet in Nuremberg. Because of a plague that was raging there, however, it was held at Worms, and the imperial insignia, deposited in Nuremberg for safekeeping, were brought to Worms.

Nuremberg, together with other cities, welcomed the decision of Charles to come to Germany in person and sent a deputation to him in the Low Countries, where it received from him a confirmation of the imperial privileges granted the city by previous emperors. Charles's chief purpose in coming to Germany at this time was to gain support for his dynastic struggle with Francis I of France. To accomplish this, he was compelled to take into consideration the situation within the empire, especially the growing power of the territorial princes, the decline of the importance of the lesser nobles, and the ambitions of the strong imperial cities. Although he wished to establish a centralized monarchical state in Germany, the princes forced him by the "capitulation of election" to promise to maintain the constitutional system of the past, make no important political decisions without consulting with the estates in the imperial diet, employ no foreigners in German public offices, use no foreign troops for dynastic purposes on German soil, and condemn no German subject without a hearing. To assure that these conditions would be respected, the princes demanded that Charles revive the Imperial Council of Regency (*Reichsregiment*), which convened in Nuremberg in 1522 and for a few years attempted to carry out imperial reforms and strengthen the administration of the empire along federal lines.

The imperial diet remained weak and incapable of solving internal tensions and maintaining law and order. Although earlier reforms included the maintenance of Eternal Peace (*Ewiger Landfrieden*), internal disorders continued, much to the dissatisfaction of the cities that looked to the emperor for support against the territorial ambitions of the princes and the depredations and plunderings on the part of the lower nobility. Because neither the Council of Regency nor the Imperial Chamber Court (*Reichskammergericht*) proved effective, Charles relied for most of the first decade of his rule on the Swabian League. Comprising south German princes, counts, knights, and cities, it proved effective in suppressing the revolt of the imperial knights in 1523 and the Peasants' Revolt in 1525. It became hopelessly ineffective, however, in solving internal religious divisions.

Nuremberg and other German cities were compelled to pay the lion's share of the costs of the Imperial Council of Regency and the Imperial Chamber Court. They might have been willing to do this if these institutions could have maintained law and order; but because they could not, the cities submitted to the emperor at the Frankfurt Fair a supplication written by Spengler.[1] In reponse to their request for greater security, the emperor and the estates did no more than declare another Eternal Peace at the Diet of Worms, a renewal of the ineffective one of 1495. In other words, law and order in the empire depended to a large degree on the military strength of the cities and the good will of the territorial princes. In Nuremberg's diplomatic discussions with the rulers of Brandenburg and the Palatinate, Spengler played a leading role, for he had become thoroughly acquainted with the details of the conflicts of the city with these principalities, especially those having to do with territorial claims. This is clear in his summary report on these negotiations to the city council.[2]

In March 1521, when Spengler still hoped that Pirckheimer and he would receive fair treatment by the papal legate Aleander at the Diet of Worms and that the pope would approach the problems associated with the evangelical movement with an open mind, there was published anonymously the clever *Dialogue at the Apothecary Shop*.[3] In it the author, believed by some to have been Spengler, portrays God as a person in charge of an apothecary shop, the Christian Church; the papacy as the *Unguentum apostolicum*, or apostolic ointment, represented in Worms by Archbishop Albert of Mainz; the priesthood as the *Unguenta*, or anointed; and those who support Luther as the *Radices*, or roots, claiming that Luther's doctrines are rooted in the *Angelica*, or the Gospel. During the verbal battle that the apothecary overhears, the *Herbae*, or herbs, seek to act as mediators, claiming that they were qualified to do so because they came from the roots and are the source of the ointments. When the *Apostolicum* states that Luther's works are to be condemned and burned, the *Herbae* answer that these works should not be destroyed without a fair hearing because they are rooted in the *Angelica*. This sets the stage for a discussion of the pride, love of luxury, immorality, misuse of church property, and false preaching on the part of the pope and his courtesans that will lead to God's righteous judgment and their downfall. But the dialogue ends on a happy note, with the pope's acceptance of the evangelical doctrine of the Lord's Supper.

Indicative of the impact that the Diet of Worms had on Spengler's attitude toward Luther and the evangelical movement is his report on the diet as a whole.[4] He divided those in attendance into two groups, those who favored the pope rather than divine truth and those who had the good of God's kingdom and the Holy Roman Empire at heart. He stated that the decision of 19 February to permit Luther to come to Worms was made because people were reading Luther's works so avidly that any acts harmful to him could easily lead to a revolt against the clergy.

Like Luther, Spengler was impressed by the young emperor, whom he considered honest and sincere but misled by those who had provided him with misinformation concerning the reformer. Spengler's patriotic and Christian fervor was directed especially against the higher ecclesiastical lords. In his report he contrasted the behavior of many of the higher clergy, some of whom had lost thousands of gulden in gambling during Holy Week, with Luther and his behavior during his "passion." While neglecting urgent business, such as providing security for merchants who were being robbed and murdered even near Worms, the estates were enjoying themselves with trifles. Spengler summarized his opinion of Luther by stating that the reformer had deported himself in the public hearings "so courageously, in such a Christian and honorable manner, that I believe that the Romanists and their secret and open supporters would have given thousands of gulden not to have demanded his presence and seen and heard him."[5] Although we do not know for certain whether Spengler attended the meetings in which Luther appeared before the emperor on 17 and 18 April, we know that he or other citizens of Nuremberg were present and that one of them, Sixt Oelhaven, was in Luther's living quarters when he returned from the second meeting and uttered the well known words, "I am through, I am through." We also know that Spengler was impressed by the large number of nobles as well as common people who became his followers because of his courage. He was thoroughly convinced that Luther was being persecuted for the basest of motives and that he would have avoided all this, including the charge of heresy, if he had accepted the divine right of the papacy, the authority of the church, and the money arrangements that supported both. The pope and his supporters, Spengler believed, were in the case of Luther plaintiffs, witnesses, judges, and executors at the same time.

In concluding his report, Spengler summarizes what he has learned from Luther's books, namely, that Luther humbles men and magnifies God; that by a strong faith man receives a gracious judge in God; that the correct attitude of the heart is more important than outward works and ceremonies; that man must obey God rather than man and the church; that the more sinful man is, the more he must call upon God; that there is a great difference between Holy Scripture and the teachings of the scholastics and the church; that the true believer is opposed to good works as a means for obtaining salvation; and that God punishes abuses of the clergy and shows man how he can free himself from them. In turning to the papal bull, he asks who has given the pope the right to try Luther without a hearing, stating that it is dangerous to order new procedures and doctrines. Such matters, he maintains, should be referred to a church council.[6] Although Aleander did not publish the bull of January 1521, the *Decet pontificem romanum*, at the diet, it was common knowledge that it included Spengler among the "four horned Lutheran beasts" with Luther, Hutten, and Pirckheimer, who now must be absolved by the pope himself. Spengler approached both Aleander and the imperial court about the possibility of obtaining papal absolution. On 26 May, Aleander reported to Rome that Spengler, who no longer was in

Worms, was completely contrite and had assured him of complete obedience to the pope. Therefore Aleander recommended that the pope absolve him and Pirckheimer, whose contrition had been reported to him. How much Aleander exaggerated the contrition of these two men we do not know. It is obvious, however, that he was aware of the fact that his solution of this difficult problem would enhance his reputation.

The representatives of Nuremberg sent their last report home on 23 May, stating that they were leaving Worms because the imperial recess (*Abschied*) had been heard by the estates. On 25 May, the few remaining members of the diet accepted the Edict of Worms against Luther. On the way home, Spengler, who had made a good impression on the elector of the Palatinate, was included among those invited to his castle at Heidelberg. Spengler, having contributed to the solution of difficulties between Nuremberg and the Palatinate, had increased his stature among his contemporaries and began to play a dominant role in the events leading to the reformation of the city. On 1 June, his handwriting again appeared in the records of the city council. The absolution of both Spengler and Pirckheimer was recognized in the papal curia but it is not known when or how it was announced in Nuremberg.

HALTING STEPS TOWARD REFORMATION

Matters of general concern now took precedence over personal issues in Nuremberg as well as throughout the empire. In Nuremberg, the city council proceeded with caution. Although it frequently demanded of the printers that they obey the Edict of Worms by refraining from printing and selling Luther's books,[7] it did not seem to enforce its demands. At the same time, it decided not to publish the Edict because of the dangerous mood of the people and because it wished to await the action of other cities. It was during this time that Spengler's sister Margaretha, wife of Jörgen von Kirnhofen, administrator at Hiltpoltstein, wrote him a comforting letter, which he answered by writing his *A Comforting Christian Instruction and Medicine for All Adversities*.[8] In it he demonstrates his confidence in the victory of the evangelical cause by quoting Psalm 126:5: "They that sow in tears shall reap in joy." He demonstrates the maturity of his evangelical views, strengthened by his contacts with Luther in Nuremberg and at the Diet of Worms. He emphasizes that one cannot have fortune without misfortune and well-being without adversity; that God sends man misfortunes to keep him good and preserve him from the dangers of sin; that God often sends plagues, illnesses, and afflictions to increase his divine glory and sanctify his holy name; and that through temptation, affliction, and misfortune, all burdens are made light and all bitterness sweet. "I must confess," he writes, "that the Old Adam often holds me by the hair and advises me to ask God to remove the cup of adversity from me, while the Holy Spirit in me says, 'Lord, not my, but thy will be done.'"

The impact of the events connected with the Diet of Worms on Spengler's circle in Nuremberg can best be expressed in the words of Albrecht Dürer. When the artist, then on a year's sojourn in the Low Countries, learned that Luther had been seized on his way home from Worms and feared that he had been killed, expressed his deep remorse and concern in his diary.[9] He had shown his interest in the Reformation and his appreciation for what Luther had done for him on numerous occasions before the Diet of Worms. As early as 1518 he sent the reformer a gift, presumably a picture. The next year he asked Nicholas von Amsdorf of the University of Wittenberg to send him one of Luther's writings.[10] In 1520, he asked Luther, through Spalatin, to care for the well-being of Frederick the Wise and announced that he intended to make a copper etching of Luther "to provide a long remembrance of the Christian man who has helped me out of great distress." He also promised Spalatin to send him Spengler's *Defense*, of which there were at that time no more copies in Nuremberg but which was being reprinted in Augsburg.[11]

It was not until 18 October 1521 that the city council reluctantly decided to publish the Edict of Worms.[12] Even the bishop of Bamberg waited until 25 October to do so. It had been sent to Nuremberg soon after it had been issued by Ulrich Arzt, captain of the Swabian League and bitter opponent of Luther. The council, however, did little to enforce it. Although it had the printers submit to it all Luther's books and those of his followers and on the surface seemed to do everything to maintain the old order, it permitted changes. Whereas it demanded of the clergy that they "adhere to the Gospel and Christian doctrine," it permitted a latitude of interpretation that favored change.

APPOINTMENT OF LUTHERAN PROVOSTS AND PREACHERS

That the majority of the members of the city council had chosen to follow the leadership of Kaspar Nützel, Hieronymus Ebner, and Lazarus Spengler by supporting the cause of reform is shown not only by the council's action with respect to the publication of Luther's books but also by its appointment of new clergymen for the parish churches.[13] An important step had been taken in the summer of 1520 when, at the death of Georg Beheim, the provost of the parish church of Saint Lorenz, the council appointed Hektor Pömer (1495-1541), a young patrician follower of Luther who was at that time studying in Wittenberg, to replace him. Because Pömer wished to complete his studies and obtain the doctor's degree in law before returning to Nuremberg, he did not assume his duties until the next year, after having been ordained as a priest by the bishop of Bamberg. In October 1521, the council induced Melchior Pfinzing, an outspoken opponent of Luther, to resign his position as provost of Saint Sebald, the other parish church. It offered the position to Hieronymus Baumgartner (1498-1565), son of councilman Bernhard Baumgartner and also a strong Lutheran, a former student and personal friend of both Luther and Melanchthon. Luther had at one time hoped that Hieronymus would marry Katharina von Bora.[14] When Hieronymus declined the offer of provost because of his youth and inexperience, the council, ignoring the wishes of the bishop of Bamberg, appointed Georg Pesler (ca. 1470-1536), another citizen of Nuremberg who had studied law and theology at Wittenberg and was a strong supporter of Luther.

The control of the city council over the two parish churches of Saint Sebald and Saint Lorenz had been well established before the Reformantion, for it had for a long time considered the maintenance of the general welfare as including the spiritual life of its citizens and had obtained from the papacy a share in the selection of the city's provosts and clergy. The bishop, residing at Bamberg, a considerable distance from Nuremberg, could offer little resistance to this growth of ecclesiastical authority of the council, especially because the council had control of church benefices and used the city's wealth to gain other advantages. Through the appointment of council members as superintendents (*Kirchenpfleger*) over the churches and other religious institutions, it controlled virtually all matters related to property, benefices, and money. Pope Sixtus IV in 1474 gave the council the right of presentation, that is, the right to nominate a candidate for the position of provost at each of the two parish churches, with the pope retaining the right of confirmation. This procedure was to be applied only when the incumbents had died during the "papal months," that is, the odd months of the year. In 1513, the council gained from the bishop the right to employ the same procedure in the event that the incumbents had died during the "bishop's months," the even months. For this right, the council paid the bishop one thousand gulden cash and one hundred gulden annually. In 1514, the council obtained from the pope a grant giving it complete patronage over the parish churches.

Because the provosts and the majority of the city council favored the Reformation, it is not surprising that the parish clergy were in time all Lutherans. One of the foremost reformers among them was Andreas Osiander (1496-1552), with whom Spengler dealt in all important ecclesiastical and doctrinal matters.[15] Born only a few miles from Nuremberg, the brilliant son of poor parents, Osiander overcame many obstacles to obtain a good education. He attended schools at Leipzig and Altenburg and then the University of Ingolstadt, where he became proficient in Latin, Greek, and Hebrew, but also in philosophy, mathematics, and medicine. It was he, as we have seen, who wrote the introduction to the first edition of Copernicus's *Revolution of Heavenly Bodies* and saw it through the press in Nuremberg. He was a forceful preacher, highly respected by Spengler and the city council, but also obstinate and intolerant of the views of others. After entering the priesthood, he came to the Augustinian monastery in Nuremberg in 1520 as a teacher of Hebrew and soon became a Lutheran. Influenced by Neoplatonism, however, he espoused the doctrine that man was justified before God through Christ, received in man through the Word of God and the sacrament of the Lord's Supper. This doctrine later was the cause of serious conflicts with other Lutheran theologians. On 20 March 1522, the council approved his appointment as a preacher at Saint Lorenz upon the recommendation of Provost Hektor Pömer.

On 23 February 1524, the council, upon the recommendation of Luther, made Dominicus Schleupner (d. 1547), a native of Silesia, the preacher at Saint Sebald for his lifetime. The contract containing the mutual rights and duties of council and preacher had been arranged by Spengler and two members of the council. It stipulated that Schleupner should, "during his lifetime as long as he was able, preach the Word of God and the Holy Gospel purely and simply."[16] Such a contract in place of an appointment to an independent church living was new. Illustrative of how rapidly the council was assuming the right of appointment was the case of a chantry priest of the altar of Saint Wenceslas in the Church of Saint Mary. As early as June 1523, the council's advisers suggested that the man be asked to resign and, if he did not comply, that he be replaced by another person without resignation, adding that, in this case, the council should not obtain the confirmation of the bishop of Bamberg but should act solely on its own authority.[17]

CHANGES IN THE MONASTERIES

Meanwhile, Lutheran doctrines spread among the monks, particularly among those of the Augustinian monastery, where the

Martinians continued to meet to discuss books and pamphlets emanating from Wittenberg and the issues raised in the indulgence controversy. Among the new leaders of this circle was the Augustinian prior Wolfgang Volprecht, who in 1518 had given Peypus the printer a sermon against indulgences for publication for which Volprecht received a reprimand from the city council. He probably was the first clergyman of Nuremberg to administer the Lord's Supper in both kinds, that is, to give the wine as well as the bread to the laity, although at first only in a small, intimate circle of trusted friends. This was in Holy Week, 1523. In May 1524, he read the Mass in German, revised to exlcude parts offensive to Lutherans. After leaving the monastery, Volprecht became a preacher at the Hospital of the Holy Spirit, together with Thomas Jäger, called Venatorius (d. 1551), a humanist friend of Reuchlin and Pirckheimer. They served under the chief preacher there, Wenceslas Linck (1483-1547), a close friend of Luther and Spengler who had returned to Nuremberg in August 1521.

Abbot Wolfgang Sommer of Saint Egidien, a Scottish Benedictine monastery founded in 1140 and the oldest monastery in the city, was detested by the Lutherans and as a consequence was replaced by Friedrich Pistorius (1486-1553), a friend of Pirckheimer and later also of Melanchthon. He became a vigorous supporter of the Lutheran movement. Leadership in the other monasteries in Nuremberg remained Catholic until later, although numerous monks began to leave them and created problems for their superiors and the city council. In addition to the Benedictines with their church at Saint Egidien and the Augustinians with the church of Saint Vitus, there were the Dominicans, who had established their monastery on land north of the city hall on the slope leading to the castle; the Carmelites, who were located south of the Pegnitz River in the parish of Saint Lorenz; the Franciscans, just north of the River and also in the parish of Saint Lorenz; the Teutonic Knights, with their Church of Saint Jakob and Hospital of Saint Elisabeth (later called "Old Hospital" to distinguish it from the "New Hospital" of the Holy Spirit), who had established themselves outside the old walls in 1200 but who now were within the new walls in the southwestern part of the city; and the Carthusians, the youngest monastery in the city, who also built outside the old walls in 1380 but later were within the new ones, on the site today occupied by the Germanic Museum.

There were two convents in the city, that of Saint Clara and that of Saint Katherine. The former, originally the Convent of Mary Magdalen, was assigned to the Clares, who had adopted the rule of Saint Francis. Numerous daughters of influential citizens entered this order, including the two sisters of Willibald Pirckheimer, Caritas (1467-1532) and Clara (1480-1533), and a daughter, Katherine. The Convent of Saint Katherine, originally endowed as a hospital, adopted the Dominican rule. Many of the nuns of this order also were from influential families, as, for example, Felicitas Tucher, its last prioress.

By the time of the Reformation, the city council of Nuremberg exercized considerable control over the city's monasteries and convents. It acted as their administrator and protector, and through the official it appointed for each monastery, the *Schaffer*, it kept itself informed with respect to what went on and kept a firm hand on all administrative matters. It took an active interest in supervising the lives of monks and nuns, and it participated in, and encouraged, reforms from time to time.

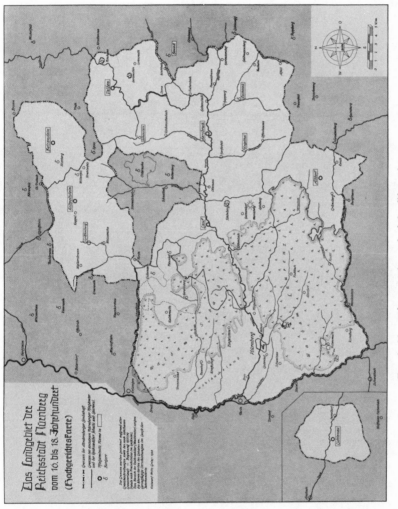

Fig. 1. Nuremberg at the end of the fifteenth century.

chapter five

THE ROAD TO REFORMATION

Prepared by legal training, religious study, and practical political experience, Spengler played a leading role during Nuremberg's progress on the road to Reformation after the Diet of Worms. He seemed able to keep all the many kinds of problems facing the city council in proper perspective and to assist it in steering a course that did not alienate it from Emperor Charles V and the empire to which it owed its allegiance and from which alone it expected support in its struggles with territorial princes. Skillful diplomat and administrator, he helped the council pursue a steady course despite the storms aroused by a determined populace supported by clergymen and intellectuals demanding religious and even social changes on the one hand and the church supported by the emperor demanding a return to the old religious order. This occurred during the critical years when Nuremberg was the focal point of virtually all the powerful political, social, economic, religious, and cultural currents of Germany as the Imperial Council of Regency and the Imperial Chamber Court convened within its walls (1521-24) and the diet of the Holy Roman Empire met there three times (1522-24).

The Council of Regency convened in Nuremberg in the fall of 1521, primarily to lay plans for the meeting of the diet in the spring of 1522. This provided an opportunity for Spengler and other influential citizens to meet its important members and those of the diet and for the latter to become acquainted with the powerful religious currents operative in a dynamic urban community. Because the diet that assembled in the spring of 1522 was poorly attended, it was ineffective in coping with such urgent questions as enforcement of the Edict of

Worms, ecclesiastical jurisdiction, demands of the cities for a greater voice in the diets, the breaking of the Eternal Peace by the robber barons, minting problems, the large number of tolls, monopolies and restrictions in business, and the threatening Turks, who had taken Belgrade.

Among the prominent members of the Council of Regency who were in close contact with the citizens of Nuremberg was Johann Freiherr von Schwarzenberg, chief steward in the episcopal court at Bamberg and later in the service of the margrave of Brandenburg-Ansbach. He was an imposing person, well educated, a highly respected jurist, and deeply religious, a layman who had opposed work righteousness and indulgences and had enunciated a doctrine of justification by faith before Luther. He became a close friend of Willibald Pirckheimer, to whom he dedicated one of his translations of Plutarch's works.[1] Elector Frederick the Wise attended the meetings of the Council of Regency during much of the summer of 1522 and was in Nuremberg again from November 1523 to February 1524, accompanied by Philipp von Feilitsch, Friedrich von Thun, and Spalatin. He became a friend of Hieronymus Ebner, Kaspar Nützel, Anton Tucher, and Lazarus Spengler. Hans von der Planitz was the influential delegate of Frederick the Wise in the Council of Regency from October 1521 to June 1524. A convinced Lutheran who maintained close contacts with Spengler and kept his prince well informed on events transpiring in Nuremberg,[2] he did much to further the Lutheran cause.

Of great significance was the presence in the Council of Regency of Albert of Brandenburg, the well-educated grand master of the Teutonic Knights, who became a friend of a number of patricians and of Andreas Osiander. Influential in developing the evangelical religious views of Albert, Osiander later left Nuremberg to serve him after the grand master had become a Lutheran and duke of Prussia (1525-68). Count Palatine Frederick, the *Statthalter*, or imperial representative, at the Council of Regency's first meeting brought with him to Nuremberg his chaplain, Martin Butzer (1491-1551), an early supporter of Luther who had good connections with the elector of the Palatinate and the elector of Trier. It was apparently not easy for the strong opponents of Luther, the bishop of Bamberg, the bishop of Augsburg, Duke George of Saxony, and the archbishop of Salzburg, to get the Council of Regency to desert its moderate religious course. The constant presence of the dominant personality of Planitz assured the continuation of the position of the elector of Saxony. As a consequence, the Council of Regency issued a weak mandate on 20 January 1522, making no reference to Luther or the Edict of Worms and urging the diet to make no religious changes until the meeting of a general church council. The diet agreed to allot for the time being a half of the amount requested for aid against the Turks and set 1 September 1522 as the date for the opening of a new diet in Nuremberg.[3]

REFORMATION PUBLICATIONS

Meanwhile, Spengler was developing his evangelical religious convictions, studying church history, humanist works, and writings of the reformers, making excerpts from his sources as well as from the sermons of Lutheran preachers.[4] From the *Ecclesiastical History* of Eusebius and the *Tripartite History* of Cassiodorus, he obtained a general view of the condition of the church during its first centuries and made comparisons between it and the church of the sixteenth century. From Marsiglio of Padua's *Defender of the Peace* he obtained many excerpts concerning limitations of papal authority. Pierre d'Ailly's *Reformation of the Church* gave him a clear conception of the need for church reforms and means for accomplishing them. Spengler found D'Ailly's demands for reform substantiated by numerous humanist works, including the well-known chronicle of Hartmann Schedel that includes the dramatic account of Emperor Henry IV's conflict with Pope Gregory VII. Important for the basic organization of his theology was Philip Melanchthon's *Common Points of Proof* of 1521, the first attempt at a systematic presentation of Luther's evangelical theology.

On the basis of these studies, Spengler wrote another defense of Luther, "Why Luther's Teaching is a Necessity and Protection."[5] Although he did not publish the work, we are familiar with its contents. Writing in a humanist style and using humanist methods, he argues that Luther, like Saint Paul, places the content, or essence, of Christianity above the person while adding a new emphasis, the use of examples of the pagan Romans in stressing the importance of the common welfare of the fatherland, stating that Christians should serve the common welfare of Christianity by protecting and honoring the Word of God. It is significant that Spengler, like the city council, insists throughout these critical years that he is following the Gospel and the Word of God, not Luther or any other person.

Spengler gave expression to his practical ethical concerns as well as his opposition to the papal church in another pamphlet, *The Main Articles Through Which Christendom Has Been Misled*, published anonymously by Nikel Schirlenz in Wittenberg toward the end of 1522. Nikolaus Amsdorf, in a covering letter sent to a friend with a copy of the pamphlet, stated that the booklet had been written by a layman and dedicated to a layman, Frederick the Wise, with whom Spengler had had many contacts in Nuremberg that summer. Like Erasmus in his *Handbook of a Christian Soldier*, Spengler's concern is for raising public morality. This is apparent in the subtitle, *Basis of and Information Concerning a Complete, Correct Christianity.*[6]

It is obvious that *The Main Articles* is based on Melanchthon's *Common Points of Proof* and Luther's *Freedom of a Christian Man.* He lists four main errors by means of which the papal church has misled Christians: (1) the doctrine of the freedom of the will, which has led people to believe that they did not need God's saving grace; (2) the emphasis on good works as merits, which has resulted in the "gathering of whole wagon loads of works and sending them up to heaven"; (3) obscuring the Word of God by emphasizing human doctrines and laws, the "vermin and corruption" that follow in the wake of scholasticism in which Saint Paul must give way to Thomas Aquinas; and (4) the division of Christ's teachings into a double standard of ethics, one for the clergy and one for the laity, inferring that the regular clergy can obtain ethical perfection by means of monastic vows, special vestments, diets, prayers, and masses. Spengler was particularly severe with monks who believed that they were more pleasing to God than laymen because of their cowls and despite their frequent moral lapses. Like Luther, Spengler frequently alluded to the original functions of monasteries as schools. Accordingly he later supported the transformation of the Augustinian monastery into a school and was instrumental in founding the new Gymnasium at the Monastery of Saint Egidien.

Spengler now became so deeply involved in the critical events transpiring in Nuremberg that for the next two years he devoted less time to writing and gained considerable practical experience in helping solve the important issues of the day. Supported by Hieronymus Ebner, Kasper Nützel, Hieronymus Baumgartner, and Hieronymus Holzschuer, he became the driving force in the city council, serving as its spokesman in the affairs touching the empire and particularly those having to do with the Reformation in the city.

SECOND DIET OF NUREMBERG

When the second imperial diet convened in Nuremberg on 17 November 1522, Archduke Ferdinand presided, with anti-Lutherans seemingly in control. Nevertheless, there was so much discontent in Germany that statesmen must have felt as though they were sitting on a volcano. Political, economic, and social motives were now added to religious demands for change among nobles, townsmen, and peasants. Widespread dissatisfaction among the nobles led to the Knights' War, 1522-23, also called the Sickingen Feud after the name of its leader, whose castle, the Ebernburg, long had been a place of refuge for persecuted humanists and reformers. During the ill-fated attack on the elector of Trier by Franz von Sickingen and the relatively few knights who had joined him, the Imperial Council of Regency was powerless to prevent either the revolutionary violence of the knights or the vicious retaliation of the princes.[7] Attempts of the knights to gain allies among the townsmen explains the fact that Spengler came into possession of a manuscript prepared by Hartmuth von Kronberg, a strong supporter of Sickingen and the knights and a consistent follower of Luther who did not, however, participate in the attack on Trier.[8] In this manuscript, Kronberg urged the imperial cities to join the knights in freeing the Gospel and thereby bringing salvation to all men as well as peace and justice on earth. But the knights could scarcely be protectors of the cities and robber barons at the same time.

To gain protection for their merchants, Nuremberg and other cities first turned for help to the Imperial Council of Regency, which, however, did little more than send mandates to the robbers. Then they appealed to the imperial diet, in which they had an ineffective voice and often little sympathy from the princes, many of whom were heavily in debt to them. They likewise received little help from the Swabian League, to which they belonged. They were therefore compelled to draw close together to form common programs of action among themselves, as they did when attempts were made to impose imperial customs duties on their trade with which to pay for the support of the Imperial Council of Regency and the Imperial Chamber Court. Spengler served as an active leader among the cities and at their assemblies. He also produced a brief outline of his thoughts on the matter for Emperor Charles V, arguing that the projected customs duty would harm the empire as a whole, the majority of the estates, and especially the cities.[10]

The imperial cities also had a strong common interest in religious developments, especially with respect to the question of ecclesiastical jurisdiction. Present at the second Diet of Nuremberg to represent papal interests was the papal nuncio, Francesco Chieregati (1478-1539), who, as Spengler informed Frederick the Wise, came with the double purpose of preaching a crusade against the Turks and suppressing Lutheranism.[11] At a combined session of the Council of Regency and the diet on 3 January 1522, Chieregati presented the papal breve demanding that the estates enforce the Edict of Worms and root out the Lutheran heresy.[12] Following this, to the surprise of all, Chieregati admitted that the pope recognized the presence of serious abuses in the papal curia that had filtered down through the entire ecclesiastical hierarchy and stated that Luther's bringing these abuses to light was a divine punishment for the sins of the papacy, prelates, and priests.[13] But later, when the estates had agreed to grant aid against the Turks, the papal nuncio represented a much less conciliatory papal position. When he demanded that the Lutheran preachers of Nuremberg be arrested and compelled to submit to trial for heresy, the committee chosen to consider the religious issues and to report to the nuncio argued that the pope's admission of abuses made it impossible to criticize Luther for having called attention to them and to enforce the Edict of Worms. It also urged that the pope answer the long-standing grievances of the estates against the curia by summoning a "free, Christian" church council comprising secular as well as ecclesiastical delegates to meet within a year to solve the religious questions. Meanwhile, Luther and his followers should do nothing to cause disturbances and should preach the Gospel according to the church fathers Jerome, Augustine, Gregory, and Ambrose, under the supervision of episcopal committees. The influential Planitz succeeded in having the names of the four fathers deleted from the instruction of the committee of the estates. It is noteworthy that the words "Gospel" and "evangelical" by now had come to denote Lutheran doctrines and that an attack on Lutheranism was considered an attack on the Gospel and the Word of God. Spengler and most of the members of the City Council of Nuremberg supported this instruction of the committee with enthusiasm.[14]

The city council, accused of harboring heretical preachers and permitting the publication of Lutheran books on religious matters, was ordered by Chieregati to publish only anti-Lutheran materials. The council selected a committee made up of the Seven Elders and Endres Tucher, Sebald Pfinzing, Sigmund Fürer, and Lazarus Spengler to recommend an appropriate response.[15] The council refused to arrest the preachers and turn them over for trial. Instead, it prepared to protect them by force, if necesesary. Like Spengler, the council consistently maintained that it was supporting the Gospel and the Word of God, not Luther or any other person. It agreed, however, to permit the publication solely of anti-Lutheran books but only after they had been inspected by the Council, that is, by Spengler, who remained the chief censor of books until 1528. The firm position of the council proved effective, for there was no further threat made by the nuncio against the preachers.

About the middle of January 1523, the committee of the estates concerned with religious matters requested of the three ecclesiastical princes present, the electors, the princes, and the cities their written memorandums concerning the religious problem. Only that of the cities is still extant, presumably written by Spengler.[16] It supported the report of the committee of the Imperial Council of Regency to the nuncio, stating that, if followed by the emperor and the pope, the main differences within the church would be solved, conflicts among the estates would be averted, and God and his Word would be honored.

Arguments of the opposing factions, however, were continued in the small committee of the Council of Regency and in the large committee of the estates as well as in the diet. Despite the objections of Chieregati and his supporters, the diet in its final decree, or recess, of 9 February 1523, included the statement that nothing should be preached or published "except the true, clear, and pure Gospel according to the doctrine and interpretation of Scripture as approved and accepted by the Christian Church." This amounted to a distinct victory for the Lutherans, for it permitted, in effect, the free preaching of the Gospel and the abrogation of the Edict of Worms, even though Luther's enemies interpreted it otherwise.[17]

Although the people of Nuremberg had been aroused by the threatened attacks on their preachers and openly showed their hostility toward Chieregati and other opponents of Luther, the council experienced little difficulty in maintaining order. Still, important questions arose in connection with Lent and Easter in 1523. The council forbade the passion play at the Hospital of the Holy Spirit and resisted the demands in the parish churches for communion in both kinds, hoping that it would be much easier to decide such important matters after the meeting of a general church council. On Maundy Thursday, however, the Augustinians solemnly celebrated communion in both kinds but with only a select few lay citizens participating.[18]

The excitement of the common man over the preaching of the Gospel with its promise of reforms and hope for the future was intensified by the publication of simple pamphlet literature, especially that written by Hans Sachs. On 8 July 1523, he published his well-known *The Wittenberg Nightingale*,[19] a poem of 700 verses in which he presents the evils of the church that have obscured the Gospel message and then a summary of Luther's theology that the people have been hearing in the sermons of their evangelical preachers and reading in the pamphlets of Spengler and others. This is done with such beautiful imagery as that in the first few lines, in which Sachs portrays the nightingale announcing with "its dulcet call" the end of the long night, the fading away of the moon and "moon creatures," and the coming of the sun. Most of the poem consists of a mechanically contrived, long-winded account of the story of salvation. But it is a simple presentation in the language of the people that did much to give meaning to the urban life of the time and to provide hope for the future, both on earth and in heaven, infusing their secular as well as religious institutions with new life and relevance. This poem, together with popular dialogues discussing issues of the day and with hymns, appeared in many editions, both in Nuremberg and elsewhere. It is no wonder that many representatives of the old order demanded that Hans Sachs the cobbler "stick to his last."

In 1523 there appeared another apology for Luther written by Spengler. It was published anonymously under the title *Responsibiity For and Analysis of Some Alleged Arguments and Causes Used Daily to Oppose and Suppress the Word of God and the Holy Gospel By Those Who Are Not Christian But Claim To Be.*[20] Repeating much that he had stated in his *Why Luther's Teaching is a Necessity and Protection*, he now addresses himself primarily to the masses in an attempt to bring them to the Word of God, using arguments raised in answer to Chieregati's attack on the Lutherans of 10 December 1522. To the charge that the church fathers, church councils, and many theologians would be in error if Luther's doctrines were correct, he answers that no authority can prevail against the clear Word of God, adding that one must not follow teachings of the fathers if they are wrong. The preaching of the Gospel does not cause unrest and revolt among believing Christians, as Chieregati claims, but only among the godless. In answer to the charge that Lutheran preaching leads to ethical decline because of the deemphasis of good works as merits, he points to the evils associated with the work-righteousness of his opponents. Finally, Spengler denies Chieregati's statement that the Bible is not unequivocally clear but needs to be interpreted by the church, the church fathers, and the church councils. Such an argument he calls a blasphemy against God.

Spengler's publication of this apology between the second and third diets in Nuremberg marked the apex of his literary support of Luther and the Reformation. Meanwhile, other events occurred that were leading Nuremberg toward her break with Rome. Political circumstances were such that Spengler and the city council could defend changes that had been made and press for more. Although most of the estates were hostile to the cities and sought to place the largest share of financial burdens on them, a few influential princes proved to be friendly to them. Frederick the Wise, for example, remained consistently cooperative with Nuremberg. Albert, grand master of the Teutonic Knights, who had quarters in Nuremberg from October 1522 to April 1524, maintained close connections with Nützel, Spengler, and Osiander. He also influenced his brother, Margrave Casimir, the traditional opponent of Nuremberg, to express his willingness to compromise long-standing differences, if only for financial and political rather than for religious reasons. Casimir's chief secretary, Georg Vogler, by now a close friend of Lazarus Spengler, cooperated with him in carrying out the Reformation in the lands of their respective governments.

THIRD DIET OF NUREMBERG

The third imperial Diet of Nuremberg opened in the parish church of Saint Sebald on 14 January 1524, Ferdinand presiding, flanked by the electors of Saxony and the Palatinate. Threatened by the advancing Turks and greatly in need of money, Ferdinand tried to mediate between the estates and the cities. The change in the political climate was demonstrated by the fact that Spengler, formerly excommunicated by the pope, now was the recipient of an outstanding imperial honor. On 15 February 1524, he received from Ferdinand a document, signed by Emperor Charles, granting him and his brother Georg an improvement of their family coat of arms in recognition of their services to the empire. The old one consisted of a shield divided vertically with the dexter field of silver containing half of a red rose with three petals and the sinister field in red containing half of a silver lily. The silver helmet at the top was closed and had two closed silver and red wings with a half-rose and a half-lily respectively. This was changed to include in the center above the shield the bust of an armless virgin in a red dress and yellow hair between the two wings of an imperial eagle, indicating the close association of the Spenglers to the city of Nuremberg and the Holy Roman Empire. As a special favor, they were permitted to use blue wax for their seals, indicating that they and their heirs were "authentic noble bearers of arms" of the Holy Roman Empire, entitled to all the rights and privileges associated with this honor.[21] In January 1547, the City Council of Nuremberg placed the Spengler coat of arms in a window of the church at Wöhrd.[22]

This act of kindness to the Spenglers on the part of the emperor did not mean that he would be lenient toward the Lutherans. As a matter of fact, in his preliminary instructions to the diet he mentioned nothing about a church council but requested the enforcement of the Edict of Worms against Luther. The new pope, Clement VII (1523-34), supported this approach as part of a program of counter-Reformation. To represent him and his concerns, Clement sent to Nuremberg the legally trained and diplomatically experienced Cardinal Lorenzo Campeggio (1474-1539), who was well acquainted with conditions in Germany. Although officially he was courteously received by the city and tactfully met with Scheurl, the city elders, and Spengler on different occasions, he could not effect a change in the attitude of Nuremberg toward the new doctrine.[23]

As the cities now began to play a more significant role in the imperial diet, Spengler's importance increased correspondingly. His views, as expressed in a memorandum written for the cities before the opening of the third diet, prevailed among them. He insisted on making clear that the cities did not support Luther or any other person but Christ and the Gospel; that they would remain loyal to, and support, the emperor but could not act contrary to their consciences by recognizing anyone as superior to Christ. They advised letting the preaching of the Gospel run its course because the use of force against it would be insane. They supported the decision of the diet in its recess of 9 February 1523, to the effect that a free, German council should meet on German soil to solve the problems raised by Luther. Finally, Spengler suggested that the cities put the papacy on the defensive by pressing grievances of the diet against it. Strassburg, Frankfurt, and Ulm expressed agreement with this memorandum although the city representatives at the diet were not bound to follow its recommendations.[24]

When the estates ignored the requests of the cities, these, encouraged by Spengler and Ulrich Rehlinger, city secretary of Augsburg, stated firmly that they would abide by the decision of the previous diet to continue preaching the Gospel according to the interpretation of the church until a final decision had been reached at a free church council. Any other course, they insisted, would lead the people to revolt, for they insisted on hearing the Word of God. Therefore, they rejected the demand of the pope through Campeggio that the Edict of Worms be enforced.

In February 1524, Archduke Ferdinand ordered the seven elders of Nuremberg's city council to appear before him. When, out of fear that they might be arrested, the council sent only four of them, Ferdinand charged them with permitting the publication and sale of heretical books and of books slandering the emperor, the preaching of heretical doctrines in the city churches, the toleration of renegade monks and nuns in the city, and preaching on the streets by peasants and other outsiders, all in defiance of the Edict of Worms.

The city council's reply to Ferdinand of 5 March, probably drafted by
Spengler,[25] contains an excellent summary of the council's official
position with respect to the religious changes it had made up to that
time. It justified its actions by answering seriatim the charges made by
Ferdinand. With respect to the accusation that the council was
permitting the sale of Lutheran books and of writings slandering the
emperor, the letter affirmed the council's steadfast loyalty to the Holy
Roman Empire as seen by the fact that it was obeying the decree of the
previous diet in every respect. But it added that it was determined above
all else to serve not its own interests but the honor and glory of God by
furthering his Holy Word and the salvation of its citizens and subjects.
To this end it had forbidden the printers of Nuremberg to publish
anything without its permission and its citizens to offer for sale books
that would encourage heresy, rebellion, or slander of the emperor. It
had punished severely those who had disobeyed. Nevertheless, because
the city was a large, public market for the exchange of ideas as well as
goods, it could not prevent all persons from surreptitiously selling
forbidden books.

With respect to the charge that the city council continued to support
its preachers, the letter assured Ferdinand that the council acted in
accord with the imperial mandate demanding that only the Holy
Gospel be preached.[26] It stated that the council had brought to its
churches able preachers who did not adhere to Lutheranism or to any
other human doctrine and that it had given them the imperial mandate
with the order to conform with it in their sermons, preaching only the
Holy Gospel according to the interpretation of Scripture approved by
the Christian Church and avoiding heresy, tumult, and slander. The
thousands of people who heard the preachers, including members of
the imperial diet, could attest to the fact that the preachers obeyed the
mandate.

The monks and nuns who had renounced their monastic vows and
were making a living in Nuremberg were not interfered with provided
that they did not commit criminal acts or act contrary to the imperial
mandate. In answer to the charges against the peasant who was
preaching on the streets of Nuremberg, the letter stated that a careful
investigation had shown that he had preached nothing unchristian or
improper. Nevertheless, because of the council's desire for peace and
order, it had forbidden him to preach in the future.

On 27 March 1524, the representatives of the cities met to discuss the
position they should take in the diet in response to Campeggio's
request for action with respect to the Lutheran problem. Spengler had
drafted a memorandum for them that probably is his best statement on

the religious issues facing the diet.[27] With respect to the important matter of Lutheranism, he stated that the cities as an imperial estate should decide "whether or not they wished to be Christians." Some persons, he said, wished to be Christians but at the same time wanted to be on good terms with the majority of persons in the other estates. This was difficult, for "one cannot serve two masters." Because the cities had decided to be Christians, this matter could be resolved readily, for Christ is lord even over his enemies and is powerful enough to maintain his honor, Word, and truth. Accordingly, Spengler insisted, first, that the members of the imperial cities should make clear to the emperor, Ferdinand, and the estates as a whole, that they were Christians, baptized in the name of Christ, not in the name of Luther or any other man, and therefore were committed to follow Christ's Gospel; second, that with respect to secular matters, they acknowledged the emperor as their sole lord and would serve him loyally as their ancestors had done; and third, that, "as far as their souls and consciences were concerned, they recognized Christ alone as their lord, master, and savior who had redeemed them with his blood and to whose Word, Gospel, and commands they cling."

Although no one could deny the propriety of these answers, Spengler stated, he was not certain what the response would be; yet he outlined five possible contingencies that the city representatives should bear in mind. One was that no action would be taken for the time being until such issues as the Turkish threat were clarified. This would be the best action for the cities because it would permit the further spread of the Word of God. The second possibility was that the authorities would use force, a method shunned by all Christians for it would lead to tyranny and rebellion. The third possibility was that a number of pious, Christian, learned, and understanding men with no secular stakes in the old order would be asked to discuss and solve the main points at issue. This, he said, would be helpful but would be opposed by the clergy "who flee the light and cannot stand the truth." The fourth possibility was the submission of the matter to a church council, a procedure supported by many people but dangerous because councils had often acted contrary to the Word of God. On the other hand, a free council held in Germany might be helpful for a while. The fifth possibility was the use of edicts of excommunication and outlawry, such as the one issued at Worms but proven ineffective.

Spengler also indicated two ways in which to approach the papal legate and ecclesiastical princes who were intending to act improperly in this matter. The first was that the imperial estates should upbraid the legate for distorting to the pope the action of the previous diet concerning the preaching of the Gospel. The second was to take a firm stand against the financial and other injustices perpetrated by the pope and clergy upon the German nation, thus placing Campeggio on the defensive. Above all, the representatives of the cities should as Christians trust in God and his Word and be alert to any attempts to force the people to forsake Christ and the Holy Gospel. The cities instructed their representatives to the committee of the diet to follow Spengler's advice.

When the diet formulated a new draft of its recess, it proved so unacceptable to the cities and nobility that it was not read publicly for fear of arousing strong resentment. Backed primarily by the secular and ecclesiastical princes, it decided to postpone certain issues until the meeting of the German nation in a council at Trier that same year, which should make plans for a general church council. The cities under the leadership of Lazarus Spengler declared that they would abide by the decision of the previous diet to the effect that the Gospel should be preached freely, for the people were so eager to hear the Word of God that its suppression might lead to revolt. Calling themselves "Christian, evangelical communes," they stated that they would, if necessary, accept a "free Christian council" as arbiter in the religious matter.[28]

Campeggio, pleased that the diet had demanded enforcement of the Edict of Worms, insisted upon the strict enforcement of its new recess and objected to the solution of religious problems by a national council in which laymen participated. He would, however, support the calling of a general church council. His adamant stand alienated many who previously had been his supporters.

On 18 April, the estates issued their final recess, stating that the Germans as a nation were determined to settle the religious problems themselves.[29] The cities, having received a draft of the recess the next day, responded that they would not accept the renewal of the Edict of Worms but would support the calling of a free, Christian council of ecclesiastical and secular representatives to consider the issues. Even Ferdinand expressed his desire to renew discussions with the papal legate. The estates, however, refused to do so while Campeggio reiterated his former position.[30] He supported the renewal of the Edict of Worms, protesting against the statement in the recess that there might be some good in the teaching of "the heretics," and opposed the calling of a general council, yet stating that he would bring the matter to the attention of the pope. He opposed outright the convening of a national council, suggesting that grievances against the papacy should be settled by sending a deputation to the pope. After accepting the recess, Campeggio left Nuremberg, an unpopular and harassed person. This departure of the papal nuncio marked the end of Nuremberg's connection with the papacy. When, at the end of April, the diet had disbanded, the Imperial Council of Regency and the Imperial Chamber Court had been transferred by the recess of the diet to Esslingen, and Archduke Ferdinand had departed, the city was left to its own devices.

Although the Catholic estates were in the majority in the diet and wished to support the emperor in his attempts to enforce the Edict of Worms "as far as possible," that is, vigorously, supporters of Luther interpreted this phrase of the recess as limiting the enforcement and excusing any failure. The Lutheran princes and cities had long insisted that enforcement was impossible for it would cause tumult and revolt. Therefore, they justified their subsequent inaction by referring to this phrase.[31]

Charles V, who had received the recess of the diet in July, that same month issued from Burgos in Spain a mandate to the estates forbidding the holding of a national assembly, demanding the unconditional enforcement of the Edict of Worms, and prohibiting the public discussion of religious matters until the calling of a general church council by the pope. This new mandate seemed to the City Council of Nuremberg to be particularly severe inasmuch as the emperor threatened those who would not live up to it with the imperial ban. For this reason, the council again turned for advice to Spengler, who responded by presenting to it a detailed memorandum in the latter part of October 1524.[32]

In his memorandum, the *Ratsschreiber* expressed the opinion that the emperor's threats were directed primarily against the imperial cities and above all against Nuremberg, of which he wished to make an example. He advised the council to do nothing by itself in response to the mandate, for the emperor could not pronounce the ban or carry out any other punishment without following proper legal procedure. Before a city could be banned, its case would have to be brought before the Council of Regency for discussion and then the Imperial Chamber Court, where it would be tried according to imperial law. Moreover, he insisted, the mandate should be directed against all the estates, not merely the cities. Failure to apply the mandate equally among the estates would be illegal. Spengler used as an example the emperor's demand that the Edict of Worms be enforced. This, he showed, had been enforced by none of the estates. The great majority of them felt that to enforce it would lead to tumult and revolt among their people. He then explained that Nuremberg and all the imperial cities should reject the mandate as a group at their next meeting in Ulm on 6 December and make known to the emperor that they had lived up to the Edict of Worms as far as possible and remained loyal to the emperor but that they could not act contrary to the Word of God. The city council did Spengler the honor of following his advice.

The pope, determined to put a quick end to the Lutheran movement, enlisted the services of the individual estates. He repaid the dukes of Bavaria for their loyalty to the church by granting them a fifth of all the income of the bishops and clergy in their lands, granted Ferdinand a third of such income in his lands, and gave the archbishop of Salzburg the right to appoint the bishops of his four dioceses.[33] In June 1524, Campeggio, supported by the capable Bavarian chancelor, Leonhard von Eck, called a convention of princes to meet at Regensburg to plan subsequent action in support of the pope's plans. There Archduke Ferdinand, the two dukes of Bavaria, and twelve ecclesiastical princes agreed to enforce the Edict of Worms in their lands but also to correct certain abuses and to improve the discipline of their clergy.[34]

Because the recess of the Third Diet of Nuremberg had appealed to the estates to have their theologians and lawyers make excerpts of Lutheran teachings for discussion at Speyer so that "the good would not be suppressed with the bad," several evangelical leaders began to formulate statements of doctrine to be used at the national assembly. Among the first of these were a memorandum written by the preachers Osiander, Schleupner, and Venatorius of Nuremberg and one by Pastor Rurer of Ansbach and Chancellor Vogler. Although the assembly did not meet, these and similar statements prepared by other Evangelicals served as the first evangelical confessions of faith.[35]

chapter six

THE BREAK WITH ROME

Lazarus Spengler's close contacts with the leading figures in Germany during the meetings of the Imperial Council of Regency, the Imperial Chamber Court, and the diet of the Holy Roman Empire in Nuremberg not only made him well known but gave him confidence to assert himself as a leader during the critical years ahead. He and the city council had frequently expressed their loyalty to the empire, whose chief representatives were present in the city, and to the papacy, whose nuncios sought to stop the Lutheran movement. Motivated by the desire to maintain peace and order in Nuremberg and its concern for the spiritual as well as temporal welfare of its people, however, the city council permitted the reformers to preach doctrines and initiate changes that inexorably led to the defiance of the wishes of the emperor and the break with Rome.

Despite Spengler's assurance that Charles V would not carry out the threat made in his mandate at Burgos on 15 July 1524 because he had promised in the Capitulation of Election to conform to the laws and customs of the empire, the city council felt that it had to conduct its religious affairs with great circumspection. Its difficulties became considerably complicated by the fact that the clergy were initiating various changes in their church services, especially with respect to the Eucharist. Volprecht, the Augustinian prior, had led the way by celebrating communion in both kinds and giving the cup to 4,000 communicants during Holy Week, 1524.[1] On Pentecost, the pastors of the two parish churches likewise administered communion in both kinds according to prior arrangements that had been made with the two provosts, Pömer and Pesler. At the same time, Isabella, queen of the exiled Christian II of Denmark and sister of Charles V, received communion in both kinds from Osiander in the castle at Nuremberg, eliciting from Ferdinand the remark that he regretted that Isabella was his sister.[2] The provosts went even further by abolishing requiems and birthdays of the saints, Masses for the dead, singing of the "Salve regina" in honor of the Virgin Mary, and consecrating salt and water. The pastors also began to baptize and read the Gospels and Epistles in the German language.[3]

Although the majority of the clergy and citizens of Nuremberg were pressing for these changes, a number of them did not hesitate to voice strong opposition to them, as the city council soon learned. For example, it ordered one Bernhart Sammat, an assistant to the provost at the Church of Our Lady, to appear before it and answer for having said that he would "defecate on the new order of the Mass," and threatened him with punishment if he continued to use obscene language unbecoming to a priest.[4]

THE BISHOP OF BAMBERG AND THE PROVOSTS

When the city council, which had cautioned the provosts and preachers to proceed slowly, realized that Nuremberg was moving faster in its reforms than any city or estate outside Wittenberg, it sent three councilmen, Sebald Pfinzing, Martin Tucher, and Christoph Koler, to the two provosts to induce them to desist from making further changes and to restore some of the ceremonies that were not contrary to the Word of God and did not endanger men's souls. Furthermore, the council requested from the provosts a written statement justifying and explaining their actions. That same day, the council, determined to avoid the accusation that it had ignored the imperial mandate, earnestly requested the provosts to restore the old ceremonies and customs but stated that it would not object to their having the Lord's Supper celebrated in both kinds and the Gospel and Epistles read in the German language.[5]

The provosts stated in their report to the city council that they could not restore the old ceremonies because they were contrary to Scripture.[6] The council then decided to send a delegation consisting of Christoph Kress, Clemens Volckamer, and Christoph Scheurl to Archduke Ferdinand and the Imperial Council of Regency, who received them at Regensburg on 25 June 1524.[7] They explained that they had appeared before them because the recess of the last diet had recommended that those estates that could not carry out the imperial decrees without great difficulties should take this action. Following closely the instructions of the council, based on Spengler's advice, they stated that Nuremberg and other imperial cities had not accepted the recess of the diet but had protested against it. Nevertheless, the council had respectfully received the imperial decree and accordingly had forbidden the publication of books by, and in support of, Luther. In those cases in which it did not carry out the decree, it was because it feared civil disturbance, revolt, and bloodshed, believing that the emperor desired peace and unity in preference to revolt and disunity.

When Ferdinand responded by calling attention to the Reformation changes that had been made in Nuremberg, the delegates stated that the provosts had made them before having received the imperial decree and without the knowledge or consent of the council. The council then had requested the provosts to rescind those changes not in harmony with the Word of God. They also referred to the recess of the Diet of Nuremberg of 1523 that demanded that the Gospel be preached according to Scripture as interpreted and approved by the church. For this reason, the council could not rescind those reforms occasioned by the preaching of the Gospel as long as a church council had not acted on them. When Ferdinand answered through his steward that he had warned the city council against permitting changes, the delegates promised that the council would do its best to obey the imperial recess.[8]

The city council sent this same delegation to Weigand von Redwitz (1522-56), the bishop of Bamberg, to explain its action and "to request instruction."[9] It explained, as it had to Ferdinand, that the changes had been made without the council's knowledge or consent and that it had requested that the old order be restored. If the preachers had erred and had taught heretical doctrines, the council would not defend them but would act according to the imperial recess of 1523.

The bishop answered that he himself had noted the changes and had ordered the provosts to restore the old order. Now that the clergy had not obeyed but had excused themselves by stating that the citizens of Nuremberg were demanding the preaching of the Word of God and the changes, he considered it his duty to proceed against the provosts and the preachers. He requested the city council to assist him.

The jurisconsults, Doctors Scheurl, Marsilius, Marstaller, and Heppstein, whom the council asked for an opinion, advised on 28 July that the provosts and preachers be carefully prepared for the coming judicial procedure and that the council continue to support them, permitting them to make use of their legal services.[10] The two provosts and Prior Volprecht were summoned to appear personally before the bishop on 2 September 1524 to answer for their misconduct. There the fiscal procurator presented the accusation and recommended that the provosts and prior be tried in the episcopal court. The men replied that this case concerned the entire city of Nuremberg, not merely them, and that they could not recognize the bishop as judge for he was party to the case. They would accept only the Bible as their judge.

The bishop then demanded that the provosts and prior answer sixteen specific questions both orally and in writing. They prepared a statement explaining their reasons for making the changes in Nuremberg and presented one copy to the bishop and one to the city council. The bishop refused to receive this explanation. Instead, he summoned them to reappear in Bamberg on 19 September to receive his verdict. The defendants, however, did not appear personally but were represented by an attorney. Although the attorney repeated the claim of his clients that they could not submit to the bishop as judge, the episcopal court charged the three men with heresy, excommunicated them, and deprived them of their offices. They, in turn, renewed their appeal before notary and witnesses, sent it to the bishop, published it, and informed the Council of Regency at Esslingen of its contents.

The city council was faced with a difficult decision because it expected the bishop to call upon it as his secular arm to execute the episcopal sentence. Therefore it again turned to Spengler for advice. In his memorandum he stated that the defendants had refused to accept the bishop as judge in this matter and had requested him to show them on the basis of Scripture that they had acted contrary to the Word of God and the Christian Church. Because he had refused to do this but had immediately pronounced judgment, he had wronged the defendants. For this reason, the council would be justified in refusing to permit the execution of the bishop's verdict. Dismissal of the provosts, Spengler explained, would solve nothing. To demand a return to the old ceremonies without justifying the action on the basis of Scripture and to expel the provosts would cause great disturbance in Nuremberg. Resorting to a calculated gamble again, Spengler stated that the council need not fear that the bishop would place Nuremberg under the interdict. If he did so, it would mean nothing. In either case, the council could protect itself and tie the bishop's hands by appealing to a church council. It certainly should not allow itself to be "frightened daily by every carnival mask it sees" but should trust in God and find comfort in his grace and justice. God will not forsake those who trust in him. He concluded by quoting Psalm 55:22: "Cast your burden on the Lord, and he will sustain you; he will never permit the righteous to be moved."[11]

When the judgment of the bishop reached the council, transmitted by the provosts, it ignored it and took the provosts under its protection. Prior Volprecht discarded his monastic garb. Dominicus Schleupner, preacher at Saint Sebald, married early in 1525. Even the bishop seems to have accepted the situation as a *fait accompli*, an evidence of the end of his jurisdiction in Nuremberg. The city had, in effect, developed a confession of faith and a church discipline based on Scripture and on the principle of a territorial church backed by territorial law.[12]

THE RELIGIOUS COLLOQUY

The official break with the papacy came early in 1525. The council's support of the excommunicated provosts assured the continuation of changes along Lutheran lines, as advised by Lazarus Spengler, the preachers, and the jurisconsults. The strongest opposition the council faced came from some of the monasteries, especially from the Dominicans and the Franciscans.[13]

Events in the Carthusian monastery were such that the city council believed it necessary to intervene in its affairs in behalf of the Reformation. Blasius Stöckl (d. 1556), the prior, had been reported to his superiors by some of his brothers as harboring heretical doctrines. He informed the visitator sent to examine him that he would submit to punishment if anyone would prove that he had preached anything contrary to Scripture. The council informed the visitator that it had been pleased with the prior and that it would be glad to have the abbot of Saint Egidien, the provosts of the parish churches, and the heads and preachers of all the monasteries in Nuremberg attend a meeting to participate in a discussion of Stöckl's doctrines, provided the visitator had no objections. The visitator replied that he had no intention of staging a disputation but that he would now await the orders of his superiors.[14]

When, in January 1525, the city council learned that Stökl had been removed from his priorate because he had been accused by his brother Martin of teaching evangelical doctrines before the arrival of the visitator, the council requested reasons for this action. When they were not forthcoming, the council as guardian of the monastery forbade the visitator to send Stökl away and to replace him with another prior. At the same time, it ordered Brother Martin to leave the city within three days. The council made it clear that it wanted to have the Word of God preached in its purity in the Carthusian monastery. If the monks did not want to listen to Stökl's sermons, the council would assign the Augustinian prior and the preacher at Saint Egidien to them.[15] When the monks responded that they would not listen to those men either, the council threatened to proceed against their leaders. Meanwhile, two Carthusians, sent by the superior of the order, appeared on a visitation at the monastery in Nuremberg. They informed the council that they intended to appoint a new vicar and other officers. Acting in accordance with Spengler's suggestions, the council answered that it would cooperate with them if they recognized it as the proper governmental authority over them and chose Christians who would not oppose the preaching of the Word of God by the Augustinian prior or any other preacher.[16]

The city council followed a suggestion made by Stökl that the charges made against him be discussed by a group of theologians. Believing that it might use such a procedure to establish unanimity of preaching by convincing the Catholic preachers of the truth of the evangelical doctrines, it summoned, on 20 February 1525, all the preachers of the monasteries and parishes to an examination of the basic Christian doctrines. To this end, the council requested that all the preachers prepare articles of faith that they believed were essential to salvation. Each of the six preachers at Saint Sebald, Saint Lorenz, the Hospital of the Holy Spirit, Saint Egidien, the Augustinian monastery, and the church of the Teutonic Knights presented such articles. Those from the Dominican, Franciscan, and Carmelite monasteries and the convents of Saint Clara and Saint Katherine presented one statement for the group. The council then had one person, presumably Osiander, produce a draft embodying the most important theological doctrines enumerated by the preachers. The finished draft consisted of twelve articles.

The council distributed these articles among all the preachers, requesting them to appear in the City Hall on 3 March 1525, on which occasion each preacher would be given the opportunity to state how his preaching agreed or disagreed with each article and to defend his position by reference to the Bible. Although the Dominicans, Franciscans, and Carmelites at first declined the council's invitation, stating that they would not attend a disputation in opposition to a mandate of Charles V, they finally agreed to have their preachers participate after they had been assured that the meeting was to be only a friendly colloquy.[17]

Spengler believed that the reluctance of the monks to participate in the colloquy was a consequence of their being "poor, miserable people without any understanding of Scripture."[18] Although he, like Scheurl, at first insisted that a discussion of differences in theology would be fruitless and merely postpone the forceful action needed to put an end to "the unequal preaching" of the Catholics, he finally accepted the will of the evangelical majority of the council, who probably wished to use the colloquy to justify their evangelical actions before the estates of the empire. In his memorandum of 3 March 1525, prepared for the city council, he emphasized that there were two problems facing the city of Nuremberg and also him as a Christian. The first had to do with those preachers who defied the council by not preaching the "pure Word of God" and by retaining all the old errors, thereby keeping many people in their old ways and causing uncertainties and doubts among them. Thus there resulted a lack of unity among those in authority, differences in religious customs, lack of civil peace, and rebellion against the clergy and the government. The second evil concerned the "devilish captivity of the poor, miserable women in the convents" administered by the city council. Most of these women were the daughters of the citizens of Nuremberg, even sisters and daughters of city councilors, who were being robbed of the Word of God and confined to the strong prisons of monasticism. It was the duty of the city council, Spengler wrote, not so much to free them from their convents as to bring the Word of God to them, which they had not previously heard in its purity. For this reason the council must forbid the preaching and hearing of confessions by the monastic clergy, who were misleading monks and nuns. To make matters worse, Spengler said, the three obstinate orders that had been asked to present their articles concerning doctrines essential to salvation had presented theological positions ignoring the twelve articles submitted to them, arguing instead concerning suggested procedure, whether to participate in a colloquy or to present their doctrines orally or in writing.

For this reason, Spengler urged the city council to establish uniformity in the preaching of the Gospel. Since the monks could not be induced to conform because their respective orders relied upon their own individual statutes, rules, customs, and human doctrines, and could not accept the pure Gospel, he advised the council to let monastic orders withdraw and select a spokesman to give a Christian answer to each of the twelve articles in the name of all the others, which then could be answered by the council.[19]

The religious colloquy began formally in the large hall of the City Hall on 3 March 1525, with the members of the small and large councils and a number of other citizens in attendance. Altogether, about five hundred people tried to attend. Spengler expressed the ugly mood of the large crowd outside the City Hall graphically in a letter to Volckamer, stating that the mob, "eager to tear the monks to pieces, wanted them thrown out of the window.''[20] Ignoring the bishop of Bamberg, the council had appointed as presiding officers Friedrich Pistorius, the provosts of the two parish churches, Georg Pesler and Hektor Pömer, and the cathedral preacher of Würzburg, Johann Grauman, called Poliander, a Lutheran whom the council had invited to Nuremberg for the occasion. It selected the jurisconsult Christoph Scheurl to deliver the opening address and pose the questions to the participants and made Lazarus Spengler lector and its official spokesman.

Representing the Lutheran party were Wolfgang Volprecht, prior of the Augustinians, Dominikus Schleupner of Saint Sebald, Andreas Osiander of Saint Lorenz, Thomas Venatorius of the Hospital of the Holy Spirit, Sebastian Fürnschild of Saint Egidien, and Jakob Dolman of Saint Jakob, the church of the Teutonic Knights. The old faith was represented by Michael Fries, guardian of the Franciscans, Konrad Pflüger, prior of the Dominicans, and Andreas Stoss, son of the sculptor Veit Stoss and prior of the Carmelites, the three who played the dominant role. Present also were the preachers Lienhard Ebner of the Franciscans, Ludwig Hirsvogel of the Carmelites, Jobst Pregler of the Dominicans, Georg Erber of Saint Katherine, and Nikolaus Lichtenstein of Saint Clara.[21]

In his opening address, Scheurl explained why the council had arranged the colloquy and asked the participants to use the German language so that all the members of the council could understand them. Because this was to be a friendly discussion, not a disputation, the participants were to refrain from abusive language and always to bear in mind their duty to serve and honor the Word of God. The Holy Gospel, Scheurl emphasized, was to be the sole and ultimate authority.[22]

Spengler then read the twelve articles that Osiander and he had selected for discussion. These dealt with such basic doctrines as the nature of and punishment for sin; the necessity of law, justification, the role of the Gospel in justification; baptism and the prevention of sects growing out of different doctrines concerning it; the Lord's Supper; good works and their importance; human laws and in how far they should be obeyed; secular government and obedience to it; wrath and how it is to be avoided; and marriage of the clergy and the right of innocent divorced persons to remarry. These articles were clearly designed to distinguish among Catholics, Lutherans, Zwinglians, and Anabaptists and also to delineate the authority of the secular government with respect to numerous matters once under the jurisdiction of the bishop.[23]

The participants met in five sessions from 3 to 14 March 1525. After the second session, on 5 May, in which barely two of the twelve articles had been discussed, the council decided that having each participant present his views on each article would take interminably long. Following Spengler's original suggestion, it asked each side to present its views through a speaker. The Lutherans selected Osiander, and the Catholics, Lienhard Ebner. Needless to state, the two parties could not agree on the basic doctrines, even though they had amicably discussed numerous theological issues. At the close of the discussions, on 12 March, the council invited the speakers of the two groups to appear at the City Hall two days later to summarize their respective doctrines.

Early on the morning of 14 March, Spengler read the statement prepared by the preachers of the Catholic party, which explained that they could not participate in further meetings because they would take on the character of a disputation, specifically forbidden by Charles V in the Edict of Burgos. Furthermore, because the participants could not be confronted by impartial judges, they requested that the council obtain the opinions of the universities of Heidelberg, Tübingen, and Ingolstadt, stating that they would abide by these opinions and the orders of their ordinary, the bishop of Bamberg, with respect to any changes. Despite this request of the Catholic participants, the council proceeded with the meeting as scheduled. Osiander gave a two-hour address, summarizing the arguments of both sides, attacking the views of his opponents by reference to the Bible, charging the Catholic preachers alone for the unrest in Nuremberg, and urgently requesting the council to wait no longer for the meeting of a general church council to settle the religious disputes but to settle them immediately on the basis of Scripture.[24] When all those present at this session had expressed their agreement with Osiander's summary, Scheurl concluded the colloquy.

The protocols of the colloquy, taken by the three persons appointed by the city council and those taken by the two persons appointed by the Evangelicals and Catholics, respectively, are lost. An account of the proceedings, written by a citizen of Nuremberg from the evangelical point of view, was published in Augsburg under the title *Action of the Honorable, Prudent City Council of Nuremberg with Respect to its Preachers 1525.*[25] The council, however, repudiated this account and tried to halt its publication because it did not wish to have the colloquy considered more than a "brotherly and friendly" discussion among the clergy of Nuremberg for the purpose of establishing unity in preaching "the Holy Gospel and clear and pure Word of God" according to the requirements laid down at the second Diet of Nuremberg in 1523. It gave a detailed official explanation of its action to Michael von Kaden on 20 March 1525, to be used by him in defending it against possible action against it in the Imperial Council of Regency.[26] It firmly maintained that it had acted legally in every respect. Although it moved persistently toward Reformation as before, it continued to proceed cautiously, reluctantly using force to attain its ends. On 17 March, it had issued an order demanding that the preachers of the monasteries and convents cease preaching and the hearing of confessions until they conformed to the doctrines accepted by the council. It assigned evangelical preachers to the convents and ordered Andreas Stoss, the Carmelite prior, to leave the city within three days. It also exiled the preachers of the Franciscans and the Dominicans. All the monasteries and convents were ordered to cease celebrating the Catholic Mass, to arrange their divine services to conform with those of the two parish churches, and to celebrate the Lord's Supper according to the form prescribed by the two parish provosts. A manual prepared by the chaplain of the Hospital of the Holy Spirit, Andreas Döber, and published under the title *The Evangelical Mass as Celebrated in the New Hospital in Nuremberg*, was retained until 1526.[27]

DISSOLUTION OF THE MONASTERIES

These steps were but preliminary to the ultimate dissolution of the monasteries in Nuremberg and its territory. As elsewhere in Germany, monks and nuns in Nuremberg began leaving their religious houses soon after Luther's first cirticism of monastic life. Lazarus Spengler's sister Ursula was among those who left the Convent of the Holy Sepulchre at Bamberg.[28] Convinced that monasticism was a great evil that threatened the church, Hieronymus Ebner, Kaspar Nützel and Spengler vigorously attacked the monasteries against the ineffective opposition of Martin Geuder, Hieronymus Holzschuher, and Jakob Muffel. The Augustinians, as early as December 1524, had asked the council to take their property, including real estate and buildings, rents, and endowments, and put it into the newly created common chest of the great alms and to provide the monks with livings or income from the chest. The council, on 22 March 1525, carried out this request, having been assured by the jurisconsults that the superior of the order and the imperial fiscal would not have prior legal claims.[29] The Carmelites handed over their property under the same conditions on 19 May, the Benedictines on 12 July, the Carthusians on 9 November, and the nuns of the Convent of Gründlach, outside the city, on 12 May. The Dominicans, who had offered the council their property in return for annuities, held out as a monastery until 1543, and the Franciscans until 1562.[30]

The most spirited, and often pathetic, resistance came from the convents, especially from Saint Clara's, where Caritas Pirckheimer (1467-1532), a sister of Willibald, had been abbess since 1503. Formerly on such good terms with Spengler that she could write him, Albrecht Dürer, and Kaspar Nützel a jovial and cordial letter on 3 September 1518, while the three men were at the Diet of Augsburg, she now condemned Spengler as a stubborn innovator who ignored the strongly evangelical teachings and high moral conduct of her convent in his determination to dissolve it.[31] This change in attitude was reflected also in the relations between Spengler and her brother, who called Spengler "a vicious man without honor."[32] Clara, sister of Willibald and Caritas and prioress of Saint Clara's Convent, even suspected Spengler of twisting the meaning of a petition of the convent to the city council prepared by Willibald. She stated: "We greatly fear that when Spengler read it, he did not read it correctly for we do not believe that we have a friend in him. Pardon my suspicion."[33]

Although the city council did not close the convents by force, it attempted to convert the nuns to Lutheranism by having them accept Lutheran preachers. When it met with determined resistance, it ordered the abbesses to have the nuns give up their distinctive gowns for conventional dress and to permit those to leave the convents whose parents or relatives desired this, to be released from their vows, and to take with them the possessions they had brought into the convents. Encouraged by this order, the wives of the councilmen Hieronymus Ebner, Friedrich Tetzel (deceased), and Kaspar Nützel, the administrator of Saint Clara, went to the convent and forced their daughters to leave against their will before a large crowd of people who had come to witness this sad affair. The apparently violent treatment of one of the daughters in an open wagon taking them to their respective homes caused many of the onlookers to sympathize with the girls.

After Melanchthon, in Nuremberg on business related to the new gymnasium, had talked with Caritas, he recommended to the city council that it proceed understandingly with the nuns under her, for they were sincere in their religious commitments.[34] The council, accordingly, permitted the convents to remain as they were but forbade them to accept novices. Caritas remained abbess until her death in 1532. Her sister Clara succeeded her but died the next year. Willibald Pirckheimer's daughter Katherine was abbess from 1533 to her death in 1563. Saint Clara closed its doors in 1590, Saint Katherine in 1596, the Convent of Pillenreuth, outside the city, in 1552, and that of Engelthal in 1565.

Following the advice of Spengler and the demands of most of the citizens of Nuremberg, the city council increased its authority over the clergy. Long considered the first estate with special privileges in the Holy Roman Empire, they now became citizens of Nuremberg with duties and obligations to match their privileges. They were compelled to be citizens, pay taxes, submit to the jurisdiction of the municipal courts, and serve the common welfare in various ways. The preachers served individually and sometimes as a group in providing memorandums on matters of religion and morals for the city council, a function ordinarily reserved to the jurisconsults and the city secretary.

The requirement that all clergy, regular as well as secular, should become citizens led to serious difficulties between the city council and the Teutonic Knights, who had a large hospital, the church of Saint Jakob, and considerable property in the city and its territory. The council demanded that all priests and vicars of the order obtain citizenship, arguing that the city in its turn was providing them with security, particularly during the Peasants' Revolt, and therefore should receive help through taxation of the clergy and its possessions. On 16 May 1525, the commander (*Landkommenthur*) at Ellingen "gratefully" received the city's request, and the local commander and the administrator of the hospital appeared before the city council and became citizens. After the end of the Peasants' Revolt, however, the commander of the order sought to free it from civic responsibilities and appealed to the Swabian League for assistance in reestablishing its autonomy. The city council refused to relax its position, with the consequence that relations between it and this Catholic island in the city remained strained.

The city council also gradually changed the church life of the city to conform with Reformation doctrines and to suit its practical needs, giving the reasons for its actions to the bishops of Bamberg and Eichstätt, other imperial cities, and Archduke Ferdinand in documents prepared by Lazarus Spengler.[35] Having abolished fasting regulations, the cult of the saints, and many holy days, it stipulated, in May 1525, the following as acceptable holy days: Sunday, Christmas, Easter, Pentecost, Ascension, Saint John's Day, Saints Peter and Paul's Day, the Annunciation of Mary, Candlemas, and the Visitation of Our Lady. Stringent laws forbade the playing of dice and cards, blasphemy, and certain carnival excesses. The end of episcopal authority at first was followed by considerable moral misconduct, leading to severe laws against bigamy and adultery.

Much progress was made in poor relief. Upon the advice of Melanchthon, the city council took over properties from churches and monasteries and money from the many endowments for masses and other religious activities for use in supporting the church, its clergy, and its functions. In the case of endowments, the council followed Melanchthon's advice in ordering that those donors who were still living be permitted to dispose of them as they wished but that all others now be administered by the council.[36] The property of Saint Mary's, Saint Egidien, the two parish churches, and the dissolved monasteries was placed in the common chest and new almonry created in 1522. Now greatly enlarged and called the great almonry, it was administered by the alms office.[37] This administrative body was divided into two parts, one for the city and one for its territory. The city alms office had supervision of virtually all church and monastic buildings, endowments, charity, pensions of monks and nuns, and payment of the salaries of provosts, preachers, sextons, and school teachers. The alms office for the territory likewise administered properties of churches and monasteries, endowments, and salaries. This reorganization of the almonry did much to improve assistance given poor and sick persons and to minimize begging. Spengler wrote the introduction to the document describing the reorganization.

The religious changes introduced by the city council provided for its direct control over the members of the clergy. It called them, paid their fixed salaries, and regulated their conduct, forcing them, for example, to give up their concubines or marry them. The first preacher appointed directly by the city council was, as we have seen, Wenzeslas Linck, a close friend of Luther and Spengler, whom it made a preacher and custodian at the Hospital of the Holy Spirit at the relatively high salary of 200 gulden a year.

IMPROVEMENTS IN EDUCATION

Although education at all levels seemed to suffer from the rapidity of change and general disorder during the first years of the Reformation, Luther, Melanchthon, and other reformers soon placed great emphasis on the importance of the development of good schools for improving learning, religion, and morals, and training for constructive citizenship. Spengler's interest in improving education in Nuremberg was greatly stimulated by Luther's widely read work, *To the Councilmen of All Cities in Germany That They Establish and Maintain Christian Schools*, published in 1524.[38]

The city council not only improved the three excellent Latin schools at Saint Sebald, Saint Lorenz, and the Hospital of the Holy Spirit but planned a new higher school, or *Gymnasium*, for the purpose of providing education for moral and political as well as religious ends and preparing young men for university studies. Hieronymus Ebner, Kaspar Nützel, Hieronymus Baumgartner, and Lazarus Spengler encouraged this project in every way. Early in 1525, Spengler went personally to Wittenberg to obtain advice with respect to procedure from both Luther and Melanchthon. In September of that year, the city council, through Baumgartner, sought the services of Philip Melanchthon to head the development of the school. Although Melanchthon declined the position, he assisted the council in numerous ways.[39] He came to Nuremberg on 12 November, where he remained for several days discussing curricular and administrative matters involved in setting up the school and suggesting able teachers for it. The council made his friend and travel companion, Joachim Camerarius (*Kammermeister*, 1500-1574), rector and teacher of Greek and history and appointed Michael Roting (1494-1588) teacher of Latin and Eobanus Hessus (1488-1540) teacher of literature and rhetoric. It was Camerarius who later gave Spengler the main credit for convincing the council that it should establish the school.[40]

Plans for the new school were completed by the spring of 1526. Melanchthon came for the festive opening at the Monastery of Saint Egidien on 23 May and delivered the dedicatory address.[41] During his visit of about two weeks, he assisted the council in selecting outstanding teachers for the school. In addition to the men appointed the previous year, it now made Johann Boschenstein teacher of Hebrew and Johann Schöner (1477-1547) teacher of mathematics. Schöner, a former priest, gained considerable reputation because of his mathematical and astronomical knowledge, the making of geographical globes, and the publication of important works by well-known scientists. All these teachers were Lutheran. Accordingly, the intellectual circle furthered by Spengler and others attracted theologians as well as humanists, and did much to bring humanism and Reformation together in a dynamic amalgam. Among the theologians who helped set the tone of this circle were Wenzeslas Linck and Thomas Venatorius.

Spengler retained his interest in the new school, seeing to it that it received adequate financial support and that the city council provided stipends for worthy students. It is not suprising that Luther dedicated his *Sermon on Keeping Children in School* in 1530 to Spengler as a leader of humanist-Protestant education in Germany.[42] In 1575 the city council moved the school to Altdorf, where students would not be distracted by the blandishments of a big city. Eventually it made the school into a university.

The new intellectual circle included the teachers at the new school together with Linck, Veit Dietrich, Wilhelm Breitengraser, composer and rector of the school of Saint Egidien, and Sebald Heyden, cantor of Saint Sebald and rector of the school of the Hospital of the Holy Spirit after 1525. They did much to encourage the development of religious music.[43] They themselves, and the meistersingers, composed hymns and encouraged the publication of hymnbooks, two of which appeared in Nuremberg in 1526. Well known is one of Spengler's hymns, *Through Adam's Fall*, of 1524, which has been included in Lutheran hymnbooks from the Wittenberg *Geistliches Gesangbüchlein* of 1524, for which Luther wrote the preface, to those of our day. Like most hymns of the Reformation, this one was doctrinal, stressing the effects of original sin, man's inability to save himself by good works, and the necessity of faith and the grace of God. Following is the first verse in English translation:

> Our nature fell in Adam's fall,
> One common sin infects us all,
> From sire to son the bane descends,
> And over all the curse impends.[44]

SPENGLER'S APOLOGY

Because Nuremberg was the first imperial city to break with the papacy and to introduce Lutheranism, others looked to it for advice and assistance. In providing this, Lazarus Spengler, with his strong religious convictions, legal training and knowledge, political expertise, and diplomatic experience, played a dominant role. From 1524 to 1528, he provided cities with summaries of Nuremberg's religious development and changes.[45]

In July 1524, the City Council of Magdeburg, urged by its parishes to join the Lutheran movement, wrote the City Council of Nuremberg, requesting information concerning its change in church services and ceremonies.[46] In March 1525, Strassburg requested similar information, which the city council answered by sending it Spengler's account of the religious colloquy, originally prepared as a defense sent to the Imperial Council of Regency.[47] In March 1528, the predominantly Catholic city of Goslar, caught between the demands of its citizens for evangelical preachers and reforms on the one hand and the threat of the Catholic Duke Henry of Braunschweig to absorb Goslar into his territory on the other, asked the city council what it had done with respect to changes in ceremonies. In response to this request, Spengler wrote his important statement (*Verzaichnus*), "Order of and Changes in the Ceremonies in Nuremberg, Prepared in the Year 1528," and sent it to Goslar with an accompanying letter in which he stated that people in Nuremberg considered it the duty of all Christian governments to act according to the Word of God and the Gospel.[48] In Goslar as in Magdeburg, the Reformation was carried out along lines suggested by Spengler.

Spengler's statement became an effective document in the spread of the Reformation largely because of its systematic and practical organization. The first part deals with the problem of establishing uniform evangelical preaching because "the main duty of Christianity is to proclaim the Word of God," a problem that Nuremberg settled in the religious colloquy of March 1525. It then shows that it is the duty of the city council to see to it that there is uniformity of preaching and peace in the city and discusses the means used to prevent the divisive incursion of Anabaptism and the Zwinglian interpretation of the Lord's Supper. In the second part it gives a detailed discussion of the order of church service on work days and church holy days and notes when changes had been made with respect to ceremonies. Finally, it shows how the city council assumed the administrative functions formerly in the hands of the bishop, such as the management of church property, care of the poor, administration of the common chest, the requirement of the clergy to become citizens, treatment of the remaining Catholic monastic establishments, and reorganization of its schools.

Spengler had requests for copies of his statement from various governments. For this reason he kept his original copy and at the end of 1528 added a section on the church visitation of Brandenburg and Nuremberg. Strassburg and Ulm obtained copies that same year.[49] From Strassburg a copy was sent to Transylvania, where it exerted a strong influence in the Reformation of that country.[50]

Of great importance in the church history of Nuremberg is the recently discovered proclamation (*Ausschreiben*) of Lazarus Spengler, known as "The Last and Correct Conception of the Honorable City Council's General Proclamation in Religious Matters, 1527. The True Announcement and Instruction of the City Council of Nuremberg with Respect to its Actions in Matters Pertaining to the Holy Gospel, How They Have Been and Still Are Willing to be Convinced by Contrary Documents."[51] It is the culmination of Spengler's attempts to make clear the reasons for the council's acceptance and promotion of the Reformation in Nuremberg and also for its political relations within the empire. Although it is an outstanding summary of the council's religious beliefs and actions as well as an apology for them, the council never published the document. As in 1526, the political situation in 1528 was such that it found it advisable not to do so. Unlike the statement of 1526, it disappeared and was not brought to light again until our own day.

Because Spengler originally prepared the apology for the general reader and was aware of Nuremberg's difficult political position, he restricted himself to the bare essentials, presenting his materials with utmost care. In his introduction he meets the accusation that Nuremberg had permitted the preaching of heresy, encouraged disturbances, caused the Peasants' Revolt, and disobeyed the emperor by asserting that the council was concerned above all with the fate of the souls of its citizens as well as with maintaining civil peace and unity, the basic duties of every Christian government. It therefore must provide its people with pure Christian doctrine and correct church services. It is the council's duty as well as right to carry out the Reformation as called for in the grievances (gravamina) of the German nation, supported by Catholics as well as Lutherans.

In the main body of the tract, Spengler reiterates the conviction that the council must concern itself with the care of the souls of its people and then emphasizes its responsibility to provide preachers who faithfully proclaim the Word of God according to the recess of the Diet of Nuremberg of 1523, to the effect that the preachers must preach the Gospel according to the interpretation of Scripture as approved and accepted by the Christian Chruch. The council also must act according to the recess of the Diet of Speyer of 1526 as it can answer for its action to God and the empire.

With respect to changes in liturgy, attacked by the bishop of Bamberg, the council followed the memorandums of Spengler and the jurists.[52] By now it had given up the fiction that it had not known about the changes because the provosts and the prior of the Augustinian Order had proceeded on their own authority according to Scripture. Now it defended them in their actions by having a memorandum by Osiander on the matter published in the fall of 1524.[53] Spengler gives an account of the events leading to the excommunication of the provosts and argues that they had correctly appealed to a church council because the bishop had not tried them according to Scripture, had acted both as plaintiff and judge, and had passed a severe sentence on them. As in his Excerpts from Papal Law, published later, he attempts to defend the use of Scripture in this case and argues that, according to canon and civil law, custom, "no matter how venerable, good, or fine," must give way to truth. He also refers to the council's strict adherence to imperial laws and mandates.

Spengler minimizes the changes made by the provosts, for he is concerned to show that they were not iconoclastic or revolutionary. Combining Erasmian conceptions of government with Lutheran teachings concerning freedom of faith, he explains the council's defense of its subjects but also its demands for civil peace and unity that had led it to hold the religious colloquy of March 1525. In arguing that the monastic preachers were responsible for the outcome of the colloquy, he gives the impression that they were not asked to answer the twelve articles under question until the last session and that when they refused to do so, the council decided to favor the evangelical cause. The council, he maintains, did not wait to make changes until the meeting of a general church council because it believed that it already recognized the true Christian doctrines and that it would be folly to wait any longer for the calling of a general council. Furthermore, the preaching of this Gospel was responsible for preventing the spread of the Peasants' Revolt in Nuremberg.[54] Here as elsewhere, Spengler is sharp in his criticism of monasticism, the large number of saints' days, clerical exemptions from civic responsibilities, and enforced clerical celibacy. To prevent the spread of evil rumors, he explains in detail the city council's control over the clergy and the appropriation and administration of church property through the common chest.

Spengler's chief defense of the church visitation conducted by Nuremberg in cooperation with Duke George of Ansbach, added to the final copy of 1528, lies in his assertion of the great need for it because of the bishop's failure to conduct visitations in the past. He bases his defense of the council's treatment of the left-wing movements on his humanist conception of government and the Lutheran doctrine of the two kingdoms.

Although this document was not published, it nonetheless is important, for it contains a summary of the actions of the city council during the critical years 1524 through 1528, provides an excellent list of theological and juristic arguments for embracing the Reformation, and helps us understand Spengler's significant role as a lay leader in the Reformation.

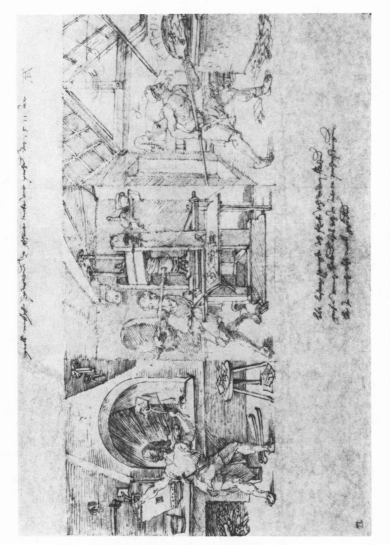

Fig. 3. Durer's facetious drawing for Spengler.

chapter seven

SOCIAL AND RELIGIOUS FERMENT

Although Lazarous Spengler consistently and vigorously supported the cause of the Lutheran Reformation in Nuremberg and elsewhere with the constant if cautious support of the city council, he was determined to avoid the preaching of social revolution and the forming of religious splinter groups that appealed particularly to dissatisfied elements of the lower social levels. The city council considered the maintenance of law and order in behalf of the general welfare its sacred trust. Accordingly Spengler did not tire of calling attention to Luther's differentiation between spiritual and secular freedom. In this he was supported by Osiander and the other preachers in their popular sermons and by Hans Sachs in his widely read pamphlets, dramas, dialogues, and hymns.

PEASANTS' REVOLT

With this support, the City Council of Nuremberg withstood the onslaughts of the widespread Peasants' Revolt of 1524-25, opposed the teachings of Carlstadt and Zwingli, and prohibited the spread of Anabaptism.[1] Realizing that many of the grievances of the peasants in its territory and of the middle and lower classes in the city were justified, the council made adjustments where it deemed them necessary and maintained relative peace and order, eventually playing a dominant role in serving as mediator between the vindictive Swabian League and the peasants. Among the many dues and services that were imposed upon the peasants, whether they were serfs or freeman, were the heavy tithes they had to pay to the secular lords and the church.[2]

These included animals, fowl, and products of field and garden. The strong animosity against the clergy stems from the fact that they seemed especially severe with their peasants. The peasants, supported by articulate leadership, demanded a new social order at the same time that many of them were demanding a reformation of the church, purporting to find in the Gospel a justificaiton for both demands.

Conditions among the peasants in Nuremberg's territory were not so oppressive as in many other parts of Germany. Nevertheless, they were dissatisfied and sought to organize armed groups to compel their lords and landowners to abolish tithes. In the spring of 1524, the city council, acting on Spengler's contention that evangelical freedom did not imply freedom from economic and social responsibilities, threatened to punish those who refused to pay tithes and disturbed the peace.[3] By carrying out this threat while at the same time doing away with some injustices with respect to ground rents and sales tax, the city council maintained law and order until the spring of 1525, when the peasants of Franconia, supported by numerous inhabitants of Nuremberg, again were prepared to use force to obtain their ends. Already in May of that year the council abolished the "living" tithes on farm animals and the death tithes on hay and vegetables, retaining only the "large" tithe on grains.[4]

Although Nuremberg was a member of the Swabian League, which decided to suppress the revolt by force of arms, and provided its share of troops, its city council preferred to settle the problem by peaceful means, believing that most of the demands of the peasants were justified. Determined to prevent bloodshed and destruction, it warned its peasants that rebellion would result in defeat and further suppression.[5] While it sent councilmen into its territory to treat with the peasants, it armed itself to protect the city and to prevent the formation of peasant bands in the country. When representatives of the peasants came to the city to ask the council whether it would join in the revolt, the council pointed out that its obligations to the empire and the Swabian League would not permit this but assured them that it had no intention of using force against them.[6] Because it had to prepare to defend itself against the Swabian League, which threatened to use force against Nuremberg if it did not give the league full support, the council at first wavered, wanting to see how the wind was blowing. It finally refused outright to support the peasants against Margrave Casimir of Brandenburg-Ansbach, arguing that he also was a member of the Swabian League. The peasants had taken Neustadt an der Aisch and Rothenburg ob der Tauber and threatened to take Nuremberg. But having failed to take Würzburg, they had to give up plans for further attacks. They now sought to negotiate with the city council, which reproached them for having used force.

When the leaders of the peasants in Würzburg and Bamberg requested Nuremberg to intervene and bring about a cease-fire, the council did its best to comply. It could do little, however, to prevent the Swabian League and Margrave Casimir from brutally suppressing the revolt and wreaking bitter vengeance on peasants and townsmen, in numerous cases punishing them and executing their leaders without trial, a particularly severe infraction of legal procedure in the eyes of Spengler. Although the council could do little to assuage the anger of the league and Margrave Casimir in most cases, it nevertheless interceded with considerable success in behalf of the cities Windsheim, Rothenburg ob der Tauber, and Dinkelsbühl. At all times the city council displayed an exceptional sense of social justice, recommending the use of moderation, legal justice, and good will in bringing the revolt to an end. All subjects who had not been accused as participants in the revolt were required to swear that they had not been present in one or more bands of rebels or had not sided with them in any other way. Those who could not take such an oath were exiled.[7]

The City Council of Nuremberg was alert to the fact that the Swabian League used the suppression of the Peasants' Revolt as an excuse for the suppression of the evangelical movements and an attack on evangelical cities. This was apparent in its letter of 10 July 1525 to Clemens Volckamer, its representative at a meeting of the Franconian Circle.[8] Because it believed that this attack was aimed also at Charles V and Ferdinand, it approached the latter in the hope that it might obtain his support for the cities and the free preaching of the Word of God. Because this attempt failed, the council sought other ways and means for counteracting the harm done by the identificaion of the Peasants' Revolt with the Lutheran Reformation.

THE RADICAL REFORMATION

The City Council of Nuremberg sought to reestablish order after the Peasants' Revolt not only by organizing the churches in the city and its territory but also by suppressing those religious groups that had deviated from the Lutheran position. The first problems arose with persons who urged more radical religious reforms than those advocated by Luther and the Lutheran preachers in the city and whom Luther grouped together under the term "enthusiasts" (*Schwärmer*). Already in 1523 there appeared in Nuremberg and its territory one Diepold Schuster, an exiled Swabian priest who posed as an illiterate peasant known as Diepold Beringer, "the peasant from Wöhrd." Although he attracted large crowds of all classes by his simple evangelical message, he appealed particularly to the peasants and lower classes in the city. The council at first defended him, but when it noted that other more radical persons began to imitate him, it compelled him to leave the city. The freedom to preach, at first maintained by the city council, led to strange excesses, such as that of a woman who, during a sermon at the Hospital of the Holy Spirit, waved a flask of wine and began delivering a sermon of her own.[9]

Much more disruptive was the presence in Nuremberg of Thomas Müntzer in 1524 and 1525, the radical spiritualist who had gained the hostility of Luther and Frederick the Wise and who eventually lost his life as a leader of the peasants during the Peasants' Revolt.[10] Having come to Nuremberg to have his most recent pamphlets published, he found considerable support there. Especially helpful to him was Hans Hut, who, after Müntzer's death, became the leading radical reformer in southern Germany. Hans Denck, the humanist schoolmaster at the church of Saint Sebald, also supported the radical reformer.[11] During his stay in Nuremberg, Müntzer saw his pamphelts through the press, meanwhile establishing contacts with numerous religious and social dissidents, especially among the city's artisans. Although he preached a radical theology, he did not yet recommend the establishment of the kingdom of God by means of the sword. Because his second pamphlet was a sharp attack on Luther, the *Defense Against the Spiritless, Soft-living Flesh at Wittenberg*, the city council confiscated the printed copies but reimbursed the printer for his loss. In January 1525, Spengler wrote to Luther, asking him how one should treat persons like Müntzer. Luther replied that the devil was carrying out his will through the enthusiasts but that Müntzer had not yet committed blasphemies. It would not be right to punish him and his followers unless they refused to obey the city council.[12]

In December 1524, the city council learned that a pamphlet of another religious radical, Andreas Bodenstein von Carlstadt, Luther's former colleague at Wittenberg, had been printed in Nuremberg. Because it propounded a symbolic interpretation of the Lord's Supper, the council ordered the printed copies confiscated and the printer imprisoned for a short time for questioning. But its presence further stirred the restless elements in the city. The incident served as a prelude to the Sacramentarian Controversy, which eventually involved Lazarus Spengler. On 8 March 1525, Spengler wrote to Clemens Volckamer, stating that "nowhere will Carlstadt's error with respect to the body of Christ persist for any length of time. It will gradually disappear because it so obviously is contrary to Scripture and the Word of God and is based alone on his personal opinion and, at best, on reason."[13] Because of the publication of pamphlets by Müntzer and Carlstadt, the city council instituted its policy of censoring books, with Spengler determining which ones should not be offered for sale.[14]

Among those citizens of Nuremberg suspected of having radical social and religious ideas were painters. The city council, in November 1524, accused one of these, Hans Greifenberger, of a shameful attack on the papacy in one of his paintings and of helping create a new, radical sect around a misinterpretation of the sacraments.[15] One suspects that the accusation with respect to the papacy was made to placate important authorities at the Diet of Nuremberg. A prolific writer of pamphlets, originally firmly adhering to Luther's theology but stressing Christian ethics as applied to urban life, Greifenberger later displayed a strong individuality and Christian mysticism, opposing outward forms while stressing inner religious experience. Accordingly, he leaned toward the symbolical interpretation of the Lord's Supper and espoused a strong anticlerical feeling. The old church, he maintained, had been replaced by a new tyranny, that of the city council and its pastors. Despite this contention, the council treated him leniently, probably hoping that Osiander would convince him of the validity of the strictly Lutheran doctrines.[16]

By the beginning of 1525, the city council became aware of the fact that most of the dissenters it had detected could be identified with a central figure, Hans Denck,[17] the schoolmaster. This was disclosed in the affair of "the three godless painters," Georg Pentz and the brothers Sebald and Barthel Behaim, students of Albrecht Dürer who were imprisoned in January and questioned in the torture chamber. It is this questioning that led the council to suspect Denck and to order its spiritual and legal advisers to question him concerning his views on justification, baptism, the Lord's Supper, and the inner voice as a spark from God. Convinced of his unorthodox views, it ordered him to leave the city immediately, on 21 January 1525.[18]

In their testimonies in the torture chamber, the three painters confessed that they did not believe in Christ, had denied civil authority, had doubted that the body and blood of Christ were present in the Lord's Supper in the form of bread and wine, believing that the sacrament was only a sign, and had maintained that water was not essential to the efficacy of baptism. In response to the council's request for advice with respect to what it should do with these men, the preachers replied that because the men were unwilling to be instructed by them they should be exiled from the city.[19] The jurisconsults answered that the three painters already had received sufficient punishment during their imprisonment of two weeks and should be dismissed after having been given further instruction by the preachers. If that did not alter their views, the council should proceed as it wished. Lazarus Spengler argued that they should immediately be exiled, for they were godless men who would take no advice from the preachers; all interrogations indicated that they intended to spread their views; fear of torture in the dungeon had forced them to state that they had altered their previous views; they denied their oaths of loyalty to the city council; their radical position was widely known and might lead to violence against them; and their presence in the city would encourage disloyalty and religious error.[20]

The city council, acting on the advice of the theologians and Spengler, expelled "the three godless painters" and employed a replacement for Denck. Whereas Denck served as leader of the Anabaptists in Mühlhausen, Saint Gall, and Augsburg until his death, the exiled painters requested a reduction of their sentence and permission to return to the city. The council finally, in November 1525, granted their request. Georg Pentz remained in the city in good standing, but the Behaim brothers left it permanently by 1528, the year of Dürer's death.

The spread of "enthusiasm" and Sacramentarianism continued despite the stern measures taken by the city council. It was accompanied by the spread of social discontent. Luther's "freedom of the Christian" was interpreted by a number of people as a permission to ignore moral and ethical laws, both secular and spiritual. One Adam Satler and a number of his companions, for example, decided to engage in bigamy.[21] Three of these men and their wives were called before the council. Following the suggestion of its jurisconsults, the council forced the men to give up their second wives and placed them in the city's tower for two weeks to discourage further bigamy among the townsmen. Two prominent patricians, Georg Kress and Hans Tucher, were placed in a tower for two weeks for having encouraged Satler. Although there were a number of cases of bigamy throughout 1525 and 1526, usually associated with radical religious views, the council passed a severe law against the practice that eventually put an end to it.

SACRAMENTARIANISM

Equally serious in the eyes of Spengler and the city council, which had assumed the functions of the bishop of Bamberg in religious matters, was the continued spread of Sacramentarianism, introduced by Carlstadt.[22] In August 1525, the council learned that a number of persons had been reading some of Carlstadt's pamphelts in the church of Saint Lorenz during one of Osiander's sermons, hoping thereby to bring about a disputation concerning the Lord's Supper. They were duly expelled from the city and its territory together with a number of Sacramentarians, including a few preachers.

On 14 July 1526, the city council enlarged the list of doctrines that it would not tolerate. At the same time, it ordered all printers and booksellers not to print or sell books written by Carlstadt, Oecolampadius, Zwingli, or their followers because they "contain nothing but the work of the devil." It also informed all the preachers that Carlstadt's doctrine of the Lord's Supper was contrary to the teachings of Christ who had stated that his body and blood were present in the Sacrament.[23] Its punishment of the radicals, however, continued to be relatively moderate, with exile, usually temporary, being its extreme form.

To prevent conventicles in which heterodox views concerning the Lord's Supper were disseminated, the council, on 16 July, decreed that it would not tolerate such assemblies, that it was its duty to ban such sects as were causing disunity in the city and to punish severely citizens who refused to be instructed by their parish preachers in the truth concerning the sacraments.[24] This edict had the effect of making the Sacramentarians aware of the fact that questioning the Lutheran position on the Lord's Supper was no longer a matter of a mere difference of opinion but constituted a heresy as interpreted by the city council and its clergy. Disobedience was an infraction of the civil law, punishable by civil penalties. This led to an increase in the number of citizens who now challenged the council's position, augmented by the influx of many homeless refugees at the conclusion of the Peasants' Revolt.

That Spengler was deeply involved in the Sacramentarian Controversy on Luther's side is apparent in his correspondence with his friend Theodor Billican, an evangelical preacher in Nördlingen, begun in the spring of 1527. At the beginning of the controversy on Luther's side, Billican gradually was influenced by the writings of Zwingli and Oecolampadius to accept the Zwinglian doctrine of the Lord's Supper, although he tried to prove to Spengler that he occupied a theological position midway between that of Luther and of Zwingli. After Spengler had obtained two memorandums from Osiander concerning Billican's views, he concluded that Billican was indeed a Zwinglian and attempted to refute him.[25]

On 4 April 1527, Spengler wrote Billican a letter in which he gave expression to his firm conviction of the correctness of Luther's theology concerning the Lord's Supper. He would cling to this, "even though Basel, Zürich, Strassburg, or Nördlingen, even the entire world, believe otherwise, for I am certain that the words of Christ will never deceive me. I would rather err with the one Christ, if it should be an error, than agree with the entire world." Yet he added that, despite Billican's errors, brotherly love dictates that he not hate him personally or persecute him but that he pray God that he show Billican the truth and keep him in it.[26] Until his death, he was convinced that the devil had influenced Zwingli, Carlstadt, and even Butzer to spread false doctrines concerning the Lord's Supper for the purpose of fomenting discord among the Evangelicals.

ANABAPTISM

Spengler and the city council came to grips with Anabaptism early in 1527, when it became apparent that this movement was making considerable headway in Nuremberg and the surrounding territories.[27] Hans Denck, the spiritualist-sacramentarian who had been converted to Anabaptism by Balthasar Hubmaier, won Huns Hut to the cause and rebaptized him in May 1526. Hut, who had obtained most of his views from Thomas Müntzer and appealed particularly to persons previously active in the Peasants' Revolt, was one of the most dynamic leaders of the movement. Having stopped at Eltersdorf in Nuremberg territory on a trip to northern Germany, he converted Wolfgang Vogel, a fanatical preacher of its parish church, to his brand of apocalyptic Anabaptism. The City Council of Nuremberg had gently reprimanded Vogel previously for having published a bitter attack on Catholic princes in 1526. Early in 1527 it charged him with a religious fanaticism requiring its special attention. During its investigation of Vogel, the council learned of the presence in its surrounding territories of a social revolutionary group being brought together by Anabaptist leaders. Vogel and two other men of Eltersdorf were arrested and brought to Nuremberg for questioning, which revealed that they had many supporters in the city as well as in its territory. It was not until late in 1527, however, that the council realized that making examples of a few of the leaders would prove ineffective against Anabaptism, and was convinced that this religious movement was closely involved in communism of property and opposition to established political authority.[28] Whether or not the movement was connected with the Peasants' Revolt and was uniformly violent, the council was certain that Vogel was advocating the destruction of secular authority as well as preaching "contrary to the Word of God." Consequently it ordered his execution by decapitation on 26 March 1527.

Vogel was the only Anabaptist whom the council executed for having taught the overthrow of the government of Nuremberg and its territory. Although it was confronted with increasing numbers of Anabaptists, many of whom had fled from persecution elsewhere and who were being protected by many of Nuremberg's craftsmen and laborers, it consistently refused to follow the Swabian League in running them down and often executing them without a trial. Instead it dealt with each individual case that came to its attention, giving the accused an opportunity to answer the charges against them, suppressing the printing of radical pamphlets, and punishing those guilty of heterodoxy by exile as the severest penalty.[29] In its letter of 30 August 1527 to the City Council of Augsburg, it stated clearly that it realized the errors of the Anabaptists but believed that the death penalty demanded by imperial law was much too severe; that no one should be coerced in matters of faith, for only the Holy Spirit could change the hearts of men; and that those who were suspected of heresy should be treated individually through normal judicial processes and dealt punishments suited to their offenses.[30] It steadfastly refused to join other South German governments in a concerted effort to exterminate the Anabaptists, even though this refusal was in opposition to the Swabian League, imperial law, and dominant Protestant opinion. It acted not only out of a certain compassion on the part of Spengler and others for poor, misled people, but also out of fear that the Swabian League was determined to use this occasion to stamp out the evangelical movement as a whole.

Although Nuremberg, like Margrave George of Brandenburg, continued to treat its Anabaptists leniently, the majority of the members of the Swabian League concurred with its harsh, indiscriminate punishments, supported by an imperial mandate against the Anabaptists, issued at the Diet of Speyer of 1529. The mandate prescribed punishment by fire or the sword with milder treatment for those who retracted. It forbade punishment by exile, the form preferred by Nuremberg, and threatened with the imperial ban governments that disobeyed it. The Swabian League went so far as to demand death by fire for those Anabaptists who would not retract, death by the sword for the men who retracted, and death by drowning for women.[31]

The Anabaptist movement in Nuremberg and its territory reached its height in 1529 and 1530, when it gained adherents in the city itself.

Compared with the movement in Augsburg, however, it was not critical.[32] Of the approximately one hundred Anabaptists mentioned in the council's protocols, none were subjects of Nuremberg. This does not mean, however, that there were none or that there was not a conventicle of them in the city. Spengler's concern in the council's treatment of the Anabaptists is shown by the fact that he copied a memorandum prepared by Osiander on the question of whether the council could compel a person to have an infant baptized. Osiander's answer, like that of the other preachers of Nuremberg, was in the negative.[33] The city council also had Spengler prepare a mandate against a particularly radical spiritualist group, called "Dreamers," which it published in printed form on 9 June 1531. In it Spengler referred to the group's "devilish theology, plural marriages, and opposition to established government."[34] On 25 January 1532, Spengler composed a work that he called "What Position One Should Take with Respect to the Radical Sacramentarians and Their So-called Doctrine, Briefly Stated."[35]

Having had some experience in dealing with Anabaptists, the city council attempted to standardize its punishments, following in the main Spengler's suggestion that Nuremberg join Margrave George in differentiating between those who remained obstinate and those who retracted.[36] On 14 July 1528, it established guidelines that it attempted to follow consistently. It divided the Anabaptists into groups that urged revolt against established authority, those who were misled by them, those who were nonviolent, and those who had only been rebaptized without having embraced a new theology. It held the leaders of revolt punishable by death, the others subject to exile. Those who remained stubborn in their beliefs were given bodily punishment or incarceration. Those who were willing to renounce their Anabaptist views after instruction by clergymen were required to announce their repentance publicly in church three times before being readmitted to the city.[37] Even though the city council acted partly for political reasons, fearing that the Swabian League might use the attack on the Anabaptists as an excuse for attacking Lutheran preachers, there seems to be no doubt that the main reasons lay in its Christian conscience, strengthened by Spengler. Accordingly, it could not permit indiscriminate punishment of all Anabaptists, the misled and repentant as well as the unrepentant leaders. It demonstrated this attitude in its instructions to Clemens Volckamer, its representative in the league, when it urged him to action that "would be considered favorable by God and all Christian, honor-loving persons."

It was the question of the fairness and value of the death penalty for

Anabaptists and other dissidents that caused Spengler and the city council the greatest concern. It led Spengler, who consistently opposed its use against dissidents, to write Johannes Brenz early in July 1528 for his opinion. Brenz answered with his well-known work, "Whether a Secular Government, by Divine or Human Law, May Condemn Anabaptists from Life to Death by Fire or the Sword,"[38] a memorandum that Spengler presented to the council early in September. In it Brenz argued on the basis of the New Testament doctrine of the two kingdoms, secular and spiritual, that heresy could be combatted only with the use of the Word of God as long as the heresy did not threaten public peace or governmental authority. This position, also maintained by Linck in Nuremberg, was not concerned with providing religious toleration to dissidents but solely with doing away with the death penalty in cases involving dissent. Influenced by these arguments, the city council assumed a middle position. It no longer considered all Anabaptists revolutionaries. Although it did not tolerate them, it did not inflict the death penalty on them after the execution of Vogler. True to the principle of the Protestant territorial states, that the government was responsible for the spiritual as well as secular welfare of its subjects, it laid great emphasis, after the middle of 1528, on having its preachers point out the errors of the Anabaptists both to the members of their respective parishes and to apprehended Anabaptists. These were usually confined to the tower or jail and instructed by capable preachers until they retracted their Anabaptist theology, primarily their opposition to infant baptism, and were prepared to make public confession of their deviation from the official theology. Those who adamantly refused to recant were exiled. Their wives and children were permitted to remain if they were not themselves Anabaptists. The possessions of the exiled persons were not confiscated. This kind of treatment helps explain the relatively small number of dissidents in Nuremberg and its territory.

Toward the end of 1528, Spengler again presented a summary of his views with respect to punishment of Anabaptists. Although he consistently opposed imposing the death penalty on religious dissidents,[39] he definitely opposed the government's toleration of "public idolators, seducers, heretics" who supported obnoxious preaching, rebaptizing, and Sacramentarianism, for this would lead to the end of law and order. His reference to Thomas Müntzer's responsibility for the Peasants' Revolt shows that he still saw a strong connection between Anabaptism and violence.

In his draft of the city council's official "Apology" (*Apologia*),[40] Spengler states that Anabaptism is inimical to God's Word, leading to the creation of many sects and cults. For this reason, the government must wipe it out, for its most important duty is to care for the souls of its subjects. Likewise, its secular duties compel it to act in order to maintain peace and order. Dissident preaching, he maintains, inevitably leads to division and revolt, as it did in the case of the Peasants' Revolt. He sincerely felt that the devil was using the Anabaptists to develop all kinds of heresy with the intention of destroying all governments. He was particularly fearful of the spread of the eschatological views of Müntzer and Hut and the communism of many Anabaptists. His belief that the government had to exercize the supervision of religion (cura religionis), that a territory could have but one religious confession, was a common belief throughout Europe in the sixteenth century and explains his lack of toleration with respect to the Anabaptists. In a letter to Veit Dietrich, written on 13 April 1534, a few months before his death, Spengler expressed his continued fear that the Anabaptists would plunge Germany into another revolt of peasants and townsmen, for "the devil has something evil and powerful in mind against Germany."[41]

Spengler and the City Council of Nuremberg had arrived at a relatively moderate treatment of the Anabaptists only after much soul-searching. The vigorous and brutal persecution of all religious dissidents by the Swabian League was questioned by numerous influential persons in Nuremberg. One of these, a friend of Spengler and a well-educated, convinced Lutheran, sent him a carefully written memorandum in which he demanded complete religious toleration for all religious groups, insisting that secular governments should maintain strict confessional neutrality in religious matters.[42] Spengler, who believed that the anonymous author's sharp distinction between the functions of the spiritual and temporal governments was unbiblical and would lead to the destruction of the state as well as the church, addressed an inquiry concerning the memorandum to Luther through Veit Dietrich on 17 March 1530, but without enclosing a copy of the document.[43] In the letter he calls attention to "a new error that is entertained in secret by several people here who are not enthusiasts but are considered good Christians" (meaning good Lutherans). These people, Spengler states, argue that "one should give religious freedom to everyone in matters of faith, irrespective of what he teaches, does, preaches, . . . and not to worry about what dangers this might entail but leave the problem to God. No government, they maintain, should make laws concerning this" as long as this freedom "does not lead to a disturbance of the peace." Luther gave his reply to Spengler's inquiry in his Commentary on the Eighty-Second Psalm, where he opposes such a blanket toleration.[44]

On 26 March 1530, Spengler wrote a letter to Johannes Brenz at Schwäbisch-Hall, enclosing a copy of the memorandum of his friend, whose name he did not disclose, a copy of the letter from this friend, and copies of two counter-memorandums prepared for him by Osiander and Linck.[45] In his letter, Spengler gives in detail his friend's arguments in behalf of religious toleration. Basing them on Luther's distinction between the spiritual and temporal kingdoms, the anonymous author insists that the basic function of the spiritual kingdom under Christ in its treatment of unbelievers is the preaching of the Word of God and that of the secular government is maintaining peace among the various religious groups, thereby enabling authorized preachers to present the Gospel. Expressing his horror over the bitter hatred evinced among the various religious cults and the "burning, butchering, and exiling of religious dissenters, he refers to Luther's statement in his *Concerning Secular Government*[46] that Christians no longer are bound by the law of the Old Testament that demands the punishment of heresy but to the Gospel of the New Testament, which does not give the government the authority to punish unbelievers. As shown by the parable of the good seed and the weeds (Matt. 13:24-30), Christ will send his angels to separate the bad from the good at harvest. Christ does not fight with the sword or have the government fight for him. As king of the spiritual kingdom, he wields the Word of God as his scepter, which not only produces true faith and the Holy Spirit but also drives out false faith and the devil. Just as it is impossible for the secular government to produce true faith and the Holy Spirit with the sword, so it cannot eradicate faith, heresy, or the devil by force. The most it can do is provide good preachers who will preach the Word of God.

The anonymous author counters the argument that tumult and revolt occur when there is no uniformity in religion by stating that these are caused by evil people among believers as well as unbelievers. A government has enough to do to suppress such rebellion when it occurs. It would be impossible for it to ascertian the inner religious thoughts of those who do not accept the religion of the majority. Attempting to do this by force drives minority opinion underground. To prove his point, he quotes a passage frequently used by Luther and Spengler, the advice of Gamaliel in Acts 5:38-39: "If this plan or this undertaking is of men, it will fail; but if it is of God, you will not be able to overthrow it." He even argues for the necessity of religious sects by quoting Paul's statement in 1 Cor. 11:19: "For there must be factions among you in order that those who are genuine among you may be recognized." He alludes to the folly of attempting to root out

Anabaptists by force, showing that such action actually increases their numbers and leads many to seek martyrdom. The example of one government using force to root out heresy will, he states, be followed by others, until there is a widespread butchery of nonconformists of all kinds. It is commendable that some governments use only relatively mild punishments such as exile; but he insists that giving a government any right to punish provides no guarantee that the punishment will remain mild. "God grant," he concludes, "that governments do their duty and do not interfere in Christ's kingdom."[47]

Spengler, in his letter to Brenz concerning this amazing document on religious liberty, agrees with the author that the government should not use the death penalty against Anabaptists because of their religious beliefs but opposes "the detested opinion" that the Bible forbids the government to punish or exile public "deceivers of Christians, false prophets, idolators, blasphemers, or despoilers of the Gospel." Although he concedes that the government does not have the right or the ability to make people change their faith by the use of force, he does not believe that it can tolerate "public enemies and blasphemers of God and despoilers of Christian women" without destroying a uniform Christian order and true religion. Without this right, it would be useless to establish a visitation and a church discipline, as Nuremberg was doing at that time. Catholicism with its "abomination of the Mass" would return to the city and its territory and the government itself would face destruction.

Furthermore, Spengler believes that it is a falacy for his unnamed friend to argue that, since the government is forbidden to kill a heretic or anyone else because of his religious faith, it cannot punish a person in any other way but must tolerate error for fear that it cannot exercise restraint or that the papacy would then be given cause for similar action against "faithful Christians." One may as well argue that the government must tolerate its political enemies and criminals as well, thereby putting an end to the further development of the Reformation in Nuremberg and preparing for its own destruction. He states that he has faithfully advised his city council "against staining its hands with the blood of poor, blind Anabaptists," despite all mandates of the empire and the Swabian League. He cannot, however, advise the council to tempt God by doing nothing to put an end to the dangerous religious divisions in the city and its territory. It is the duty of the government to exercise the *cura religionis*, its religious responsibilities, by protecting God's Word and its preachers, eradicating false doctrines, and helping its subjects obtain salvation. He also calls attention to the formation of the Schwabach Articles, which are based on Luther's doctrines and are designed to hold together those who believe in the Word of God as well as to militate against the Zwinglian conception of the Lord's Supper that has been accepted by a number of Christians in southern Germany. He concludes by stating that Christians must commend these problems to God. He asks Brenz to return to him the enclosed statement of his unnamed friend and also to send him his opinion concerning it.

In view of the great difficulties facing the Protestant estates in 1530, it is not in the least surprising that Brenz, like others whom Spengler had asked for their responses to the arguments raised by his anonymous friend, refused to accept complete religious toleration.[48] The City Council of Nuremberg, like territorial states throughout Europe, was beset with threats from the outside as well as with internal problems involving law and order that, it believed, it could solve only by maintaining uniformity of religious belief. It felt that it was by tradition and secular and divine law responsible for the spiritual as well as the political, economic, and social welfare of its people. It had come to this conclusion during its protracted difficulties with the radical religious movements in which it had detected social as well as religious motives. This was apparent in its action of 14 July 1528, decreeing the death penalty for those Anabaptists who planned to overthrow the government.[49]

chapter eight

NEW STRUCTURES

The medieval device for ascertaining the religious and social problems within the parishes of a bishopric was the visitation. Encouraged by the example of Electoral Saxony's general visitation, begun in 1528, Spengler urged the City Council of Nuremberg to conduct a similar one in the parishes of the city and its territory. To expedite such a visitation, he suggested that Nuremberg cooperate with Margrave George of Brandenburg-Ansbach, who was planning a similar visitation in his lands, which were contiguous to those of Nuremberg.[1] Such a cooperative venture, Spengler reasoned, would help solve the religious and social problems in its parishes and at the same time ameliorate the long, bitter political rivalry between the two Lutheran states, thus enabling them to present a united front against their chief enemies, the bishops and the Swabian League. Spengler presented his views in a memorandum prepared for the city council and for Margrave George. In it he argued that a visitation was necessary because of the dilatoriness of the bishops in putting down dissident preaching and to stop tendencies toward revolt.[2] Georg Vogler, the margrave's chancellor and a good friend of Spengler, had similar hopes. Spengler approached the margrave through Johann von Schwarzenberg, the latter's steward. The margrave, who agreed with the plan despite considerable opposition to it in his lands, suggested a meeting of representatives of both states at Schwabach to work out the details. The City Council of Nuremberg, immediately upon receipt of the margrave's cooperative letter of 22 May 1528, asked its jurists and theologians for a memorandum on the matter. When they responded, advising such action, the council agreed to the meeting and selected as its representatives Kaspar Nützel, Christoph Kress, Martin Tucher, Osiander, Schleupner and Spengler. The margrave's representatives were Chancellor Vogler, Wolf Chr. v. Wiesenthau, the margrave's bailiff at Schwabach, and three preachers of Ansbach, Andreas Althammer, Johann Rurer, and Adam Weiss.

THE CHURCH VISITATION

The sessions at Schwabach began on 15 June 1528. There the delegates accepted twenty-three articles that had been formulated by the pastors of the margravate and amended by Osiander. These were intended to serve as the basis for carrying out the visitation and came to be known as "The Schwabach Articles of Visitation." The delegates also approved thirty examination questions to be used by the visitators. Finally, the delegates of Nuremberg suggested that the margrave and the city issue a common church order based on the findings of the visitation. Although there were differences of opinion concerning the excommunication of church members, the delegates solved these differences and accepted the proposal. They also agreed on the parishes that were to be examined by each of the visitation commissions.

The brief church order agreed upon at Schwabach contained only a few basic guidelines for establishing and maintaining some uniformity in the churches of the two governments.[3] It dealt with questions concerning baptism, the Lord's Supper, confession, and church organization. It also explained the need for the use of German in church services and the great importance of the sermon. A number of problems were raised by the delegates that were not solved until the acceptance of the Brandenburg-Nuremberg Church Order of 1533.

After the return of Nuremberg's delegates on 18 June, the city council ordered the pastors of its two parish churches to work out the details of the visitation and to submit these to the counselors of the margrave. The visitation of both the city and the margravate began on 3 September 1528. The margrave's commission ordered each pastor in the area assigned to it to appear before it in Ansbach, accompanied by a member of his parish. The commission selected by the City Council of Nuremberg for its territory consisted of three city preachers and two councillors, Christoph Koler and Hieronymus Baumgartner. The commission for the visitation of the city's parishes consisted of the five city preachers, councillors Koler and Baumgartner, the head of the alms office, Bernhard Tucher, and the head of the common chest, Lucas Sitzinger. The commissions visited the pastors in their homes to ascertain their living conditions and habits. Then they asked the clergy living near Nuremberg to appear there for a public examination and the remainder to appear in other cities. Parishes in the country in which there was much dissatisfaction with the clergy were ordered to send from five to seven representatives to the public examinations.

Because the bishop of Bamberg considered Nuremberg's projected visitation a usurpation of his ecclesiastical authority, he informed the Swabian League to this effect. On 16 July, the city council answered the charge by informing the officials and representatives of the league gathered at Ulm that it had no intention of depriving the bishop of his authority but, as protector of the spiritual as well as physical welfare of its subjects, it felt obliged to see to it that able pastors and preachers provided them with good examples of conduct, preached the pure Word of God as demanded by the Diet of Nuremberg of 1524, maintained peace and order in their parishes, and prevented religious error and the formation of religious sects. Because neither those bishops who had jurisdiction in the parishes of Nuremberg's territory nor a church council, universal or national, had done away with the errors and abuses, the city council intended to make use of the visitation as the only feasible means for preparing to carry out those functions assigned to it by the Diet of Speyer of 1526 in accord with its obligations to God and the emperor.[4]

Meanwhile, the Swabian League, meeting in Augsburg, issued a mandate to the City Council of Nuremberg and the margrave forbidding them to carry out the visitation. Nevertheless, the visitation was begun as planned on 3 September. To further objections by the bishop of Bamberg, the city council replied that it was only carrying out its proper duties, which the bishop had failed to do. As far as the council knew, neither the bishop nor his predecessors had ever conducted a visitation in these parishes.

Although a number of the clergy caused the visitation commission of Nuremberg difficulties, frequently by order of their bishops, the visitation proceeded according to plan; and the commission kept the margrave's officials informed concerning their progress, especially in the parishes belonging to the margravate. In those few reports of the Nuremberg visitation that have survived, the main emphasis seems to have been on retaining those clergymen who gave evidence of the desire to lead respectable lives, preach the Gospel, administer the sacraments according to their institution by Christ, and cooperate with the city council in seeing that they had sufficient income for decent living conditions. Only those who appeared incorrigible or hopelessly obstinate were recommended for dismissal. The visitation commission completed its task on 22 October 1528, when it submitted its report to the city council. Early in December, the council acted on the recommendations of the commission, dismissing a few of the clergymen, filling their places with able men, and rewarding deserving persons. Like the visitators, the council was lenient in its treatment of the clergy.

At the meeting of the Swabian League in Augsburg in December, the bishop of Bamberg again submitted a detailed complaint against Nuremberg, demanding that the city cease its infringements on the bishop's authority. The matter was postponed, however, until the meeting of the league in Ulm in February 1529. On that occasion, the bishops of Augsburg, Würzburg, and Eichstätt joined the bishop of Bamberg in an attack upon both Nuremberg and the margrave. In this way they were supported by the influential Bavarian chancellor Leonhard von Eck, a bitter opponent of the Reformation who was determined to counteract the effects of the visitation. A committee of three submitted eight charges against the margrave and his visitation commission: that the clergy in his lands no longer were permitted to celebrate the Mass in its traditional form; that they were urged to marry; that they were placed under secular authority and compelled to assume the duties of citizens; that they were forced to accept the interpretation of Scripture prescribed by secular counselors; that they were bound by oath to obey secular authority with respect to endowments; that they were given endowments only if approved by the margrave's officials; that the margrave appointed the clergy; and that the margrave compelled all the clergy, including those who were subjects and vassals of the bishops, to appear before his visitation commission.[5]

The margrave, who was requested to give answers to these eight charges at the next meeting of the Swabian League, turned to the City Council of Nuremberg for a memorandum containing suggestions for answers. The council in turn asked Lazarus Spengler to prepare the memorandum and asked other cities to support it in denying the league the right to decide questions of faith that belonged solely to a church council.[6] Spengler, basing his arguments on the Bible and recognizing the importance of the continued close cooperation of Nuremberg and the margrave, produced a carefully conceived and strongly worded memorandum in which he attacked what he considered the false accusations against Nuremberg and the margrave and justified the actions taken at the suggestion of the visitation commissions. In unequivocal statements, he threw down the gauntlet to those who threatened to use force to stop the spread of the Reformation. He asserted that no clergyman had been denied the right to celebrate the Lord's Supper according to its institution by Christ; that priests who openly kept concubines should move to parishes where vices, vexations, and evil practices were not considered sins; that it was disgraceful that bishops considered adultery on the part of their clergy as belonging to their jurisdiction, tolerated it, and accepted money for condoning it; that if the clergy wished to be under the protection of the government, they should obey it; that the government should see to it that intelligent and devout preachers were put in charge of their parishes; that if the bishops had appointed faithful preachers in their dioceses, one would gladly have had them conduct visitations; that the imperial edicts of 1523 and 1524 and subsequent imperial mandates required the clergy to preach the pure Gospel; that the Swabian League, created to maintain peace, had nothing to do with the Word of God, man's salvation, or faith; that God alone was the Lord of man's conscience; and that the margrave and Nuremberg had done only that which the bishops had neglected to do.

At the meeting of the Swabian League in Augsburg on 11 July 1529, the chancellor of the bishop of Bamberg presented orally the accusations of the bishop. The margrave's representatives answered these charges in a written statement containing many of Spengler's suggestions. After the reading of this statement, the bishop of Bamberg was asked to prepare a written account of his charges against the margrave and Nuremberg to be read at the next meeting of the league. When this meeting took place at Ulm, the bishop did not present such an account but alleged that the charges were obvious enough yet too difficult to enumerate in detail. Therefore, the matter was again postponed.

Nuremberg's cooperation with the margrave continued with respect to religious matters, even though political and territorial differences remained so acute that enemies of the Reformation almost succeeded in driving a wedge between the two and inducing the margrave to withdraw from the group of estates that had protested the recess of the Diet of Speyer of 1529. Spengler was highly effective in carrying out the delicate negotiations needed to maintain a solid front. His success was attributable in no small degree to his long friendship with the margrave's chief counselor, Georg Vogler. Spengler wrote to Vogler on 21 November 1529, expressing his fear that the margrave might be led to desert the cause of the Reformation.[7] Spengler's persistence was rewarded by the continued cooperation of the margrave during the trying religious and political crises that followed. The margrave expressed his determination not to let any threats cause him to desert the cause of the Reformation.[8] While the bishops and their supporters were doing their utmost to undo the work of the visitation committees, the Swabian League disbanded and the Religious Peace of Nuremberg of 1532 provided a truce between the hostile forces.

THE BRANDENBURG-NUREMBERG CHURCH ORDER

Meanwhile, Lazarus Spengler continued to work for the formation of a church order for Brandenburg and Nuremberg.[9] Because Margrave George was aware of the considerable opposition to the Reformation in his territory, he was at first reluctant to compel his clergy to accept a new church order. Nevertheless, he was not opposed to having the City Council of Nuremberg proceed at once.

The council appointed a commission for drafting the church order. It consisted of Osiander, Schleupner, Linck, and Georg Koberer, the able preacher at the Carthusian church. Osiander, whom the other members of the commission permitted to assume the leading role, postponed action for a long time, for he realized the many difficulties involved. When, however, the margrave changed his mind and urged them to action so that he could have a church order for his territory at an early date, Osiander began the first draft of the order but without consulting the other members of the commission. Upon its completion, at the beginning of February 1530, he submitted the draft to the city council. Spengler found the draft inadequate, for it contained only an order of service and discipline, omitting a summary of doctrine for the poorly educated clergy. Because he believed that the church order established by the margrave and Nuremberg would be one of the first in Lutheran lands and therefore would exert an important influence in the church as a whole, he felt that it should not be the work of only one man, regardless of how able he was. He accordingly advised the council to submit the draft to the other members of the commission, with Koberer assuming the initiative. This group completed its additions and revisions in May.

As Spengler had foreseen, Osiander was deeply hurt by the council's action. As a consequence, a bitter correspondence between the two men ensued in which Spengler urged Osiander "to conduct himself as a Christian" and to "think of the salvation of thousands of people" rather than of "his honor and reputation." He stated that basically Osiander's difficulty stemmed from his *"ambitio* and *pertinacia."* Eventually, Osiander agreed with Spengler that the task was much more important than any one man and assumed the task of revising the work of the other preachers.[10]

At this point, a majority of the members of the city council began to fear the consequences of the city's assuming the lead in the Reformation while political conditions seemed especially unfavorable to the Protestant cause and preparations were being made for the meeting of the Diet of Augsburg. For this reason, it postponed the completion and publication of the church order. Now it was Margrave George who was eager to have Nuremberg complete its draft. Not until June 1530, when the margrave stated that he was in great need of the church order because of negotiations at Augsburg with respect to doctrine, did the council accede to his wishes, although it stated that it had not yet come to a common understanding with respect to some of its provisions. The continued preoccupation with doctrines at the Diet of Augsburg, however, did not leave the margrave and his theologians time to consider the church order. Not until November could they return to it. Then they urged Nuremberg to send delegates to a meeting of Protestants called by the elector of Saxony, to be held at Schmalkalden, to discuss the matter. But Spengler saw that, after the emperor's demand that the Protestants return to the Catholic fold, it would be highly impolitic to make known the nature of the church order.

Although theologians of all the Protestant estates were not brought together in Nuremberg to consider a common church order, as the margrave had proposed, the theologians of Ansbach and Nuremberg invited Johannes Brenz, reformer of Schwäbisch Hall, to prepare a memorandum on the church order and discuss it with the margrave's clergy in Ansbach. Brenz accepted the invitation. The resulting draft was sent to the City Council of Nuremberg late in the spring of 1531. At the same time, the margrave urged Nuremberg to cooperate in the completion and publication of the church order to prove to Emperor Charles and King Ferdinand that they were determined to adhere to the Augsburg Confession and not be influenced by religious radicals and enthusiasts. After having made further additions and revisions, Brenz and the theologians of Ansbach suggested the creation of a permanent commission to assure adherence to the church order and a church synod to represent the congregations.[11]

When all the parties concerned were satisfied with the draft, they agreed to send it to the Wittenberg theologians for their opinion. Lazarus Spengler wrote Veit Dietrich, his friend and Luther's close coworker, urging that the theologians send their opinion of the draft as soon as possible.[12] This they did. The city council, however, again postponed its final acceptance another three months after it had discovered that Osiander had attempted to place the right of excommunication into the hands of the clergy alone. The council, supported by a majority of its jurisconsults, insisted that it must have the ultimate authority in this important matter. Spengler, agreeing with Osiander, finally solved the problem for Nuremberg by suggesting the omission of the article on excommunication but allowing the clergy to deprive grave moral offenders of the Lord's Supper. The sincerity of Spengler in stressing the necessity of having the clergy to be able to induce sinners to amend their lives is apparent in one of his letters to Vogler in which he states, "Not for the possession of the entire principality, with all that belongs to it, would I despise God's Word by being responsible for doing away with the punishment of sins."[13] Brenz and the Ansbach clergy agreed to drop the article on excommunication but insisted on retaining for the clergy the right to give private absolution and on creating an ecclesiastical commission to supervise church discipline and the church order.

Closely related to the problem of discipline was that of the necessity of the announcement by church members of their intention to participate in the Lord's Supper. The problem was whether the clergy could maintain discipline by withholding the sacrament from the unworthy, which they could not do without requiring such announcement. For this reason, the clergy demanded the right to decide who could attend the Lord's Supper and stressed the necessity of the announcement. The city council, however, supported by its jurisconsults Scheurl and Heppstein, refused to permit the clergy to have this right.[14]

Another serious problem arose in Nuremberg over the question of whether the Lord's Supper could be celebrated without communicants, as was the case before the Reformation. Whereas the liturgy of the Catholic Mass, which usually contained the Eucharist, was retained in both parish churches in Nuremberg, Margrave George's theologians substituted for it in the first draft of the church order the simple service consisting of the reading of Scripture, the sermon, prayer, litany, and congregational singing, with the clergy not wearing the eucharistic vestments. Whereas the council insisted on retaining old usages, Osiander, supported by Luther and Melanchthon and the margrave's theologians, suggested the retention of the daily service but the omission of the Lord's Supper if there were no communicants present. Spengler succeeded in winning the council over to this view, although it insisted that the clergy wear the eucharistic vestments and retain the elevation of the consecrated bread and wine. The divisive question of the elevation was solved by omitting it from the church order, thereby permitting everyone freedom to do as he felt proper.[15]

Finally, on 17 July 1532, the representatives and counselors of Margrave George, eager to establish religious unity in the margravate, sent the revised copy of the church order to the Wittenberg theologians with a statement drawn up by Spengler on behalf of both the margrave and the City Council of Nuremberg, requesting a memorandum from them concerning the draft, especially on the article concerning excommunication. The Wittenberg theologians sent their memorandum, stating that the church order conformed in general to the Word of God. In a separate memorandum on excommunication, they stated that electoral Saxony exercised discipline against obstinate public transgressors only by denying them the right to participate in the Lord's Supper, adding that the main duty of the government was to provide people with pure doctrine, evangelical sermons, and ceremonies that ensured unity and order. These memorandums were signed by Luther, Bugenhagen, Justus Jonas, and Melanchthon. They also advised the abolition of the many lesser Masses previously celebrated even without communicants, suggesting that these might encourage the revival of private Masses.[16] Because the church order appeared to be a patchwork of articles produced by many persons, they suggested that one man, presumably Osiander, be appointed to write the final copy. This Osiander did, with the help of Johannes Brenz, who came to Nuremberg at the invitation of Osiander and the city council.

When the final draft of the church order was completed, the City Council of Nuremberg again dragged its feet by hesitating to publish the document, for a large number of councilmen still were reluctant to take such a decisive step. At Vogler's suggestion, Spengler, who continued to be the chief force behind its formulation and acceptance, drafted a letter for Margrave George to send to the city council to induce it to have the church order published and immediately put into effect. This letter contained the previously used argument that the margrave needed the church order to overcome opposition to the Reformation in his lands, especially in Ansbach, where the Catholic practices continued to such an extent that the city council began to doubt whether the margrave seriously intended to introduce the church order. Influenced by this letter, the council informed George on 5 December 1532, that it had approved the church order and had given it to Jobst Gutknecht, the printer, with the commission to publish about 1,000 copies for the margravate.[17] On 22 December, the preachers of Nuremberg announced that they would conduct services according to the order beginning on 1 January 1533. On 9 February, it was introduced in the congregations in the territory of Nuremberg, and in March in the margravate.

Because the governments of Nuremberg and the margravate were fundamentally different, the church order could not serve as a constitution. For this reason, each government was compelled to develop its own means for administering the church. On 20 May 1533, Nuremberg created a permanent commission consisting of representatives of both the church and the state to administer and interpret the church order. The ultimate authority over the church rested with the city council, which had assumed the authority of the bishop in conducting the visitation, appointing and dismissing the clergy, and establishing the church order. Unlike Luther, who insisted that his elector served in this capacity only as "an emergency bishop" (*Notbischof*), the city council considered it its function to serve the common welfare of its people, spiritual as well as secular. Spengler, agreeing that the state was responsible for the salvation of its citizens, supported the government in this assumption of ecclesiastical functions.[18]

The church order was accepted throughout the city and its territory. Only the Teutonic Knights refused to do so. It proved to be valuable not only in providing a simple doctrinal statement for the many uneducated clergy but also in establishing uniformity in church services and in the administration of baptism, the Lord's Supper, confession, Communion of the sick, weddings, and funerals. A helpful feature was its catechetical supplement consisting of the sermons for children preached by Osiander in the winter of 1531-32.[19] The church order was so well organized that it became the model for a number of orders in Germany.

Despite acceptance of the church order, differences over ceremonies and doctrines appeared from time to time. In sermons preached in the spring of 1533, Osiander stirred up a bitter controvesy by attacking the use of common confession in connection with the administration of the Lord's Supper as "worthless, harmful, and godless." The city council did its best to stop the controversy but to no avail at first. Spengler, thoroughly incensed by Osiander's adamant position, wrote to Veit Dietrich on 9 August to ask that he urge Luther to correct Osiander in unmistakable terms, stating that "this horse must be ridden with sharp spurs."[20] When Luther and his colleagues at Wittenberg replied, in a memorandum of 8 October, that private confession was as Christian as common confession, and when Dietrich wrote to Spengler, urging him and the Council to put the best construction on Osiander's attack, the controversy subsided for the time being, to emerge again in 1536.[21]

chapter nine

NUREMBERG AND THE DIETS OF SPEYER, 1526-1529

Lazarus Spengler's thorough familiarity with the political activities of Nuremberg's city council during the critical years leading to the formal break with Rome, his experience in diplomatic matters, his personal involvement in the religious issues of his day, and his close contacts with the political and religious leaders of Germany help explain the increased reliance that the city council placed on him as well as his success in helping surmount the difficulties raised by the city's adherence to Lutheranism. From 1526 to 1529, the council did not request the opinion of its clergy with respect to matters pertaining to the diets of the empire or the Swabian League or questions concerning a Protestant alliance but seemed to rely almost entirely on Spengler's advice.[1]

The opposition to Nuremberg was formidable. The bishop of Bamberg, who saw his authority in Nuremberg and its territory gradually eroded by the city council, was supported in diets of the Swabian League and the empire by the papacy and powerful neighboring bishops such as those of Würzburg and Eichstätt. The majority of the members of the Swabian League adhered to the old order and used every opportunity to bring Nuremberg back to Catholicism. The dukes of Bavaria sided with the majority of the imperial estates in supporting Charles V and Ferdinand in their determination to enforce the Edict of Worms against Luther. The imperial cities, restricted to a tenuous role in the affairs of the empire, in general tended to support the Reformation but were divided with respect to details. Spengler was particularly apprehensive with respect to the loyalty of the smaller cities to the Reformation, for they were inclined to look for support "to a gracious emperor rather than to a gracious God. . . . We must either remain Christians or deny Christ." He repeated the statement of Gamaliel that he had often used: "If God is for us . . . who can prevail against us?"[2]

To make matters more complicated, Spengler, like Luther, was basically opposed to the use of force in protecting the Reformation, especially against the emperor. For a long time, both believed that Charles V was opposed to the evangelical movement because he was being misinformed concerning it by the higher clergy and that he would come to its support if he were correctly informed by a formal delegation or during a visit to Germany. Furthermore, Spengler and the city council were conscious of Nuremberg's dependence upon the good will of the emperor for its continued autonomy and prosperity in the face of the ambitions of the territorial states surrounding it. Yet they remained adamant in their support of Lutheranism, taking full advantage of the growing number of evangelical princes and cities in the empire, the constant threat to Charles V by his powerful dynastic rival Francis I of France, the successes of the Ottoman Turks both in the Mediterranean Sea and the Balkan Peninsula, and the emperor's long periods of absence from Germany.

Early in 1526, however, Charles believed that he could come to the support of the papacy in its determination to stamp out Lutheranism. He had defeated Francis I at Pavia in 1525, had kept him in Madrid as a prisoner for a while, and had forced him to sign the Treaty of Madrid in 1526. Moreover, Charles was supported in his plan by a number of German princes, including Duke George of Saxony, who, after the suppression of the Peasants' Revolt in Thuringia in July 1525, had organized the League of Dessau of Catholic princes, similar to the Catholic Regensburg Union of the previous year, for the purpose of enforcing the Edict of Worms. It comprised Duke George of Saxony, Elector Joachim of Brandenburg, Elector Albert of Mainz, and Dukes Erich and Henry of Braunschweig.[3] Charles and Ferdinand were convinced that they could enforce the Edict of Worms at the next diet of the empire.

Before the imperial estates gathered for the meeting of the diet in Speyer in 1526, however, the political situation had changed to such an extent that Charles was compelled to alter his plans. When Francis I was released from captivity after the Peace of Madrid, Pope Clement VII absolved him from his oath to uphold its terms. Clement himself joined the enemies of Charles in the League of Cognac. At the same time, the Turks invaded Hungary, defeated and killed King Louis of Hungary and Bohemia, brother-in-law of Charles, at the Battle of Mohács, and threatened to invade Austria and Germany. Beset with these problems, Charles needed the support of the evangelical estates and cities. Nonetheless, he continued his policy of suppression of Lutheranism. Accordingly, he ordered his brother Ferdinand, who represented him at the diet, not to permit a discussion of doctrinal or ecclesiastical matters, which he considered solely within the province of the papacy.

The Lutheran princes, Elector John the Constant of Saxony and Landgrave Philip of Hesse, aware of the plans of Charles, formed the League of Gotha-Torgau in May 1526, enlarged to become the League of Magdeburg in June.[4] The members of this league were determined to defend the changes made by the Lutherans with force, if necessary. They invited Nuremberg to join them. Its city council, however, replied that it could not as an imperial city join an armed alliance against the emperor. The religious question, it maintained, should be settled for all the German lands at a meeting of the imperial diet or of a free church council. On the other hand, Nuremberg and other imperial cities had agreed at an assembly of cities in Speyer in September 1525 to oppose the emperor by bringing up the religious issue at the forthcoming imperial diet for the purpose of pressing for a clear statement establishing a uniform mandate "based on the Word of God" for all Germany.[5]

THE DIET OF SPEYER OF 1526

Although the Imperial Council of Regency had set the time for the opening of the diet at Speyer for 1 May, the estates arrived so tardily that Ferdinand could not open it officially until 25 June.[6] On that date, the imperial proposition was read. It stated that it was the duty of the diet to determine how to preserve the Christian faith, together with inherited customs and ceremonies of the church in Germany, until the calling of a universal church council; what action to take against those Lutheran doctrines that had been declared heretical at the Diet of Worms; and how to enforce the Edict of Worms. It specifically demanded that the estates should consider ways and means for correcting abuses in the church, make provisions against further insurrections, consider the Turkish problem, and provide money for maintaining the Imperial Council of Regency and the Imperial Chamber Court.[7] It was clear that the emperor, supported by the bishops, was determined to restore the old order by force if necessary.

Despite these bleak prospects for the Evangelicals, the situation changed when a Catholic prince, Margrave Casimir of Brandenburg-Ansbach, recommended that the estates turn first to the discussion of the serious religious question, beginning with the recess of the Diet of Nuremberg of 1524 and resuming the discussions that had sought ways for handling the religious problems until a church council could be called to solve them. He suggested bringing up once more the grievances (*gravamina*) of the German nation against Rome and the clergy,[8] for he was convinced that there could be no religious peace without far-reaching reforms. Without such a peace and unity, it would be impossible to deal with the other issues mentioned in the proclamation of Charles. The majority of the estates accepted the recommendations of the margrave.

As was customary, the electors, princes, and cities deliberated on the emperor's proposals separately. The electors at their meeting declared that questions of doctrine and faith had to be decided at a church council but that the estates were obliged to preserve the faith and inherited religious customs, abolish abuses, and enforce the Edict of Worms. Yet they advocated moderate punishments for those who had made unauthorized changes. The princes agreed with the electors but wanted to discuss also the feasibility of carrying out the Edict of Worms, which, many felt, would cause much unrest. The cities, not full-fledged members of the diet, were led in their deliberations by the representatives of Nuremberg, Strassburg, and Ulm, all supporters of Lutheranism. Bernhard Baumgartner, Nuremberg's representative, wrote to his city council on 3 June to request advice on how to counter the actions of the electors and princes and to ask for advisers and secretaries to assist him.[9] The assembly of the cities declared the enforcement of the Edict of Worms impossible, for it would lead to disunity in the empire. Spengler and the City Council of Nuremberg were well aware that the supporters of Luther had a difficult struggle ahead of them, especially because the princes would pay little attention to their opinions.[10]

Nuremberg, sensing the possibility of the enforcement of the Edict of Worms, on 2 July sent Johann Müller, the jurist, as adviser and Jorg Höpel, a secretary and good friend of Spengler, to assist Baumgartner. Later it also sent Christoph Kress, its most experienced diplomat, as a second delegate. At the same time, the city's jurisconsults prepared a memorandum that the council had Kress bring to the delegates as its own instructions to them. The memorandum made it clear that it would be impossible to enforce the Edict of Worms and that the delegates should oppose adamantly its enforcement only as a last resort. Furthermore, they should oppose the emperor's proposition, take their stand on the recess of the last Diet of Nuremberg, and appeal to both the emperor and a church council for a solution to the problem.[11]

Shortly before the arrival of this memorandum, the cities, fearing that a postponement of an answer might encourage the princes to ignore them completely, submitted their report. They stated that because Christian governments should not act contrary to Christian doctrines, they should retain their Christian practices and ceremonies that were not contrary to Scripture until the meeting of a general church council. They expressed their hope that the electors and princes would no longer tolerate unchristian practices or attempt to enforce the Edict of Worms.[12]

The answer of the cities did not fail to impress the majority of the princes. They appointed a committee of eight to study religious abuses and recommend action to the diet as a whole. Because the cities were not represented on the committee, they assigned Höpel the task of preparing another report that was handed to the princes but also to the counselors of the electors on 14 July. It demanded that the cities be included in the deliberations of the diet. It accused the emperor of indirectly causing the Peasants' Revolt by refusing to call a church council and permitting the continuation of abuses in the church. The reformation of the church, it stated, was an absolute necessity and the enforcement of the Edict of Worms an impossibility.[13]

When opposition to this report became strong and the evangelical cause seemed hopeless, Landgrave Philip of Hesse and Elector John of Saxony arrived at Speyer. Philip encouraged the cities through Christoph Kress, for whom he had a high regard, to remain firm in making their demands for reform and to join the Lutheran Union of Magdeburg. When Kress reported this to the City Council of Nuremberg, it responded that it still could not join the evangelical princes, but it carefully left the door open for such an alliance in the future.[14]

Meanwhile, the city council, conscious of the political strength of its religious opponents at the diet and concerned about the disconcerting false rumors spread among its friends, prepared a justification of its political as well as religious actions. This concern, which preempted much of its time during the next two years, involved Lazarus Spengler at every step.[15] Prompted by the request of the city representatives at the diet for advice from Nuremberg, Strassburg, and Ulm with respect to how they should respond to the memorandum of the electors in answer to the emperor's proposition, it appointed a committee of councilmen to deliberate on the matter. The committee, in turn, called on the jurisconsults and Spengler for assistance. Following their advice, it recommended to the city council that it publish an apology not only for the use of its representatives at the diet but also for the general public. The council then appointed Spengler to prepare such an apology, which he completed 16 July 1526. Although it sent a copy of this statement to Baumgartner and Kress at Speyer, it now decided that such a publication might provoke strong opposition on the part of Nuremberg's enemies and requested its representatives to show it to no one. For this reason, it eventually disappeared in the archives.

Meanwhile, the estates of the diet took up the question of aid in the struggle against the Turks. The cities immediately formulated their response to this, stating that they could not deliberate on new matters before having received an answer to their demands concerning the religious question. But even before they delivered this response, they learned that they would be represented on the committee concerned with religious matters by Christoph Kress of Nuremberg and Jakob Sturm of Strassburg. Inasmuch as Elector John's chancellor and Philip of Hesse also were on the committee, the cities felt assured of a certain measure of support.

On 2 August, a supplementary instruction from Emperor Charles was read before the committee at its first session, stating that he was planning to go to Italy to discuss with the pope the calling of a general church council designed to eradicate heresy and correct abuses in the church. Therefore, he demanded that no decisions on religious matters should be made before his personal appearance in Germany. When this instruction was submitted to the estates and the cities, it caused general resentment. The electors agreed not to deal with the religious issues for the time being. If, however, these issues should come up for discussion, each estate should act in accord with its obligations to God and the emperor.

The cities, determined to oppose the demand of Charles, formulated a memorandum that they submitted to the committee on 4 August together with a list of grievances.[16] In it they asserted their continued loyalty to the emperor but stated that it would be impossible for them to enforce the Edict of Worms. They were encouraged in their boldness by the fact that the pope was now allied with enemies of the emperor and would be unlikely to call a general church council. They therefore recommended sending a letter or a delegation to the emperor, informing him of the true state of affairs in Germany and asking him to call a national council as requested in 1524. If he refused to do that, he should annul the Edict of Worms until the meeting of a general council in order to maintain peace and unity in the empire. In their list of grievances, the cities complained about the rapacity of the friars and called for dissolution of the monasteries. The governments, they maintained, should appoint the clergy, pay their salaries, compel them to assume responsibilities of citizens, make them subject to the jurisdiction of secular courts, and permit them to marry.

The committee agreed to send a delegation to the emperor. It also prepared a memorandum of its own emphasizing that the failure to clarify the religious question would lead to new violence. Therefore, it recommended the calling of a church council at the earliest possible time, annulment of the Edict of Worms, and war against the Turks. More significant still, it followed the formula enunciated by the electors requesting an imperial decree stating that, until the meeting of a church council, each government should conduct its religious affairs in accord with its obligations to God and the emperor.[17] This important provision, which appeared to give the evangelical estates and cities the right to continue their church reforms, was incorporated in the recess of the diet.

Although Catholics and Evangelicals agreed that the estates should send a delegation to the emperor, important differences arose concerning details. The City Council of Nuremberg, fearing that the Catholics would use it against the Evangelicals, urged the cities to be firm in insisting upon trustworthy representatives who would not be duped by the Catholics but would bring the cause to the emperor.[18] Evidence of its sincere concern in the matter is apparent in its letter of 6 August to Christoph Tetzel, its representative in the Imperial Council of Regency, in which it stated that in matters concerning the Gospel, Nuremberg's representatives at Speyer should rely "more on God's help than on the deeds of men."[19]

Because the Turks had penetrated deep into Hungary, Ferdinand, on 17 August, urged the estates to settle their differences with respect to the delegation to the emperor and to turn to the urgent matter of aid against the Turks. The two sides reached a compromise with respect to the delegation. But the delegates selected by the estates and instructed by them were never sent to the emperor by the Imperial Council of Regency. Nor did this body send a written explanation to the emperor, as it had promised to do.

During and after the diet, Elector John of Saxony and Landgrave Philip of Hesse sought to draw the imperial cities into a defensive alliance that would assure each member of protection against attempts to attack it for religious reasons, but not against attacks on the part of the emperor. Nuremberg took the lead among the cities in urging caution in taking a step that it considered neither necessary nor feasible at the time. The cities were careful, however, not to make their refusal appear final, for they needed the protection of the evangelical princes.

Although the City Council of Nuremberg was reluctant to enter an alliance to provide security in the event of an attack, it was determined to defend its religious reforms against its enemies, especially the Swabian League. It believed that it could do so without a formal alliance simply by reference to the recesses of the diets of Nuremberg and Speyer. This confidence was apparent in a letter writen by Spengler to the City Council of Memmingen, which also had been accused by its bishop of having usurped his jurisdiction. Spengler urged that "in the face of such action, those who are Christians and fear God more than men must vigorously oppose it. Christ says, 'He who loves father and mother more than me is not worthy of me.' . . . What can you experience that is more honorable than suffering for your Savior?" He advised the city council to defy the command of the Swabian League to reinstate a Catholic preacher whom it had dismissed. As he had expected, the league did not dare to use force to carry out its command.[20]

Postponement of the settlement of the divisive religious problems by the recess of the Diet of Speyer late in August 1526 until the meeting of a general church council brought a temporary respite to those rulers and cities that had embraced Lutheranism. Confident that they had a legal right to continue reforming their religious institutions, the evangelical reformers and political leaders occasionally evinced relaxed attitudes, as Luther did in a letter of early May to Wenzeslas Linck. In it he expressed his hope that Mrs. Linck would "bear a healthy child," announced that his Katie "had nausea again from a second pregnancy," and thanked him and Spengler for the garden seeds they had sent him, "all of which have sprung up, although the melon and gourd seeds are sprouting in other people's gardens."[21]

THE DIET OF SPEYER OF 1529

The continued spread of Lutheranism following the Diet of Speyer of 1526 was accompanied by increasing hostility between Catholics and Lutherans. This hostility was exacerbated by the Pack Affair of 1528. Otto von Pack, an official of Duke George of Saxony, showed Landgrave Philip of Hesse a forged document that purportedly indicated that Duke George, the archbishop of Mainz, and other Catholic princes and bishops had made an alliance at Breslau for the purpose of attacking the elector of Saxony and the Landgrave of Hesse. This caused the two Lutheran princes to prepare for an armed attack.

Philip even threatened to invade the lands of Bamberg and Würzburg in a preventive war. Although it soon became known that the two Lutheran princes had been duped, the Catholics accused them of starting hostilities. They submitted their complaints to the Swabian League, which, in turn, accused Nuremberg of having supplied Philip with arms.[22]

Meanwhile, Charles V, successful in his conflict with Francis I, was making negotiations with the pope that finally, on 29 June 1529, led to the signing of peace between them at Barcelona. For this reason, he decided to call a new diet for the purpose of raising money for troops to stop the Turks in Hungary and to find a solution to the religious problems facing Germany.[23] When the estates appeared at the Diet of Speyer in Feburary 1529, the Catholic princes were decidedly more hostile toward the Lutherans than they had been in 1526. Encouraged by this, Ferdinand presented in the name of Charles, who could not be present at the diet, a proposition much more antagonistic to the Evangelicals than the proposition prepared by the emperor himself, which arrived much later. It demanded aid for the war against the Turks and also suppression of heresies that, it claimed, had been responsible for revolts in the empire and for the success of the Turks. Furthermore, it demanded financial support for the Imperial Council of Regency and the Imperial Chamber Court. Because the pope was now willing to call a general church council, the proposition forbade any changes in faith and church administration, threatening with the imperial ban those who disobeyed. Finally, it nullified the recess of the Diet of Speyer of 1526 that had given each government the right to act in religious matters in accord with its conscience and responsibility to God and the emperor.[24]

Nuremberg reacted vigorously against this proposition. The city council sent Christoph Tetzel, its regular representative at the Council of Regency, to Speyer, with Michael von Kaden as his adviser and secretary. On 9 March it added Christoph Kress and Bernhard Baumgartner to the delegation.[25] After these men had read the document, they requested advice from the city council with respect to their response in the event that an attempt was made to carry out its provisions. The council submitted this request to its theologians and jurisconsults for memorandums.

The memorandum of the theologians reflected the same convictions expressed by Spengler in his letter of 21 May 1526 to Peter Butz of Strassburg, in which he urged the Evangelicals to be "manly and courageous, for he who has overcome the world still lives . . . and knows how to save his people from adversity." The theologians stated that the Evangelicals "should not permit themselves to desert the Word of God because of fear, threat, or danger. . . . If we fear the emperor's ban, we should fear God's ban all the more." The Word of God, they stated, demands obedience to the government, but it allows one to be disobedient if the government commands something contrary to the Word of God. No one must be forced to believe something contrary to his conscience. If the estates should order men to act in defiance of what Christ and the apostles have commanded, they demonstrate to the world that they are not Christians.[26]

The jurisconsults prepared their memorandum in a similar spirit. They likewise stated that it would be wrong for the delegates to permit any power to deprive one of the Word of God and that the delegates were forced to choose between the kingdom of the pope and that of the Gospel. If the majority of the estates should decide to reinstate Catholic practices in evangelical lands contrary to the Word of God, the Evangelicals would be obliged to protest and to appeal to the emperor and a church council.

On 24 March 1529, the city council sent these two memorandums to the delegates at Speyer with instructions to follow them and, if possible, to win others to their point of view. They were widely distributed and exerted a great influence on the cities and Margrave George of Brandenburg-Ansbach. Spengler played a dominant role in every communication with the delegates. We know, for example, that he personally wrote to Kaden, explaining one of the perplexing religious problems.[27]

Meanwhile, the estates formed a committee of eighteen for the purpose of discussing the religious matters. Of these committee members, only three were Evangelicals: Elector John of Saxony, Jakob Sturm of Strassburg, and Christoph Tetzel of Nuremberg. (Tetzel later was replaced by Christoph Kress.) All agreed at their first meeting that a church council alone could solve the religious question, but they disagreed sharply over what should be done until the meeting of this council. This question was submitted to a subcommittee of four, which announced that a church council should be called within a year to meet in a German city. Those estates that had remained Catholic should continue Catholic, and those that had accepted "the new doctrines" might continue to retain them if abolishing them would cause revolt. It recommended the death penalty for Anabaptists but less severe penalities for those who revoked their heresy.

When the committee of eighteen expressed its determination to put the Edict of Worms into force, the evangelical princes and cities agreed to follow the main principles enunciated in the two memorandums presented by Nuremberg and submit a protest to the emperor. Ferdinand, however, demanded that the evangelical cities put an end to the religious changes that they were making or he would cite them before the emperor. The cities responded through Jakob Sturm of Strassburg that they would remain obedient to the emperor in all secular matters but that they would follow the Word of God in spiritual matters. The religious reforms that they had made were not responsible for revolts among the people, as their enemies were charging, but laid the basis for peace and unity. The majority of the cities, Sturm stated, adhered to the recess of 1526 as necessary for the maintenance of peace. They promised to provide ample aid against the Turks if the recess of 1526 would be kept in force.[28] The objections of the cities were to no avail, however, for at the meeting of the estates on 10 April Count Palatine Frederick, in the name of Ferdinand, reproved them for the stand they had taken. When it appeared that the harsh provisions advocated by the committee of eighteen would be accepted by the diet as a whole, Jakob Sturm, in the name of the cities, requested the estates to adhere to the recess of 1526. If they would not do so, the majority of the cities would be forced to protest against the decision and appeal to the emperor.

When, on 13 April, a deputation of the committee of the diet asked the evangelical princes to join the majority in presenting the report to Ferdinand, the latter agreed to do so in the hope that he might bring about a compromise between Catholics and Evangelicals on the divisive issues. When they received no reassurance along these lines, they assumed that the report of the committee would be adopted and enforced. Therefore, following the persistent urging of Philip of Hesse and Jakob Sturm, they pursued the matter of a defensive alliance with the cities that might make its wishes felt by legal means, that is, protest and appeal, the means previously suggested by the City Council of Nuremberg.[29]

Ferdinand called all the estates and cities together in the assembly room of the city hall early in the morning of 19 April. There he had his spokesman explain that even though Ferdinand did not feel that the estates had gone far enough in solving the religious issues before them, he accepted their report and would make it the basis for the recess of the diet for it redounded to the glory of God, obedience to the emperor, and preservation of the faith. He stated that he expected the evangelical estates to accept the recess decided upon by the majority and approved by the emperor. At this point, the evangelical estates left the assembly room for a short time to discuss their projected protest. This they presented upon their return, explaining that they could rightfully expect their opponents to consider their objections and to keep in force the recess of 1526 until the meeting of a church council, as they believed they were bound to do because the unanimous acceptance of that recess in the previous Diet of Speyer could not be abrogated by a mere majority. They requested that their protest be incorporated with the recess of the diet, stating that they would send a copy of it to the emperor.[30] Jakob Sturm added the protest of the cities that likewise favored retention of the recess of 1526.

On 20 April 1529, the counselors of the evangelical princes handed Ferdinand an expanded copy of the protest, signed by Elector John of Saxony, Margrave George of Ansbach, Duke Ernest of Lüneburg, Landgrave Philip of Hesse, and Prince Wolfgang von Anhalt. The protest of the cities was signed by representatives of Nuremberg, Strassburg, Ulm, Constance, Lindau, Memmingen, Kempten, Nördlingen, Heilbronn, Reutlingen, Isny, Saint Gall, Weissenburg, and Windsheim.[31] Because the diet did not include the protest in its recess, the evangelical princes formally prepared it in proper legal form before representatives of the protesting cities and before notaries, appealing from the recess to the emperor and a free, Christian church council.[32] While this appeal was pending, the resolution of the diet was *de jure* ineffective. Before departing, the evangelical estates arranged to send their own delegation to the emperor with the protest, the delegation to be selected at a meeting in Nuremberg.

With this protest, or Protestation as it was called, the Evangelicals, later called Protestants, presented a solid political front for the first time, believing that they stood on firm legal as well as sound religious ground. Just as Luther eight years before had told the emperor and the estates at Worms that he could not act against his conscience, so now these princes and fourteen cities stated to the same authorities that they as political units could not do so, because "in matters concerning God's honor and our soul's salvation everyone must stand before God and answer by himself, nobody can excuse himself in that place by the actions or decisions of others, whether they be a minority or a majority."[33] On 3 May, Spengler wrote to Vogler, stating that "the sheep had been separated from the bucks," that even though events did not turn out well for the Protestants at Speyer, he was pleased to see that the "small band of God-loving" Protestants had stood firm in their support of the Gospel, adding that "one must seek peace, unity, and tranquility, so far as possible, and also God's honor and the common welfare of our subjects. . . . If God is on our side, who can be against us?"[34]

When the emperor learned of the Protestation from Ferdinand, he immediately demanded that the Protestants accept the imperial recess. That the Protestation was to some degree serving its purpose is apparent in Ferdinand's reluctance to present Charles's mandate to the Protestants. Nuremberg learned of it much later from Kaden, its representative on the delegation to the emperor. Luther learned of it from Melanchthon upon the latter's return from Speyer, inferring that the Protestants had been successful in resisting their opponents at the diet. In a letter to Wenceslas Linck at Nuremberg, he wrote "that those who chastise Christ and tyrannize the soul were unable to vent their fury."[35]

An important consequence of the strong opposition of the Catholics to the demands of the elector of Saxony, the landgrave of Hesse, and the cities Nuremberg, Strassburg, and Ulm at the Diet of Speyer was the "special, secret understanding," a tentative draft as a preliminary step toward a defensive alliance formed on 22 April 1529, designed to provide armed assistance to any member attacked by the Catholics for reasons of faith in the Word of God, provided that this did not involve armed resistance to the emperor or the Swabian League. The broad basis of the alliance was made possible by reference to the defense of the "Word of God," not to theologically divisive doctrines. Thus, alliance took precedence over confession for the time being. The nature and constitution of this alliance were to be determined at a meeting in Rodach. Nuremberg, having resisted taking such a step for a long time, reluctantly joined. On the other hand, the Catholic cities and also Augsburg refused to join. This marked the end of the coalition of cities.[36]

The Wittenberg reformers still continued to reject such a use of force, as Melanchthon revealed in a letter to Spengler on 17 May, in which he urged him "to block any further action toward the alliance planned by Philip of Hesse."[37] Luther strongly urged Elector John, in a letter dated 22 May 1529, to have nothing to do with such an alliance under the leadership of Philip, who, he stated, had almost caused a conflagration in the Pack Affair and might readily use a defensive alliance for aggressive purposes. Such an alliance, he stated, rests not on trust in God but on man's reason. Therefore, it can bring no good results. In the second place, the alliance would include the Sacramentarians, "enemies of the Word of God," a disgraceful situation. Finally, both the Old and the New Testaments condemn such alliances and demand that Christians cast all their cares on the Lord.[38]

As early as 10 April, the City Council of Nuremberg had determined to place its reliance on God rather than on alliances, choosing to proceed along legal lines in defending the city against force: "The council today unanimously and clearly stated that it would adhere faithfully to the Word of God and accordingly support the Christian [meaning evangelical] estates at Speyer in the Protestation, Appellation, and Provocation as they see fit. We must continue to assure our representatives that the council would be agreeable to having the princes set a date for a meeting to establish unity in matters concerning the Gospel and to send a delegation to the emperor."[39] This is not to say that no councilmen supported the Gospel for wrong motives. The general spirit of the council, however, was that of Spengler, whose sincerity does not seem open to question.

As suggested by the City Council of Nuremberg, which believed that the proposition presented by Ferdinand at the opening of the diet had been falsified by him, the evangelical estates decided to deliver their Protestation and Appellation to the emperor by means of their own delegation.[40] To make arrangements for this, Elector John called a meeting of the Protestants at Nuremberg for 23 May 1529. It was attended by the representatives of electoral Saxony, Hesse, Brandenburg-Ansbach, and Nuremberg.[41] The delegation chosen to appear before the emperor comprised Michael von Kaden of Nuremberg; Johann Ehinger, burgomaster of Memmingen, whose brother Ulrich was a trusted counselor at the imperial court; and Alexius Frauentraut, secretary of the margrave of Brandenburg-Ansbach. Spengler drew up the detailed instructions for the delegation on 27 May 1529,[42] providing a carefully worded statement to be presented to the emperor. If the emperor would not receive them graciously, they should declare that their princes and cities were willing to carry out all their obligations to the empire but felt constrained to submit their Appellation for the security of their faith.

The delegation left Nuremberg 14 July 1529. It traveled across Lyons to Genoa, where Kaden became ill with a high fever and was cared for by a son of Hieronymus Ebner and other citizens of Nuremberg who were in that city at that time. Ehinger and Frauentraut arrived at Piacenza on 4 September, where they met several imperial officials to whom they presented their credentials as well as their request for an audience with the emperor. They finally were received by the emperor on 12 September, when Frauentraut presented the oral statement and the written instruction in Latin, German, and French, a copy of the imperial recess of 1529, a copy of the Protestation in Latin and German, Adrian VI's confession of 1523 of the need for reforms, the list of grievances against the papacy prepared by the estates at the Diet of Nuremberg in 1523, and the imperial recess of 1526. Although the emperor promised to study these materials and give them an answer, he did not do so.[43] Therefore, the delegates, again joined by Kaden, prepared in legal form the Protestation and Appellation to present to the emperor. Not until a month later, on 13 October, were they received by the emperor's secretary, who presented them with the emperor's statement that he regretted the fact that the evangelical estates had caused division among the estates over the recess of 1529 when they should have accepted the will of the majority. If they would not now accept the recess, he would be forced to punish them.[44]

After the delegates had formally presented their notarized Appellation on 13 October, they prepared to return home. At that time, however, the emperor's secretary appeared at their inn and announced that the emperor, angered by the formal presentation of the Appellation, declared them under arrest in their inn and forbade them to inform their respective governments of the arrest. Kaden, who had sensed trouble, had left the inn and was thus able to inform the City Council of Nuremberg of the turn of events through Nuremberg merchants. Having done this, he returned to his fellow delegates. The next day the delegates appealed from the imperial decree and recess to a free, universal, Christian church council and then requested the right to return home. They were not given an answer, however, until 25 October, the morning before the emperor's departure from Piacenza, when they were informed that they would be released after having traveled to Bologna with the imperial court. Ehinger and Frauentraut, however, were released at Parma, Kaden, fearing for his life, later fled by horseback, returning home via Venice. Soon after their return, the three delegates appeared at the meeting of the Protestant estates and cities at Schmalkalden to report their experiences with the emperor. After having discussed what they might do in response to the emperor's action, the estates decided not to send a new delegation to him.

chapter ten

THE QUESTION OF A PROTESTANT ALLIANCE

With the rejection of the Protestation of 1529 by Charles V, the City Council of Nuremberg faced an entirely new situation with respect to maintaining the Reformation changes it had made.[1] It no longer could rely on a legal justification of its actions by reference to the recess of the Diet of Speyer of 1526, believing that the emperor needed only to be better informed concerning the religious situation in the empire before agreeing to defend the Protestants against the Catholic opposition or at least to remain neutral in the struggle. Having consistently professed its loyalty to the emperor in secular matters, it now was compelled to face the question of whether it had the right to resist him by force if he attacked the Protestants for their religious faith. That this was no simple decision can be seen by examining the protracted negotiations for an alliance among the Protestant estates.

Complicating the matter still further was the question of whether an alliance should include Zwinglians, a question raised by Melanchthon after his return to Wittenberg from Speyer, for he believed that the emperor would have been more lenient in his treatment of the Evangelicals if they had not included the Zwinglians. Margrave George likewise became convinced that one could form an alliance only on the basis of agreement in doctrinal matters, for which reason he was urging a common church order.[2]

MEETINGS AT RODACH, SCHWABACH, SCHMALKALDEN, AND NUREMBERG

Differences of opinion concerning an alliance occurred at the meeting of Protestant rulers and cities at Rodach in Franconia on

6-8 June 1529, called by Elector John of Saxony to work out details of the alliance agreed to at Speyer on 22 April.[3] As early as May 1529, the City Council of Nuremberg had requested Lazarus Spengler to prepare as a basis for discussion a statement for this occasion.[4] It embodied his optimism with respect to the open-mindedness of the emperor. Accordingly it emphasized that the alliance should not be aimed at the emperor but only against an estate or city that would attack another estate or city because of its religious convictions. Although Spengler believed that no alliance should be made with the Zwinglians, the city council still felt that they should be included. For this reason Spengler considered unnecessary Philip of Hesse's plan to work out doctrinal differences between Lutherans and Zwinglians at a religious colloquy.[5] Christoph Kress and Christoph Tetzel, who represented Nuremberg at Rodach as they had at Speyer, used Spengler's statement as the basis of their discussions. The representatives of electoral Saxony, Hesse, Brandenburg-Ansbach, Strassburg, and Ulm accepted the statement for submission to their respective governments. Elector John, however, had begun to reflect Luther's opposition to the inclusion of Zwinglians in the alliance, for which reason he ordered his representative, Chancellor Hans von Minckwitz, to make no binding agreement for the time being.

Elector's John's position was complicated by the fact that at Speyer he had urged Strassburg and Ulm, who were leaning toward Zwingli's doctrines concerning the Lord's Supper, to join the princes in an alliance. His caution was reflected in the final decision reached at Rodach, namely, that the alliance should not be directed against the emperor, the Swabian League, or cities that were not hostile to the Protestants. The representatives agreed to come to the assistance of any one of their estates and cities in the event of an attack for religious reasons and to work out the details of such an alliance at a meeting to be held at Schwabach, beginning on 24 August.[6]

Because Philip of Hesse was eager to include the Zwinglian cities in the alliance and realized that Nuremberg would not join if Strassburg and Ulm were not included, he sought to work out differences of opinion with Elector John. Meanwhile, the empire and France had concluded the Treaty of Cambrai, making an attack of the emperor on the Protestants a distinct possibility. For this reason, the question of armed resistance to the emperor became a live issue that Elector John especially had difficulty in resolving in the face of Luther's strong conviction that it would be contrary to the Word of God.

Spengler, in a letter to Peter Butz, secretary of the City Council of

Strassburg, written on 13 September 1529, stated that he did not fear an attack from the emperor, for he believed that Charles had been led to threaten action against the Protestants by hostile ecclesiastics. In any case, Spengler stated, the Protestants should act like Christians, being "brave in the Gospel and remaining firm in the truth, for God still lives."[7]

Philip of Hesse failed to solve the religious differences between Lutherans and Zwinglians at the Marburg Colloquy, October 1 to 3, although the two sides found agreement on all theological doctrines except that of the real presence in the Lord's Supper and evinced a feeling of Christian love at their departure. It was this spirit that eventually led the Lutherans and the south German cities to agree on the doctrine concerning the real presence in the Lord's Supper at Wittenberg in 1536. But for the time being, this division over doctrine kept the two groups apart politically as well as theologically.

As a step toward the political cooperation of the Lutherans and Zwinglians, Luther and Melanchthon formulated for the representatives of the Protestant estates and cities a confession of seventeen articles based on those articles agreed upon by Lutherans and Zwinglians at Marburg, to which, however, they added their interpretation of the Lord's Supper. These Schwabach Articles were later used as a starting point for the formulation of the Augsburg Confession, but also to convince Charles V that the Lutherans were orthodox in their theology.[8] The representatives of Strassburg and Ulm understandably refused to accept the articles as a condition for joining the alliance. Because Nuremberg would not join if these two cities were excluded and because Margrave George would not join without Nuremberg being a member, the meeting at Schwabach adjourned after the participants had agreed to meet again at Schmalkalden on 28 November 1529.[9]

News of the arrest of the Protestant delegation to the emperor at Piacenza convinced Philip of Hesse and some others that the emperor would soon use force against the Protestants. For this reason, Philip, Elector John and his son John Frederick, and Dukes Ernest and Francis of Lüneburg appeared in person at Schmalkalden. Margrave George, who was ill with kidney stones and to whom Spengler had sent two works of consolation because of the illness, was represented by his chancellor, Georg Vogler, and his counselor, Christoph von Wiesenthau. Christoph Kress and Clemens Volckamer represented Nuremberg; Jacob Sturm and Matthis Pfarrer, Strassburg; and Bernhard Besserer and Daniel Schleicher, Ulm.[10] After having heard the report concerning the experiences of the representatives at Piacenza, they turned to the question of the religious prerequisites for membership in the alliance. The representatives of Strassburg and Ulm, asked by the princes for their opinions concerning the Schwabach Articles, replied that the princes had not previously made such a statement of faith a condition of admission to an alliance; that making minute distinctions in doctrine among the Protestants might encourage the Catholics to divide and suppress the Protestants piecemeal; and that they therefore opposed accepting them as a condition of membership. They added, however, that they would agree to the provision that the alliance would come to the assistance of any threatened estate or city whose preachers sought to substantiate their doctrines by reference to the Bible.[11] When the princes asked the delegates of Nuremberg whether their government would accept the articles, they responded in the affirmative but stated that their city would not join if Strassburg and Ulm were not permitted to do so. Brandenburg-Ansbach's representatives asserted that Margrave George would not join if Nuremberg would not do so. Spengler, however, considered the emperor's threat of the use of force God's warning to the Lutherans that they had gone too far in cooperating with the Sacramentarians.[12]

Because the representatives of the princes and cities had arrived at an impasse, all agreed to take the Schwabach Articles back to their courts and city councils for reconsideration and to discuss the matter further at a meeting in Nuremberg scheduled for 6 January 1530.[13] During the discussion of differences between the princes and the cities inclined toward Zwinglianism, there developed heated arguments. For example, the delegates of Nuremberg accused the Saxon Chancellor Bayer of having treated them with a complete lack of consideration. Bayer answered that what he had said against the Sacramentarians had been taken from a memorandum written by the preachers of Nuremberg, thereby trying to place the blame for the division on Nuremberg. Spengler wrote a letter to Vogler, dated 12 December 1529, in which he explained that the preachers who had written the memorandum had not addressed themselves to the question of an alliance but to the advisability of participating in the Marburg Colloquy, adding that the City Council of Nuremberg, which originally had opposed participation in the colloquy, now agreed to do so and to send Osiander to Marburg at the urgent request of Landgrave Philip.[14]

Elector John and Margrave George were greatly displeased that Lutheran Nuremberg would not join the alliance without Strassburg and Ulm, especially since Nuremberg had been the first city to join the princes at Speyer and had played a dominant role in the events leading to the Protestation. But they failed to understand that the City Council of Nuremberg considered it most important to maintain unity among the cities. Accordingly, Spengler explained to Vogler that, "even though [the Lutherans] could have furthered the spread of the Gospel if they had excluded those cities that earnestly desired to be Christian [yet differed with the Lutherans in some matters] . . . they would have offered up as victims these Christian cities for the sake of the Gospel. I suggest that you consider this."[15] In other words, Spengler here expressed the conviction of the city council that the princes should have admitted the Zwinglian cities despite their "Sacramentarian error." The princes, however, believing that this would force the alliance to defend theological errors against their Catholic opponents, invited to the meeting at Nuremberg only those estates and cities that had accepted the Schwabach articles.[16]

THE RIGHT TO RESIST THE EMPEROR WITH FORCE

In the discussions at Schmalkalden, it had become apparent that the problem of a defensive alliance had come to involve the more serious and disturbing question of the right of resistance to the emperor. Landgrave Philip had raised this question with Margrave George as early as 3 December 1529.[17] Luther and his prince faced the same problem. The jurists to whom the elector turned for advice argued that according to both canon and civil law anyone who was attacked unjustly had the right to defend himself. Luther, however, argued that according to the Bible one could not resist the emperor, the highest political authority in the empire, by force but had to suffer an unjust attack by him.[18]

Spengler arrived at the same conclusion as that of Luther. Like him, he previously had assumed that the emperor would not attack the Protestants because of their religious convictions but would eventually see the justice of their position. In a memorandum prepared for his city council during the first half of November 1529 and in one prepared for Margrave George in January 1530, Spengler definitely denied that the city and the margrave had the right to resist the emperor by force.[19] According to human reason, he states, man finds it difficult to believe that a Christian must suffer injustice and not oppose evil with force. According to divine law, however, one must obey his government as long as one is not compelled to act against the Word of God or his conscience to the damnation of his soul. If the emperor commands a Christian to retain religious errors and evils of the past, he must respond by passive resistance and not with force. He may use only the Word of God in his resistance. The estates of the empire owe allegiance to the emperor as their legal lord or ruler the same as a private person owes allegiance to his superior.

Spengler enlarges on this position by stating that Christ, the apostles, and the Christian martyrs demonstrated that tyranny and persecution could not destroy faith and the Gospel by the use of force. The Apostle Paul, he says, made it clear that he who resists the government resists God's order and that he who takes up the sword will be overcome by the sword. He emphasizes this point when he states:

> I have said before that no Christian, whoever he may be, must assent to this unchristian action on the part of the emperor but must oppose it directly with the word of truth and by risking his body and life. To go beyond that and to use the sword or the fist is not only not demanded of him but definitely and unequivocally forbidden by God's command and Word and also by all natural and rational order.[20]

Spengler denies the contention of many jurisconsults that the relation between the emperor and the imperial estates is determined by a contract that permits the estates to disobey the emperor if he acts contrary to its terms. He contends that a Christian cannot appease his conscience by using this argument for he cannot find it substantiated in the Word of God or in reason. To oppose the emperor by force of arms would constitute disobedience and rebellion, which are contrary to imperial as well as divine law. The proper, constitutional, and Christian way for the estates to deal with an emperor who acts contrary to the contracts and the rights of his people is to dethrone him and elect another. The claim of some estates that they have the right to use force against the emperor infers that their own subjects have this same right against them. Such reasoning would lead to complete disorder and anarchy, "for then no prince would be able to retain authority, power, or control, nor would any burgomaster have authority over citizens, or lord over his servants, or housefather over his children and domestic servants."[21] Finally, Spengler maintains that no emperor or tyrant can deprive a Christian of the Gospel or his salvation by the use of force. Likewise, no Christian can justify the use of force against the emperor by reference to the Word of God.

That the City Council of Nuremberg accepted Spengler's arguments with respect to the question of armed resistance to the emperor is apparent in its letter of 8 November 1529 to Philip of Hesse in which it explains that it would be better to respond to the emperor's arrest of the Protestant delegates at Piacenza by placing the matter in God's hands than to resort to human aid and opposition.[22] Spengler sent a copy of his memorandum to his friend Vogler, who passed it on to the reformer Johannes Brenz, both of whom agreed with him in the matter. Brenz also wrote a memorandum on the subject on 27 November 1529 that, together with that of Spengler, convinced Margrave George that it would be wrong to resist the emperor by force of arms.[23] It is this point of view that George presented to Philip of Hesse in answer to the latter's inquiry of December 29. Although Margrave George followed Elector John and Nuremberg in refusing to support armed resistance against the emperor, he remained firm in his commitment to Lutheranism. Accordingly, he instructed the representative whom he sent to the Diet of Augsburg to cooperate with Saxony and Nuremberg with respect to doctrinal matters. With respect to politico-ecclesiastical matters, the representative was instructed to follow the works of consolation that Spengler had sent him, and also his *Excerpts from Papal Law, the Decretum and Decretals*, two copies of which Spengler had sent to Chancellor Vogler on 2 January 1530.

In the *Excerpts from Papal Law*, written in German at the request of Margrave George and dedicated to him, and published anonymously in 1529, Spengler following the lead of humanists like Erasmus and reformers like Luther, differentiates between Gratian's *Decretum* and the decretals added by the popes and church councils. He lists, as requested, those sections of canon law that conform with the Word of God and can be used effectively by evangelical governments. He goes on to show that the popes had falsely interpreted the *Decretum* and had added decrees that served their selfish interests. On the basis of these decrees, they and their supporters accuse their evangelical opponents of heresy and hastily condemn them to death without hearings and evidence. As in the case of Luther, they punish them before having given them a trial. Spengler's main thrusts are against the primacy of the pope, enforced clerical celibacy, and corruption of the clergy, subjects that he developed more fully in his response to the attacks made on him by Johannes Cochlaeus, former rector of the school of Saint Lorenz. Luther was so well pleased with the *Excerpts from Papal Law* that he provided it with a foreword and had it published in Wittenberg in 1530. It played a significant role in the subsequent development of evangelical ecclesiastical law.[25]

Because Elector John still followed Luther's memorandum with respect to resistance to the emperor, even though the Saxon chancellor argued that the princes as well as the emperor had their authority directly from God, Philip of Hesse stood virtually alone. Consequently, the meeting in Nuremberg in January 1530, attended by representatives of electoral Saxony, Hesse, Brandenburg-Ansbach, and Nuremberg, also failed to produce a defensive alliance, even though all the Protestants now expected the emperor soon to use force to bring them back into the Catholic fold.[26]

All attempts at an alliance having failed, the Protestant estates and cities were divided at the very time that the Catholic estates appeared united. Cardinal Campeggio, the papal legate, demanded the extirpation of Protestantism by fire and the sword at the same time that Charles V seemed to have solved his major differences with Pope Clement VII and Francis I of France. Yet the various attempts to create an alliance of Protestants provided their leaders with valuable experience in cooperation while laying the basis for the formation of the Schmalkaldic League after the Diet of Augsburg of 1530.

THE DIET OF AUGSBURG OF 1530

The Peace of Cambrai of 1529 and the establishment of harmonious relations between Charles V and Pope Clement VII, who had crowned him at Bologna, posed a new situation for the Protestants. Charles, after an absence from Germany of nine years, felt confident that he could return and at the Diet of Augsburg begin to carry out his promise to the pope to bring the Protestants back into the church, for he did not seem to be aware of the extent and depth of their break with Rome. The threat of the Turks continued, even though they had failed to take Vienna in 1529, for which reason Charles believed that he could easily gain the support of all the imperial estates for this struggle concerned them all.[27]

When, early in March, Nuremberg received the emperor's proclamation of 21 January 1530 summoning a meeting of the diet at Augsburg, it was impressed with his conciliatory reference to the religious question and his desire, supported by that of the pope, to reestablish the unity of the church by peaceful means.[28] Consequently, when Strassburg and Ulm suggested the calling of a meeting of the imperial cities, Nuremberg discouraged this for fear of stirring up conflict. Nevertheless, the city council expressed certain reservations with respect to accepting the emperor's conciliatory statements at their face value, urging caution and suggesting that only time would tell whether the emperor was sincere.[29] Elector John, also impressed by the emperor's conciliatory statements, urged all Protestant princes to attend in person.

At Innsbruck, on his way from Bologna to Augsburg, Charles met Cardinal Lorenzo Campeggio, the papal legate. Campeggio gave him a memorandum sent by the pope, demanding the renewal and enforcement of the Edict of Worms, strict censorship of books and pamphlets, close supervision of preaching, removal of all evangelical clergy, introduction of the Spanish Inquisition in Germany, and dealing with all Lutheran heretics by fire and sword.[30] The emperor remained in Innsbruck more than a month, making plans with Ferdinand and leading Catholics for procedures against the Protestants.

Immediately upon his arrival at Augsburg, on 15 June, the emperor forbade evangelical princes to have evangelical church services and sermons and insisted that they participate with him in the Corpus Christi procession the next day. Although they agreed to respect the wishes of the emperor with respect to evangelical preaching, they refused to take part in the procession.

The City Council of Nuremberg considered the events taking place at Augsburg so important that it established its own postal system, a kind of "pony express," with relays for speedy, nonstop communication that covered the distance in about two days. The council's role was an especially difficult one because it had not agreed to join the Lutheran princes in an alliance and therefore was isolated politically. Although it had ordered Kress and Volckamer, who arrived in Augsburg 15 May, to get in touch with Elector John of Saxony and Margrave George of Brandenburg-Ansbach to ascertain how to proceed in religious matters but to have nothing to do with the Zwinglians, it warned them against making any commitments in matters of faith without its prior approval.[31] Still the evangelical princes suspected Nuremberg of having accepted the recess of the Diet of Speyer of 1529 and of following the wishes of the emperor, assumptions encouraged by members of the imperial court for the purpose of causing distrust among the Protestants. They had failed to establish a defensive alliance because of basic differences. Philip of Hesse had been willing to unite for political purposes without complete unity in religion, but Elector John insisted upon acceptance of the Schwabach Articles as a condition for membership. Strassburg and Ulm, therefore, declined, whereas Nuremberg, following Spengler's advice, insisted upon the illegality of armed resistance against the emperor and also declined. Suspicion of Nuremberg's loyalty to the Protestant cause had been increased when, in January, its city council had sent Sebald Haller and Leonhard Stockheimer to the imperial court at Bologna to attempt to reestablish good relations with the emperor after his harsh treatment of Kaden and the other Protestant delegates at Piacenza. In their eagerness to placate the emperor, however, Haller and Stockheimer had made statements that led members of the imperial court to believe that Nuremberg was weakening in its determination to support the

Protestant cause. The city council had instructed them to assure the emperor that Nuremberg had never supported the views of the Sacramentarians and Anabaptists with respect to the Lord's Supper.[32]

The City Council of Nuremberg aroused still further the ill will of John the Constant when, on 13 April, it refused to permit Luther and his amanuensis Veit Dietrich to stay in the city during the Diet of Augsburg and to send them a letter of safe conduct for that purpose. Because it was embarrassed by this refusal, it asked Spengler to write a memorandum explaining the necessity for its action. He explained that the city council, by giving Luther the right of asylum in Nuremberg despite the emperor's determination to enforce the Edict of Worms, would in all probability subject Luther to seizure by the emperor, thereby bringing great harm to him and his cause. The elector could avoid this dilemma, said Spengler, by keeping Luther in his own territory. The council, however, should assure the elector that Nuremberg remained steadfastly loyal to the Gospel. In view of this faint-hearted response of the council, the elector had Luther stay at one of his castles, the Coburg.[33]

Because the Protestant princes and cities were eager to prove to the emperor that their religious beliefs and ecclesiastical changes were not heretical but were based firmly on the Bible, they prepared detailed statements for this purpose. The City Council of Nuremberg, accordingly, asked its jurisconsults for memorandums.[34] They pointed out that the Catholic estates would not agree to discuss matters of faith but would make a determined effort to reestablish episcopal jurisdiction in Protestant lands and cities. The Protestant cities could counter such action best by protesting against it, pointing out that it would lead to turmoil and revolt, appealing to the recesses of 1524 and 1526, referring the matter to a church council, and demanding for their preachers the right to preach the Word of God freely. The theologians gave the same advice, presenting biblical proofs for such teachings as the freedom of the Christian, giving the cup to the laity in the Lord's Supper, denying that the Mass was a sacrifice, administering baptism in the German language, permitting marriage of the clergy, opposing laws regarding fasting, abolishing monasteries, and denying the jurisdiction and authority of bishops and other prelates where they were in conflict with the Word of God. Elector John and Margrave George likewise prepared statements of their beliefs. Luther, Melanchthon, Jonas, and Bugenhagen prepared a statement that they presented to Elector John at Torgau and that came to be known as the "Torgau Articles." The elector then asked Melanchthon to prepare a defense of the Lutheran doctrines based on these Torgau Articles.[35]

Christoph Kress, eager to learn the contents of Melanchthon's defense, obtained a copy from the elector, sending him Nuremberg's statement in return. Meanwhile, Eck's publication of a list of more than four hundred theses taken from Luther's writings and called heretical led Melanchthon to preface his statement with a part summarizing the main articles of Christian faith to show that Lutherans were not heretics. This enlarged statement became a confession of faith, the Augsburg Confession (*Confessio Augustana*).[36]

On 3 June 1530, the representatives of Nuremberg sent their city council a copy of Melanchthon's confession in Latin, which Hieronymus Baumgartner translated into German. They expressed their hope that the council would join Margrave George in asking Elector John to submit the confession at the diet in behalf of all the evangelical princes and cities.[37] The theologians and jurisconsults of of Nuremberg were unanimous in praising the excellence of Melanchthon's confession, but they advised against joining Elector John in presenting it to the diet because the Protestant estates had not yet agreed to act as a unit and also out of fear of offending the emperor. The city council did not accept this advice but decided to support the confession. On 15 June, it wrote to its delegates, authorizing them to join the elector, the margrave, and others "who want to be Christians" in supporting it.[38] Kress and Volckamer immediately obtained the cooperation of Margrave George and induced the elector to accept the role of leader of the evangelical cause, even though he was aware of the dangers involved. The confession appeared in the name of the evangelical estates in consequence of this action. Strassburg, Constance, Lindau, and Memmingen, who could not accept the Lutheran doctrine concerning the real presence in the Lord's Supper, presented their own *Confessio Tetrapolitana*, written by Martin Butzer, assisted by Caspar Hedio, and Wolfgang Capito.[39]

The chancellors of Elector John, Landgrave Philip, Margrave George, and the dukes of Lüneburg asked the City Council of Nuremberg through Kress to send a theologian, preferably Osiander, to Augsburg to help produce the final copy of the confession. Osiander, the jurisconsult Heppstein, and the councilmen Christoph Koler and Bernhard Baumgartner left Nuremberg on 26 June. But because the emperor had requested that the Protestants present their confession in both Latin and German on 24 June, Osiander arrived too late to assist with the final version.[40]

The estates of the diet met in the assembly room of the city hall in the afternoon of 24 June. The protracted discussion of the Turkish question, however, gave the emperor the excuse to demand that the

Lutherans present their confession only in writing. He finally gave in to their persistent request that they be permitted to present it orally, which they did the next day but in the small chapter room of the bishop's palace, which could accommodate only a few of the estates and no outsiders. The Saxon Chancellor Bayer, however, read it in German in such a loud, clear voice that people in the court could hear him.[41] The confession was signed by Elector John of Saxony, Margrave George of Brandenburg, Dukes Ernest and Francis of Lüneburg, Landgrave Philip of Hesse, Duke John Frederick of Saxony, Prince Wolfgang of Anhalt, and the cities of Nuremberg and Reutlingen. Emperor Charles demanded that the confession not be published, a condition that the Protestants accepted for the time being.

Contrary to the expectations of the Protestants, the Catholic opposition did not present its confession and the emperor did not play the role of mediator, as he had promised to do. As a matter of fact, the estates as a whole did not discuss religious matters at the meetings of this diet. The emperor merely informed the Protestants that they must accept the Confutation, or Catholic answer to their confession, renounce their heresies, and return to the Catholic church or face his wrath. The Protestants did not accept the Confutation but requested a copy of it for their examination and response. Although the emperor would not at first give them a copy, Camerarius reconstructed a working copy from notes he had taken during the reading.[42] The representatives of Nuremberg sent a copy of this to their city council to be used by its jurisconsults and theologians in preparing memorandums. On 5 August, the emperor informed the Protestant estates that he would give them a copy under the condition that they accept it as a final statement, make no reply to it, and refrain from publishing it. This they refused to promise.[43]

While the Protestants were preparing their answer to the Confutation despite the emperor's order that they not do so, their opponents made numerous attempts to divide them for the purpose of leading them piecemeal back into the Catholic church. The representatives of Nuremberg countered this attempt by having the Protestant cities cooperate with the princes in providing an answer to the Catholics in which they stated emphatically that their actions stemmed not from disobedience to the emperor but from the fact that they could not act contrary to the Word of God. When the opponents spread the lie that Nuremberg was planning to accept the demands of the emperor, Kress assured the counselors of Elector John that this was not true. The princes likewise were not induced to give up their Protestant commitments.[44]

The emperor made an especially determined effort to separate Margrave George from the other Protestants by refusing to pay him a large sum of money that he owed him and also to recognize certain hereditary rights in Silesia. It was during these trying times that Spengler wrote Goerge a well-known letter of consolation in which he gave beautiful expression of his faith and loyalty to his cause. "We are all members of one body, namely Jesus Christ," he wrote. "When one member suffers, all the others suffer; and if one member is glorified, all the others rejoice. Therefore," he stated, "there must be no doubt that all pious Christians are with your princely grace . . . in your time of difficulty, suffering with you, making loyal intercession for you, and offering you comfort and encouragement." Accordingly Spengler admonishes him "to remain constant to the Word of truth as a courageous Christian." It is characteristic of Spengler that he devotes the entire letter to religious, not political, affairs in the assumption that the solution of the former will lead to the solution of the latter. The letter had the desired effect.[45]

The answer of the City Council of Nuremberg to reports from its representatives to the effect that the emperor would use the imperial ban and armed force to achieve religious unity reflected Spengler's strong religious faith:

> There is no doubt that a severe recess, including the imperial ban, would work much hardship on us and other Protestants. . . . But it would be much more dangerous to soul and body intentionally to deny God and his Word. . . . We realize that the time has come to decide whether to remain with Christ or to withdraw from him. Therefore we are determined to adhere to that which we have confessed before the emperor and the imperial estates and which we do not fear to confess before the entire world. . . . God will still bring this matter to a conclusion quite different from that which our opponents expect and believe to have achieved to their advantage and to satisfy their pride and vanity.[46]

The emperor had called the Catholic estates together on 11 July to ask them to supply him with a memorandum concerning the various statements given him by the Protestants. He was in a difficult position, for he had led the Protestants to believe that he would give them an impartial hearing while at the same time he had promised Clement VII that he would bring the Protestants back into the Catholic church by force. Because the pope did not pursue the calling of a church council with vigor or show an inclination to carry out his threats against the Protestants by force, Charles resorted to diplomacy rather than to being caught in an internal imperial conflict in which his enemies could play an important part. To mollify the Protestants he urged Archbishop

Albert of Mainz and Elector Joachim of Brandenburg to get them to change their attitude toward the emperor and continue their discussions with the Catholics. Although the representatives of Nuremberg reported to their city council that this move was made to obscure the fact that Charles had not acted according to his original promises, they and the city council agreed to do their best to reach an understanding with the Catholics but not to defy God and invite his wrath.[47]

The Protestants selected a committee, to which Kress belonged, to meet with a committee of Catholics on 16 August. They declared on this occasion that they did not consider their Confession refuted, for which reason they would defend it as well as their appeal for the calling of a church council, whereas the Catholics remained adamant in their demand that the Protestants accept the Confutation as based on Scripture. When they stated that the emperor could not support the calling of a church council as long as the Protestants insisted that church councils could err, the latter prepared an answer, which Kress helped formulate and which they submitted on 14 August.[48]

Despite their basic differences, the two groups began their discussions on 16 August in a conciliatory spirit. Even John Eck made concessions in doctrine, and Melanchthon was willing to consider the restoration of the authority of the bishops and of the Catholic Mass. As a matter of fact, tentative agreement was reached on fifteen articles of the first part of the Protestant Confession.[49] When the representatives of Nuremberg learned of these concessions on the part of Melanchthon, they reacted vigorously and informed their city council of the new turn of events. The city council asked them to remind Elector John and Margrave George that such matters concerned not only one's temporal but also spiritual welfare, adding: "If we are deeply concerned not to arouse the disfavor of the princes in these matters, we should be even more solicitous about acting contrary to God, our consciences, and our souls. . . . We hope that the Saxons will not make the concessions as we understand them and that our opponents will not accept them."[50]

Spengler's memorandum of 25 or 26 August for the city council reflects this same determination, as evinced in his correspondence with Luther at this time. He speaks out against any denial of the Gospel and especially against the reintroduction of the Mass, which the papists had made "a shameless shopkeeper's business." Reestablishment of episcopal authority, he states, would amount to turning the Protestants over to the bishops and to the suppression of the Gospel. He was especially incensed over the fact that Melanchthon had not asked Luther for his opinion, for surely Luther would not have concurred with the "pious, peace-loving Melanchthon" in this matter. Therefore, the city council should inform Elector John and Margrave George that it could not accept the concessions and that such weighty religious matters should be submitted to a church council.[51] The committee informed the diet on 22 August that it had reached an impasse with respect to any compromise.

Largely because Spengler and the City Council of Nuremberg reacted vigorously in opposing the conciliatory action of Melanchthon, whom they nonetheless highly respected, the Protestants rallied in reviving strong support for the Confession as well as opposition to the Confutation and the concessions suggested by Melanchthon. This unity was further strengthened by Luther, who answered the request of the evangelical estates for his opinion in a spirit similar to that of Spengler and the City Council of Nuremberg.[52]

When the Protestants asked their opponents to express their views concerning the calling of a church council, Eck answered that the emperor and the estates would not support it unless the Protestants first returned to the Catholic church. To this the Protestants responded, on 28 August, that all the changes they had made in doctrine and ceremonies had been based on the Bible. This had been approved by the Diet of Nuremberg in 1524 and the Diet of Speyer in 1526, whereas their appeal to a church council had been approved by both the emperor and the estates. Therefore, the Protestants insisted upon their right to proceed as in the past until the meeting of such a council. This answer to the Catholics was signed by Elector John, Landgrave Philip, Margrave George, Dukes Ernest and Francis of Lüneburg, and the cities Nuremberg, Heilbronn, Kempten, Reutlingen, Weissenburg, and Windsheim.[53]

Because of the obvious impasse, Nuremberg now suggested that both sides agree to tolerate each other. This approach finally seemed acceptable to both Catholics and Protestants. The emperor and the estates were encouraged in this by the appearance in Augsburg of Cardinal Loyosa, who expressed the interest of Pope Clement VII in tolerating the heretics for the purpose of obtaining their support against the Turks.

Spengler became directly involved in the events at Augsburg again when, on 10 September, another attempt was made to obtain concessions from the Protestants through Melanchthon and Chancellor Brück of Saxony. It was suggested that the Protestants restore the Catholic Mass and monasticism in return for a postponement of the settlement of such issues as the celibacy of the clergy until the calling of a church council and that they agree to the handling of religious matters through their respective governments. Particularly distasteful to Nuremberg was the suggestion that monasticism be continued and that the property of dissolved monasteries be administered by imperial officials. It was Hieronymus Baumgartner who wrote to Spengler from Augsburg on 13 September decrying such negotiations as devilish tricks to deceive the Protestants. He thanked God that the Protestants now had the Augsburg Confession to keep their weak theologians, especially Melanchthon and Brenz, and also Chancellor Sebastian Heller of Ansbach, from deserting Scripture. In concluding, he gives us another glimpse of Spengler's position in such matters by stating, "I have written you all the above details in strictest confidence, for I did not want you, who see these things as I do, to be without all these facts." In another letter, written two days later, Baumgartner urged Spengler to write to Luther to ask him to prevent Melanchthon from making dangerous concessions and to admonish Elector John to remain firm in the faith. He complained that Melanchthon was "more childish than a child, that Brenz was not only stupid but also coarse and rude," and that Heller was "full of fear." No matter how much he thought of Luther and Melanchthon, Baumgartner would "not follow them if they went against the Word of God."[54]

Spengler then wrote a letter to Luther, asking the Reformer to send him letters addressed to both Melanchthon and Justus Jonas requesting them to refrain from making concessions. But because Spengler meanwhile had received the news that the emperor was planning to issue the recess of the diet the next day, he returned both letters to Luther, for he did not wish to distress these men more than necessary. He retained the highest regard for Melanchthon, whom he considered to be a deeply religious man who would not act contrary to his conscience but also a human being who at times lacked courage.[55]

On 22 September, the emperor summoned the evangelical princes, but not the cities, to meet with the Catholic estates. On this occasion, the Count Palatine Frederick presented to them the first recess of the diet with respect to religious affairs. It stated that the emperor had heard the case of the evangelical princes and cities as expressed in the Aubsburg Confession as he had promised to do at the time of his convocation of the diet. He had declined to accept it, however, because it had been refuted by the *Confutatio* as contrary to Scripture and the Gospel. For the purpose of maintaining peace in the Empire, he had graciously given the elector, the five evangelical princes, and the six cities who had signed the *Augustana* until 15 April 1531 to decide whether or not to recognize the errors in their confession and to unite with the Christian Church, the pope, and the emperor pending the convocation of the church council. Meanwhile they were to print or sell no evangelical books, make no further changes in their churches, bring no new adherents into their sect, or hinder no Catholic in his faith or worship. A church council would be convoked within six months to make a final disposition of the religious issues.[56]

Clearly, a threat of the use of force against the Protestants was implied in this recess. Again the Protestant princes and cities, including Nuremberg, protested against the imperial resolution. On 22 September, Dr. Brück, speaking for the Protestants, stated that they could not accept the recess, for the emperor and the estates had not proven that the Augsburg Confession was not based on the Gospel. Accordingly they requested permission to present to the emperor and the estates a statement, their Apology, proving that it was based on Scripture. The Protestants, he said, were not a sect that had separated from the church. Because the Word of God and the salvation of men's souls were at stake, he added, the princes requested for themselves and the cities, which were not represented, the opportunity to consider the emperor's request until 15 April and as Christian estates of the empire to give their answer to the recess. But the emperor did not accept this declaration.[57]

THE APOLOGY

Melanchthon, encouraged by the firmness shown by the Protestant princes and cities, produced his Apology, which excluded political considerations but defended and supplemented his Confession in an unambiguous manner. Chancellor Brück presented it at the first reading of the recess on religious affairs on 22 September.[58] Although the City Council of Nuremberg was disappointed over the contents of the recess, it was gratified to learn that the Lutherans were firmly united and "were trusting him who can make a cure out of poison or friends out of enemies."[59] In answer to the expressed hope of the delegates that it remain firm, even if Margrave George and others seemed to waver, the council wrote to them in the same spirit so frequently expressed by Spengler, that "the evangelical estates must now decide whether they will adhere to the Word of God or deviate from it and become faithless. . . . It is of utmost importance that we look to God, in whose hands our living, dying, and destruction rest, rather than to the entire world. We intend to trust in his help."[60] It did not waver in its determination despite the threats of its bitterest opponents at Augsburg, even when the emperor made it unmistakably clear that he would punish the Protestants by force if they did not accept the recess. Luther wrote to Spengler on 28 September, stating that he was glad that his elector "had left the hell" of Augsburg, announcing his receipt of the recess, and expressing his determination "to follow divine rather than worldly wisdom."[61]

Nuremberg, Elector John, and Margrave George had frequently attempted to gain concessions in the form of a religious peace until the meeting of a general church council by withholding their aid against the Turks. When this tactic did not have the desired results, they agreed to supply the aid, for they did not consider this a matter of conscience. Therefore they planned a meeting to be held at Schmalkalden to discuss the possibility of coming to a common agreement with respect to this aid and also of maintaining religious peace despite the threats of the emperor.

The diet ended on 19 November when those princes and cities still in Augsburg met in the city hall to hear the recess in its final form. Among those present were the representatives of Nuremberg, who sent their last report to their city council on 21 November. With respect to the religious question, the recess declared that the Protestants, who had not accepted the imperial demands of 22 September, had disobeyed the Edict of Worms, thereby causing the disdain of the emperor, contempt of government, spread of heresy, disregard for Christian morals, and hatred of one's neighbor. It maintained that the emperor had, with the assistance of competent theologians, proven the Luthern Confession in error according to Scripture. It repeated that the emperor would give the Lutherans until 15 April 1531 to consider whether they would accept his judgment concerning the Confession and live in unity with him, the pope, and the imperial estates until the meeting of a church council. Meanwhile, they should make no changes in doctrines or ceremonies and cooperate with the Catholic estates in suppressing the Sacramentarian and Anabaptist movements.

The recess also stated that the emperor and the estates would propose to the pope and all Christian rulers the calling of a general church council within six months for the purpose of reforming the church. As guardian of the church, the emperor wished to restore it to its original condition, abolishing all changes in doctrine and ceremonies, restoring clergymen who had been deprived of their offices, and punishing those who disobeyed. The recess closed with the ominous statement by Charles that, after 15 April 1531, those electors and princes who support it "should have the right to seize the persons and goods of those who disobeyed it, treating them as they saw fit . . . for they should consider them deserving of the most severe punishment and outlawry because of their unchristian, disobedient transgression. Their bodies and possessions, land and people should be declared free to everyone."[62]

It is interesting to observe that during the stress and strain of the serious issues being discussed at the Diet of Augsburg, Spengler and Luther took the time to work out the Reformer's coat of arms. In a letter of 8 July 1530, Luther replied to Spengler's question of whether the coat of arms or seal that the latter had sent to Luther at the Coburg had turned out correctly, giving a detailed interpretation of the Luther rose that he considers a compendium of his theology. A black cross, he states, is located in a red heart as a reminder of faith from the heart in the Crucified Lord. This heart is in a white rose, which symbolizes joy, confidence, and peace, and in turn is placed in a sky-blue field that symbolizes heavenly bliss. The golden ring surrounding this field symbolizes that this heavenly bliss has no end and is a precious thing. He gives the place from which he writes this letter as "Grubok," that is, Koburg (Coburg) spelled backward. In a letter to his wife, Katie, written on 8 September 1530, Luther informs her that he had a delicious piece of sugar candy that Cyrus Kaufmann, his nephew, had brought from Nuremberg.[63]

chapter eleven

DIPLOMACY OF NUREMBERG, 1530-1534

When Charles V left Germany after the Diet of Augsburg, political circumstances in Europe were such that he was unable to return for nine years. His need for united German support for his wars with France and the Turks became greater than his desire to cooperate with the pope in suppressing Protestantism by force. Furthermore, because the Augsburg Confession seemed less dangerous to the pope than previously, he apparently reverted to his position of leniency toward the Protestants. The majority of the imperial estates supported the emperor in his basic desire to suppress Lutheranism, but only Elector Joachim of Brandenburg and Duke George of Saxony were willing to risk internal strife to do so. For the time being, therefore, Charles contented himself with attacking the Protestants with legal weapons, that is, by means of litigation in the Imperial Chamber Court.

The recess of the Diet of Augsburg provided for a reorganization of the court, an increase in the number of judges, and the dismissal of those judges friendly to Protestantism. The attack against the Protestants began by challenging their right to appropriate church property. This was followed by an order of the emperor that permitted the court to proceed against those who had not signed the recess of Augsburg. At the same time, the emperor was determined to have his brother Ferdinand made king of the Romans, his successor. To this end he had distributed well-placed bribes and promises at the Diet of Augsburg and had made plans for holding the election in Cologne on 29 December 1530, actions that Elector John considered detrimental to the Protestant cause.[1]

THE SCHMALKALDIC LEAGUE

Faced with the threat of legal action against the Protestants and election of Ferdinand as king of the Romans, the Protestants who had signed the Augsburg Confession met at Schmalkalden on 22 December 1530 for the purpose of formulating a common program of action.[2] Elector John first took up the matter of the election of Ferdinand as king of the Romans, for he considered Ferdinand an enemy of the Gospel undeserving of the position. The City Council of Nuremberg, however, which previously had agreed not to protest the election, complied with the emperor's request to send the imperial regalia to Aachen for the coronation of Ferdinand by appointing Christoph Tetzel and Christoph Koler to perform this task. Elector John, incensed by this compliance, accused Nuremberg of betraying the Protestant cause and seeking a separate peace with Charles. Nuremberg responded by stating that it had obeyed the emperor in this political matter as an obedient imperial city. Whereas several cities joined Nuremberg in refusing to protest the election, all the Protestant princes except Margrave George joined Elector John in his stand on the issue.[3]

Even though Charles apparently was involved in difficult political problems outside Germany that would preclude the use of force against the Protestants, as threatened in the recess of the Diet of Augsburg, the princes and representatives of cities attending the meeting at Schmalkalden could not feel certain that circumstances might not soon cause him to change his mind. For this reason, the question of the right to resist the emperor by force again was raised. Whereas most of the theologians, drawing their arguments from the New Testament, continued to advise against armed resistance,[4] the jurisconsults in increasing numbers maintained that imperial estates and cities had rights as well as duties in the empire and that the emperor was bound by the imperial constitution and law to respect these rights that he had sworn to uphold. If he did not act accordingly, if he ignored a legal appeal and threatened to punish with force those who had presented such an appeal legally, the estates had a right to resist such an action. Far from being an absolute monarch, the emperor ruled only with the cooperation of the estates.[5] Luther and his colleagues at Wittenberg reluctantly accepted this view, being moved to a large extent by the argument that the emperor was acting in religious matters as a tool of a corrupt papacy and its supporters.[6] Whereas the City Council of Nuremberg began to express greater differences of opinion with respect to the right of armed resistance, Spengler consistently maintained that, according to the Bible, a Christian must obey his government, whether it is good or bad. Yet he consistently sought to defend the Reformation in Nuremberg by legal means.

When the representatives of Nuremberg made it clear that Nuremberg would continue to refuse to join a military alliance against the emperor, the representatives of the princes accused the city and also Margrave George of deserting the Word of God and seeking a separate peace with Charles. The City Council of Nuremberg denied this allegation, asserting that it had acted on the advice of outstanding theologians who had based their arguments on the Word of God, which made it clear that one did not have the right to resist the emperor by force, a position maintained previously also by Elector John and his theologians. The city did not seek the good will of the emperor but the grace of God and the guidance of his Word, preferring to live in temporal danger rather than in eternal damnation.[7] Although most of the Protestant princes disagreed with the position of Nuremberg and Margrave George, they did not break relations with them but continued to try to convince them that it was right to resist the emperor by force. They also brought the two into other discussions of such questions as ways and means of stopping the actions of the Imperial Chamber Court against Protestants, cooperation of Protestants in the event a prince or city should be brought to court, and the formulation of a joint appeal against the recess of Augsburg.[8]

The recess of the meeting of Schmalkalden provided for a league of Protestant princes and cities for the purpose of resisting attempts to bring them back into the Catholic fold by force; the presentation to the emperor of an appeal requesting the modification of the harsh provisions of the recess of the Diet of Augsburg, especially with respect to legal processes against Protestants in religious matters; cooperation among the members of the league in responding to legal processes; cooperation in producing a common church order; the planning of common action against the Anabaptists; and requesting the support of the emperor and other European rulers in convening a church council in Germany to solve religious differences.[9]

The recess of Schmalkalden was accepted unconditionally by electoral Saxony, Hesse, Braunschweig-Lüneburg, Braunschweig-Grubenhagen, Anhalt-Bernburg, Mansfeld, Madgeburg, and Bremen. The representatives of Strassburg, Ulm, Constance, Lindau, Kempten, Memmingen, Heilbronn, Reutlingen, Biberach, and Isny agreed to recommend its acceptance to their respective cities and to inform Elector John of their action within six weeks. Margrave George and the cities of Nuremberg, Windsheim, and Weissenburg refused to accept it. Elector John and Landgrave Philip, however, believed that they could induce Margrave George and these cities to change their minds and join the league.

The margrave, however, was inclined to oppose resistance, for he maintained that "no Christian had the right to oppose the imperial majesty as the highest temporal authority and sovereign power with the sword or in any other way." Although he was sincere in this religious commitment, there can be no doubt that George did not wish to jeopardize the receipt of the two principalities, Opel and Ratibor in Silesia, from the emperor.[10]

At the conclusion of the meeting at Schmalkalden, the City Council of Nuremberg asked its theologians and jurisconsults, and also Spengler, to analyze the recess. Spengler consistently stated that divine law took precedence over human law. He wrote to Vogler on 10 January 1531, stating that the city council and he continued to oppose armed resistance against the emperor, even though the Saxon theologians had changed their minds in support of it. No one could convince him, he insisted, that it is Christian to take up the sword against one's government. His city council found it difficult enough to face threats of the emperor, the Swabian League, and the Imperial Chamber Court without making outright enemies of them by joining the Schmalkaldic League, especially since some of its members held erroneous doctrines with respect to the Lord's Supper. Spengler believed that in solving such difficult problems it was most important to have a clear conscience and trust in the mercy of God.[11]

The theologians of Nuremberg could not come to a common agreement with respect to the right of resistance. Osiander, in response to the city council's request for another memorandum on the subject, concluded as previously that there might be instances in which the estates and cities could resist the emperor, but the decision to do so should rest with the jurisconsults. With respect to the question of whether an individual Christian could resist an unchristian action of the government by force, however, he answered firmly in the negative.[12]

On 20 January 1531, the City Council of Nuremberg wrote Margrave George that its advisers were still divided on the question of armed resistance to the emperor, although it could assert that the majority opposed it. Because of the seriousness of the situation, it did not wish to make a hasty decision, especially because an open split among the Protestants would encourage the emperor to act against them.[13] When counselors of Elector John and Landgrave Philip arrived in Ansbach on 16 Feburary to induce George to join the alliance, he gave them his final refusal, thereby following the advice of the majority of his advisers and those of Nuremberg. He expressed his willingness to cooperate with the elector, however, in seeking legal means of resisting attacks upon Protestants in the Imperial Chamber Court.

When Elector John's counselors Hans von der Planitz and Werner von Waldenstein arrived in Nuremberg on 18 February, they emphasized before the city council that failure to be prepared for an attack by the emperor would be tantamount to admitting that the preaching of the Word of God and support of church reforms had been wrong. The council answered through Kress and Volckamer that it had no thought of deserting the Word of God and the Protestant estates, but it could not act against its conscience by resisting the emperor with force or joining an alliance against him. It promised, however, to continue to consider the matter and also to stand by the Protestant estates in support of all the other articles of the recess of Schmalkalden. Although it promised to let Elector John know the outcome of its further deliberations, Nuremberg, like Margrave George, never joined the Schmalkaldic League.[14]

Before the Protestant estates had left Schmalkalden they had made arrangements to meet again to attempt to work out the military provisions of the alliance. When they assembled in Schmalkalden on 29 March 1531, Nuremberg and the margrave had not been invited, and feelings between them and the other Protestants were strained. Because the Protestant princes in the recess of Schmalkalden had inferred that Luther supported their views concerning armed resistance to the emperor, the city council was especially disturbed. Spengler accordingly approached Luther through Veit Dietrich to warn him of this inference.[15] Luther answered Spengler on 15 Feburary, stating that as a theologian he could not decide this question. In a confidential memorandum prepared for Spengler on 18 March, Luther stated that he left the question of resistance up to the jurists as a matter of conscience, although he admitted that if the emperor attacked one because of his religion, he could resist the emperor not as a Christian but as a citizen.[16]

Spengler and the city council also were disturbed by the fact that the elector apparently had made a compromise with Butzer with respect to the Lord's Supper that would enable the South German cities to join the League. Spengler distrusted the irenical Butzer, who had softened Luther's attitude toward the German Zwinglians during a visit with him at the Coburg. Spengler called him "a very tricky and sly little fellow.[17] In Augsburg, where the city council likewise worked for the compromise, the preachers Agricola and Frosch objected and were forced to leave the city. Spengler wrote these two men letters of consolation and induced the clergy of Nuremberg to do likewise.

Frosch came to Nuremberg, where he became the preacher at Saint Sebald, replacing Schleupner, who had retired.[18]

Of considerable interest at this time was the visit of Queen Mary of Hungary, the widowed sister of Charles V and Ferdinand, on her way to the Low Countries to take the deceased Margaret's place as regent there. The Protestant preacher who accompanied her administered the Lord's Supper to her in both kinds. When she was compelled to replace him with a Catholic priest, Spengler asked Luther to try to induce her to retain this Protestant preacher so that he could help spread the Reformation in the Low Countries.

Although Nuremberg and Margrave George of Brandenburg-Ansbach were not represented at the second meeting of the Schmalkaldic League, where the members decided to maintain the alliance for a period of six years, that is, to 18 Feburary 1537, they were asked to attend the third meeting that convened in Frankfurt a.M. on 5 June 1531, particularly because of the plan to discuss financial matters. There the members also took up the question of the treatment of the Anabaptists, the representatives of Nuremberg asking for mild punishments and a differentiation between the leaders and the misled. Nuremberg and Brandenburg-Ansbach also suggested the formulation of a common church order to be used by all the Lutherans, a proposal opposed by the majority.[19]

By remaining aloof from the Schmalkaldic League, which became a powerful political as well as religious force, Nuremberg relinquished its dominant role in the spread of the Reformation. Henceforth, the league became virtually an *imperium in imperio*, joined by all the Lutheran estates and cities in northern Germany and by the four South German cities that had leaned toward the Zwinglian interpretation of the Lord's Supper. Meanwhile, the period of grace of the recess of the Diet of Augsburg expired on 15 April 1531, without an armed attack on the Protestants. The league's constitution was finally accepted by its members on 23 December 1535, more than a year after Spengler's death.[20]

THE RELIGIOUS PEACE OF NUREMBERG, 1532

Whether or not the City Council of Nuremberg was justified in its refusal to join the Schmalkaldic League in defense of Protestantism, it was consistent in adhering to a political philosophy originally maintained by Electoral Saxony. For the immediate future at least, its judgment with respect to the emperor's policies appeared correct. For Spengler, the Peace of Nuremberg was the culmination of a policy of long standing that kept his city from a direct confrontation with the emperor.[21]

Soon after the Diet of Augsburg of 1530, it became apparent that Charles could not carry out the threat against the Protestants contained in the recess. For one thing, the pope refused to call a church council for the purpose of solving the question of heresy and its suppression. Furthermore, the Turks again threatened Hungary and the empire. It was obvious that Charles and Ferdinand could not stop the Turks without the support of all the Germans, including the Protestants, whose assistance they could not obtain by carrying out the recess of the Diet of Augsburg.

When Charles and Ferdinand approached the Protestant princes for the purpose of resuming the negotiations begun at Augsburg, the latter now insisted that they would not give aid against the Turks without the recognition of their Protestation of Speyer and their Augsburg Confession until decisions on religious matters were made at a church council and without the quashing of the cases pending against the Protestants in the Imperial Chamber Court. Following the advice of Pope Clement VII that he work toward a religious peace with the Lutherans before it was too late, Charles agreed to continue discussions with them at the coming Diet of Regensburg.

Meanwhile, Charles had two electors, Archbishop Albert of Mainz and Count Palatine Louis, as his negotiators schedule a meeting with the Protestant estates at Schweinfurt at the end of April 1532, for the purpose of getting support against the Turks and discussing a religious peace. To demonstrate his sincerity, the emperor ordered quashed the cases against the Protestants in the Imperial Chamber Court. Nuremberg, unhappy with its isolation from the Protestant estates, was pleased with the invitation of Elector John to attend the meeting and sent as its representatives Bernhard Baumgartner and Leo Schürstab, who also represented Weissenburg, Windsheim, Heilbronn, and Schwäbisch-Hall.

The negotiators appointed by Charles presented the Protestant representatives with a number of articles to serve as the basis for the discussions: that until the meeting of a church council, (1) the Protestant estates and cities were to make no further religious changes; (2) that they were not to support either Zwinglians or Anabaptists; (3) that neither side should attempt to force the subjects of the other side to change their religious faith; (4) that the adherents of the Augsburg Confession and the Apology were to assert publicly nothing pertaining to faith not contained in them; (5) that neither side should attack the other orally or in writing; (6) that the Protestants were to make no further changes in episcopal jurisdiction and appropriate no more ecclesiastical property and income; (7) that both sides were to work for peace, the early calling of a church council, and aid against the Turks; and (8) that the Protestants were to obey the emperor and the king of the Romans and give up their alliance against them and the Catholic estates.[22]

After lengthy discussions, the representatives of the Protestants responded (1) that they would adhere to the Augsburg Confession and the Apology and would publicly state nothing pertaining to faith not contained in them; (2) that they would keep those changes in ceremonies and customs made according to the Word of God until the meeting of a free, univeral, Christian church council held on German soil; (3) that they would adhere to the recess of Speyer of 1526 and to their Protestation and Appeal of 1529 until the meeting of the council; (4) that they would permit Christians who differed from the majority in their beliefs to have their own preachers; (5) that they sought the right to have their own clergy preach and administer the sacraments to their soldiers in the armed forces; (6) that in the selection of imperial judges and officials no differences should be made because of their religious faith; (7) that they should be permitted to retain the changes made in episcopal jurisdiction and church property until the meeting of a church council; (8) that cases concerning matters of religion pending against them in the Imperial Chamber Court and other courts be quashed; and (9) that in return for their aid against the Turks, the emperor should assure them that peace would be maintained among the estates.[23]

Obviously, the emperor could not give in to all these demands. When his two negotiators realized that they could achieve no peace with the Protestants unless he made some concessions to them, they communicated this to him and requested new instructions. In response to this, Charles stated that he wished to conclude the peace at the coming Diet of Regensburg and ordered his negotiators to continue discussions with the Protestants in Nuremberg, closer to Regensburg. When the discussions were resumed in Nuremberg on 8 June 1532, it became apparent that the emperor's new conditions for peace contained no significant change from those presented at Schweinfurt, the Protestants cleared the way for compromise and peace by requesting the emperor to include them in the general peace of the land (*gemeiner Landfrieden*), from which they had been excluded in Augsburg in 1530, and to protect them in their faith as well as in secular matters.[24]

Once more, at a critical time, a problem arose that threatened to divide the Protestants, namely, aid against the Turks. It was Lazarus Spengler who was most responsible for the determination of the City Council of Nuremberg to give the aid without reference to the granting of peace to the Protestants. Margrave George agreed with Spengler with respect to the aid. The emperor, angered by the fact that the Catholic estates were trying at the Diet of Regensburg to weaken his authority by blocking his peace efforts, instructed his negotiators on 1 July to arrange a simple armistice with the Protestants. After Luther had expressed to his prince his opinion that the Protestants should be grateful to the emperor for offering them peace, all the Protestant princes except Philip of Hesse agreed to accept it. Spengler went so far in his unwarranted optimism as to write Veit Dietrich a letter praising the "peace-loving and pious emperor" and his negotiators for their efforts to bring about peace.[25] The emperor, convinced that the Catholic majority at the diet would not in the least cooperate in obtaining internal peace, decided to act without them.

The Peace of Nuremberg, granted by Charles and signed by his negotiators and the Protestants on 23 July 1532, provided that the emperor would summon a church council within six months to meet within a year; that until the council convened, the estates were not to resort to arms for reasons of faith; and that all cases against the Protestants pending in the Imperial Chamber Court be quashed until the meeting of the church council or the next diet, whichever came first. That these provisions applied specifically to the members of the Schmalkaldic League, Nuremberg, and Brandenburg-Ansbach subsequently caused many problems when the Imperial Chamber Court again prosecuted cases involving church property and income. Because the Catholic majority of the diet would not agree to stop legal processes against the Protestants, the emperor did not include the Peace of Nuremberg in the recess of the Diet of Regensburg. On 6 November he ordered the Imperial Chamber Court to quash the cases pending against the Protestants without giving an explanation for his action.[26] Despite the uncertain nature of this peace, or temporary armistice, Nuremberg profited from it and cooperated with Ferdinand by sending him troops and military equipment for use against the Turks. Spengler continued to his death two years later to believe in the ultimate good intentions of Emperor Charles, agreeing with Luther that God would see to it that the Reformation would continue for the good of all.[27]

While Spengler and the city council were concerned primarily with maintaining peace with Charles V, Philip of Hesse was laying plans for a major coup against Catholicism and Habsburg power by helping put the Lutheran Duke Ulrich back on the throne of Württemberg, which had been given to Ferdinand as a fief in September 1530. To achieve this, he sought the assistance of the kings of France and England. The increase in diplomatic activity disturbed Spengler greatly, for he feared that it would lead to a general war. He likewise believed that giving support to King Henry VIII of England in his request for Nuremberg's approval of his plans to set aside Queen Catherine for Anne Boleyn would constitute an attack on Charles V rather than on the pope.[28]

Aware of the fact that it would be easier to arouse Germans against the pope than against Charles V, Spengler opposed both the forceful return of Württemberg to Duke Ulrich and the support of Henry VIII's separation from Catherine. The city council hesitated to give Henry VIII its opinion with respect to the case and also refused to assist Landgrave Philip in his seizure of Württemberg, although it increased its own military strength to be ready to protect itself in the event of a general war. It likewise was reluctant to come to the aid of Ferdinand, who had requested its support. In a letter of 24 May, Spengler informed Dietrich that Philip of Hesse easily had defeated and dispersed the forces of Ferdinand at Lauffen in Württemberg and had seized the entire territory without further resistance. This, he stated, he greatly regretted, for he feared that the landgrave would continue the fighting to recoup his expenditures and acquire buffer lands for himself and the duke, thereby causing Ferdinand and Charles to bring foreign troops to Germany and start a general conflagration. He added in a letter of 12 June that he feared an immediate French attack on the emperor in Germany as well as an attack by Philip on Hapsburg lands.[29]

Spengler's consistent resistance to pursuing policies detrimental to the empire and to peace gained him the ill will not only of Philip of Hesse but of friends of the excommunicated Albert of Prussia, in whose behalf King Sigismund of Poland had requested Nuremberg's support in the Imperial Chamber Court.[30] He also lived to see his loyal friend Georg Vogler replaced as chancellor of Margrave George by Sebastian Heller, who apparently influenced the margrave to give up his friendly attitude toward Nuremberg. Spengler nevertheless still hoped for the resumption of good relations between the two governments, observing that "for two governments whose lands adjoin there must be rain and storms as well as sunshine."[31]

FIG. 4 Spengler's home, "Zum Einhorn" and "Zum Rosenbusch."

chapter twelve

SPENGLER'S LAST YEARS

Although there is no necessary causal connection, the decline of Nuremberg's leadership in the political and religious affairs of the Holy Roman Empire following its refusal to join the Schmalkaldic League coincided with the decline of Lazarus Spengler's health. Like the other German imperial cities, Nuremberg could not resist the growing strength of the territorial princes even though it retained its relative autonomy until its absorption by Bavaria in 1806.

HIS ILLNESS

As early as 1529, the year in which his wife Ursula died, Spengler suffered a debilitating attack of the stones that prompted the making of his first will and testament, supplemented by a confession of faith. Nevertheless, he continued to work hard. On 19 July 1530, the city council, in recognition of his outstanding service as *Ratsschreiber* and in the hope that he would continue to serve in this capacity, gave him "a horse with a little wagon built to his specifications" and provided him with oats for a horse. It also instructed the housekeeper of the city hall and his wife to supply him with meals and other needs while he was at work there. It selected Hieronymus Ebner, his good patrician friend and coworker in bringing the Reformation to Nuremberg, to supervise the carrying out of these arrangements.[1] The previous December it had provided him with a gift of fifty gulden to help defray his expenses.[2]

Two years later, the illness returned. On 24 July 1531, Spengler wrote Veit Dietrich that he had experienced a deadly illness "from which a just and faithful God" had saved him, "without a doubt because of the earnest prayers of many pious Christians," adding that he had been "in the Lord's school of discipline" where he had learned "how sweet, good, and compassionate the Lord is to those who trustingly call upon him." He complained that he was physically so weak and exhausted that he feared that he might have consumption. He did not know "what God intended to do with him" but requested Dietrich, Luther, and others at Wittenberg to pray for him. He said that he now knew "what great power could be derived from the communion of saints."[3]

Spengler informed Dietrich, in a letter of 16 September 1532, that he had been exceptionally weak for about a month. His illness was complicated, he thought, by the fact that "our pious Christian patron, Hieronymus Ebner," who had been particularly helpful to him in recent years, had died, depriving his fatherland not only of an experienced Christian leader but also of an able statesman. But he trusted that God would continue to protect his small band of faithful followers and not permit the destruction of his Word. Spengler also expressed concern over Luther's difficulty with a leg of his, to which the *Ratsschreiber* had referred in a letter of 29 July and which he again mentioned, stating that he was very pleased to learn that the open sore had healed but noting that this was a serious ailment for which doctors did not seem to have found a cure.[4] In April, he wrote that he was happy that Luther had recovered completely and thanked God for having "spared this hero." He hoped that God would "grant us his grace so that we may have this useful man with us for a long time."[5]

At the beginning of the sixteenth century, large cities, especially important trading centers, suffered epidemics of various kinds. On 12 November 1533, Spengler wrote Dietrich that about forty people, mostly children, were dying daily in Nuremberg and that during the previous four months about five thousand inhabitants of the city had died. In his next letter, written on 24 November, he reported that the number of deaths was declining but that the epidemic had claimed as its victim one of his sons, Christoph, only twenty-seven years of age. The next month he informed Dietrich that his good friend and able coworker Jorg Höpel had died of jaundice while under the care of doctors in Augsburg.[6] His own continued poor health and disheartening personal losses led him to draw up a second will and testament and revise his confession of faith during the last days of 1533. In February of the following year, he wrote that his illness would soon make it impossible for him to retain his office as secretary. He asked Dietrich and Luther to pray to God for him as he prayed for them.[7]

Sorrow over Vogler's replacement at the court of Margrave George by Sebastian Heller also caused him considerable grief.[8] On 7 August Spengler evinced a ray of hope and excitement in writing to Dietrich that he and his friends at Nuremberg were greatly interested in the publication of Luther's translation of the Bible and in receiving copies as soon as possible. In his last letter to Dietrich, written on 26 August 1534, Spengler, after discussing numerous politico-religious problems, referred to his increasing weakness, particularly in his legs, which now kept him confined to his home.[9]

After Spengler had had his last wishes fulfilled, that is, to see in print the completed Brandenburg-Nuremberg Church Order and Luther's translation of the Bible, he died, on 7 September 1534, at the age of fifty-six, in the evening during the ringing of the church bells. Veit Dietrich wrote at the bottom of Spengler's last letter to him, "Die post has scriptas XIII. mortuus est hoc est Septembris 7. post vesperas." Melanchthon commented, "He has departed in blessedness from this vale of tears into eternal life, yet with the deep sorrow of myself and the city who have lost such a true citizen and friend." Camerarius wrote, "Few people can judge this early how much we have lost by the death of this man." Camerarius and Eobanus Hessus wrote funeral poems, and later a medal was struck in his memory.[10] Georg Vogler sent Christoph Kress his condolences, stating that the city council had lost in him "a faithful Christian and constant servant of the common welfare whom it could not soon replace."[11]

Spengler's reputation as a political leader is reflected in the opinion expressed by Dr. Konrad Peutinger, humanist secretary of the City Council of Augsburg, in a letter to the City Council of Memmingen in 1524, in which he stated that he would refer the problem submitted to him "to Lazarus Spengler, the *Ratsschreiber* of Nuremberg, who is very well versed in matters of this kind and in whom I have especially great confidence." As late as 8 March 1530, Peutinger, in a letter to Pirckheimer, asked him to "greet our Lazarus Spengler."[12] Although criticized by some of his contemporaries and also scholars of our time for not having urged the council to join the Schmalkaldic League, it must be stated in his defense that he, like Luther, came logically to the conclusion that the Bible did not sanction the use of force in resisting the emperor, and he clung consistently to this conviction to his death. Furthermore, he consistently adhered to Nuremberg's basic policy of loyalty to the emperor, from which it never deviated, recognizing that the imperial city's very existence depended upon his good will and support. Only a strong king or emperor could protect it against the territorial princes and keep the countryside and highways open for its merchants. It is indicative of Spengler's persuasiveness that he convinced not only the city council but also Margrave George of Brandenburg-Ansbach of the validity of this position.[13]

That Spengler's influence extended beyond political and religious matters is indicated by his numerous contacts with humanists, educators, scientists, and artists. Paracelsus (1493-1541), the well-known Swiss alchemist and physician, for example, was with him frequently while he was in Nuremberg in 1529 and 1530 and dedicated to him his well-known work *Concerning the French Disease*, written in 1529. Spengler was one of the few persons to whom Paracelsus dedicated a work.[14]

After Spengler had made his will and testament in 1529,[15] his health gradually improved to the extent that he could continue his activities for nearly five years. Because of the changed circumstances in his personal life and of deaths in his family, he wrote a second will and testament toward the end of the year 1533, which remained in effect at the time of his death.

In the first will and testament, he expressed his wish that he be buried in the cemetery of Saint John under a stone that he and his brother Georg had ordered that bore the family coat of arms. Lazarus's wife had recently been buried there. The plot and stone exist today, located near the grave of Albrecht Dürer. Spengler wished to have the traditional burial service, not because he considered such a ceremony necessary but because he wished to demonstrate his faith in, and hope for, a blessed future life.

Significant also is the fact that he arranged to have his executors, his brother Georg and his sister-in-law, Georg's wife Juliana, pay twenty gulden in his name into the Common Chest that he had helped organize in 1522. He stipulated that each of his sons then living, Lazarus (b. 1504), Christoph (b. 1506), Hieronymus (b. 1512), and Sebald (b. 1516), should receive an equal share of his estate. He made an exception, however, in the case of his son Lazarus. Because he had spent considerable sums of money on this sons's education and training, he stipulated that his brother Georg deduct a hundred gulden from his inheritance to be distributed among the other surviving brothers.[16]

The first will also throws light on Spengler's relations with his son Christoph (1506-33). Because Christoph was a frail young man who was unable to perform any kind of work, Spengler specified that he be given for his lifetime the income from a benefice that he had originally given to his son Lazarus. In addition to his share of the inheritance and the income from the benefice, Christoph was to receive a hundred gulden and his father's best suit of clothes. Christoph, however, died before his father, a victim of the plague of 1533.[17]

In the first will, Spengler specified that his friend and colleague Jorg Höpel should receive his library because none of his sons showed an interest in books. When Höpel died in 1533, he stipulated that the library be given to Paulus Spengler, son of his brother Georg. He willed to his patrician friend Hieronymus Ebner his little Bible bound in velvet and having gold clasps, but Ebner also preceded him in death. The clock in his study, the "Schlag-Hörlein," he wanted placed in the chancery for "the use of the secretaries as a remembrance of me." When his close friend Hans Lochinger, an influential citizen, died, he bequeathed the gift intended for him, a valuable white porcelain dish decorated in gold on silver and having a gilded cover containing his coat of arms, to Stefan Bayer.[18]

Of considerable interest is Spengler's disposition of his share of the two houses that stood side by side on the Zisselgasse, today Albrecht Dürer Strasse 19, that Georg and he had inherited from their parents.[19] They stood much as they were in Spengler's day until they were destroyed in a bombing raid during World War II, after which they were completely rebuilt as one house. They were located on a street leading directly from the parish church of Saint Sebald on the south to Dürer's home on the north. The city hall was across the street east of the church, and Spengler walked the short distances to these places that were so important in his career. He wanted his brother Georg to have half of these houses and to give the other half to his children, whom Georg and Juliana had helped raise.

The main features of the first will were retained in the will of 1533, but we have much greater detail in the testament of the latter concerning the disposition of Spengler's personal property because of an accident of history. Although the *Ratsschreiber* prepared a detailed inventory of his personal possessions, designated the recipients of each at his death, and had as witnesses Georg, who died shortly afterward, Georg's wife Juliana, and his sister Ursula Weigel,[20] he did not state the value of the items listed or have his testament notarized, largely because he was impressed by the honesty of and the good will among the members of his family. This apparently naive attitude was best illustrated by the fact that he loaned his brother Georg four hundred florins at interest but without stipulating the conditions of the loan in legal form. Normally, the members of the prominent citizenry of

Nuremberg had such inventories notarized before the municipal court but for business and social reasons kept them secret within their families. Spengler's inventory was made public because his son Sebald (1516-58), a weak problem child whom Juliana and other members of the family had helped far beyond the line of duty, later sued her and Stefan Bayer, a secretary of the city council who had replaced Georg as guardian, for a larger share of the inheritance before the municipal court in 1546. When the court refused to change the will, Sebald appealed the case to the Imperial Chamber Court at Speyer, which, after a long period of time, also decided against Sebald. This drawn-out case left him penniless. Because the Imperial Chamber Court had to have an official inventory of Spengler's real and personal property, it now rests in the State Archive in Munich.[21]

In the introduction to this testament, Spengler tries to make clear to his sons that he and his wife had not squandered their inheritance and income but had worked hard to add to the amount of inheritance customarily left untouched by citizens of Nuremberg in the sixteenth century, that is 800 florins for a man and 1,000-1,200 for a woman.[22] Despite the fact that he had received a good dowry of 2,000 gulden in 1501, he lost much of his money because of conditions beyond his control. His parents had died young, and therefore he had been compelled to care for his brothers and sisters; his wife, Ursula Sulmeister, was ill and often bedridden for about ten years; his mother-in-law, Margaretha Sulmeister, lived with the Spenglers several years but was unable to do housework and was frequently ill; and the cost of educating and caring for his children was exceptionally high.

Despite Spengler's emphasis upon his inability to save money, he does not appear to have been in financial difficulties. He had an excellent salary with numerous good perquisites; he had retained the normal part of his dowry, which he had added to the inheritance from his parents; he had owned a half of the valuable home in which he had lived, some land on the Fürreuth at Steinbühl, and income from a mill; and, as his inventory shows, he had accumulated valuable books, furnishings, and luxuries, including a valuable collection of rosaries. The clock that he willed to the municipal chancery, the gold-plated travel clock that he willed to Wenzeslas Linck, the copper and gold-plated lamp that he willed to Andreas Osiander, and the "four-cornered glasses used for reading" that he willed to Dominicus Schleupner were items of considerable value.[23]

Spengler also remembered the members of his family with valuable items. He still had three living sisters, whom he included in his will: Martha Spengler, to whom he gave a golden spoon containing the family coat of arms; Margaretha von Hirnkofen, to whom he gave a gold chain and a little gold heart; and Ursula Weigel, to whom he gave a gold-plated cup with a cover on which there was a figure of a soldier. He was particularly generous with his sister-in-law, Juliana Spengler, for she had cared for him and his children in many ways after his wife's death. His affection for her is evident in one of his last letters to Georg Vogler, written on 26 December 1533, which he closed by stating, "My sister-in-law and I wish you and your wife (of whom my 'geschwey' often speaks fondly) a very blessed New Year full of God's grace. Amen."[24]

HIS FAMILY

Of the nine children born to Lazarus and Ursula Spengler, only three outlived him: Lazarus (1504-47?), Hieronymus (1512-before 1545), and Sebald (1516-58). He was ambitious for all his sons, but especially for his namesake. After young Lazarus had demonstrated that he had no inclination to become a scholar or to follow in his father's footsteps, he sent him to the Netherlands to become a merchant. He showed his concern for his son's future in that vocation by writing for him in 1526 a detailed set of instructions to serve him as a guide, his "Notes for Reflection for Lazarus Spengler, My Son, Which I Gave Him at His Departure for the Netherlands." In this guide he reminds his son "how faithfully and paternally I have dealt with you in the past, what expense, care, and work I have showered on you for the sole purpose of educating you and bringing you up to be an honorable and good Christian." As in similar testaments of advice, popular in his day, Spengler urges his son to "love and trust God as your Creator, Savior, Preserver, and Giver of salvation"; to follow the law of nature in "doing to others that which you would have them do unto you"; to "be faithful in all the things you do and say for, as the wise man says, 'One day's honor is worth a thousand marks'"; to "obey those ordained as your task masters and supervisors in all honorable, godly matters"; to "flee frivolous, evil women, for many a decent man is seduced by them to the destruction of body and soul, as many historical accounts show"; not to "be hostile and quarrelsome"; to "shun all idleness," for it "is an especially strong poison for all young people"; to "speak evil of no one"; to "consider a shilling as valuable as a gulden and a pfennig as valuable as a shilling"; to be careful to "borrow from no one or to loan money to no one"; and to "beware of all games of chance for from these come much harm and evil." Spengler assures young Lazarus that if he follows these instructions, "all good fortune and salvation will follow, God willing."[25]

Spengler wrote a similar set of notes for reflection for his nephew Franz Spengler (1517-64), for whom he served as a father after Georg's death. Franz was leaving for Augsburg to study and work as an apprentice in preparation for becoming a merchant. Again, his advice reflected his conviction with respect to the importance of common sense to the sixteenth-century burgher, of the Stoic ethics of the humanists, and the strong morality of a devout Christian, pointing out the things that are "Christian, divine, and honorable."[26] Franz served as apprentice also in Lyons, France, and later returned to Nuremberg as a merchant. Because Franz was a teenager when he left Nuremberg, Spengler wrote in a much sterner parental tone than he had to his son Lazarus.

It was young Lazarus who showed the most promise as a merchant and had the most adventurous career.[27] After having given up university studies in favor of business training in Nuremberg, he served as an apprentice and later, agent in the Netherlands, probably with the Welsers of Augsburg. Here he was in touch with members of the Tucher family, with one of whom, Hans, he joined in a business partnership for the purpose of carrying on trade in Cuba in the New World. Since trade in the American colonies of Spain and Portugal opened up to the nationals of other countries in the 1520s, Nuremberg found an outlet there for a number of its products, including scientific instruments, tools of various kinds, guns, armor, horseshoes, and nails. It imported primarily gold, pearls, and sugar. From Antwerp, Lazarus wrote to the executors of his father's estate in June 1535, requesting 400 florins of his inheritance of 700 florins to prepare for the venture. His aunt, Juliana Tucher Spengler, at first refused his request but finally sent him 500 florins. Each partner put 300 florins into the venture and paid for his own provisions and passage for the journey. Hans Tucher knew Spain and the Spanish language well, and the Tucher family provided the two men with a letter of recommendation to the Fugger business establishment at Antwerp, thereby smoothing the way for them. They traveled on a Fugger ship under imperial protection, arriving in Seville in October 1535. On 26 November, Lazarus informed his aunt Juliana that their goal in the New World now was the Rio de la Plata, "the land of gold, pearls, and precious stones," indicating that Lazarus and Hans apparently had been influenced by the accounts of the fabulous wealth being brought back from this region to give up the venture in Cuba and seek their fortune in what amounted to a plundering expedition in recently opened lands, for Lazarus wrote of bringing back "booty." As he wrote to Hieronymus Tucher at Antwerp on 1 April 1536, the fleet of seven ships with which he and Hans were sailing was headed for *Tierre Firme*. The fleet landed on "the Island of Baru," near Cartagena in present Columbia, where there were numerous merchants from Seville and where Lazarus apparently remained. Although he maintained contact with Juliana, we know little about his activities in the New World. It is assumed that he died there or on the sea some time before 1547.

Hieronymous Spengler (1512-34 or 1535) was active in Carinthia, probably as a merchant, at the time of his father's death. The executors of Lazarus's will sent for him, but he died in Landshut, Bavaria, on the way to Nuremberg. Georg (1503-before 1529?), like young Lazarus, was a merchant with a venturesome spirit, but we know little about him. He died, a victim of the plague, soon after his return from a business trip to Damascus in the service of Nuremberg merchants stationed at the Fondaco dei Tedeschi in Venice.[28] Sebald (1516-before 1559), as we have seen, lacked the ability to provide for himself but lived with one of his father's sisters for three and a half years and then with Juliana. To the consernation of his relatives, he married Katharina Schmid, a propertyless woman who apparently coveted his inheritance and induced him to sue the executors of his father's estate for a larger share of the money. Despite the fact that Lazarus and Ursula Spengler had had nine children, each one of them was childless. The family name was perpetuated through the family of Georg, brother of Lazarus.

Lazarus Spengler's concern for the welfare of the members of his family was evinced not only by the terms of his will but by letters of consolation to his brother Georg and sisters Margaretha and Martha. In 1521, as we have seen, he dedicated to Margaretha, wife of Jürgen von Hirnkofer of Hiltpoltstein, the pamphlet *A Comforting Christian Instruction and Medicine for All Adversities*.[29] In it he states that human beings can give a person in tribulation poor comfort because the real physician for such a person is God for he uses the only effective medicines for believing Christians: "temptation, affliction, grief, suffering, persecution, and every adversity that comes to man."

In 1525, Spengler dedicated to his brother Georg in Venice his *Short Statement on How a True Christian Must Deport Himself Before God and His Neighbors in All His Being and Actions*.[30] In answer to Georg's question concerning the chief characteristics of a Christian, Lazarus explains that this is a matter of the heart as well as of the mind, stating that Christians should not trust alone in their good works, for these are vitiated by man's corrupt nature. If they are good, they are the work of God through the Holy Spirit, whom we embrace by faith. Man, he concludes, must despair of doing good works and trust only in the work, grace, and mercy of God given him in Christ so that he can do to others in love what God has done for him for Christ has fulfilled the law and the prophets.

In 1529, Lazarus sent Martha the little work called *How a Christian Can Comfort Himself in Tribulation and Affliction and Where He must Look for Help and Medicine.*[31] Martha, who at that time was living with her sister Margaretha, had written to Lazarus about a number of matters that had caused her considerable anxiety. In this pamphlet he lists six "medicines" for her consideration: the example of the Lord and Savior Jesus Christ, the comfort of Holy Scripture, contemplation of antidotes against sin, consideration of the evil that grows out of mere temporal happiness, the mercy and grace of God as seen in the Cross, and the comparison of temporary tribulation with eternal bliss.

HIS CHARACTER AND INFLUENCE

The best statement of Spengler's Christian faith is contained in his confession, his *Ratio fedei mei*, composed as early as 1527 and revised until appended to his last will and testament.[32] In the introduction, he states that he was moved to make a public statement of his faith by the accusations not only of those of his enemies "who hate divine truth" but also by those "who want to be Christians" but say that he embraces teachings contrary to correct Christian doctrines and Holy Scripture. Accordingly, he makes public his confession, not to obtain temporal honor but to inform everyone who reads his statement what he believes and on what he bases his hopes. This he does "by God's grace before the entire world."

Beginning each doctrinal point with the words "I believe and confess," he covers the articles of faith contained in the catechisms and catechetical sermons of his day, including the nature and work of God the Father, God the Son, and God the Holy Spirit; the universality of the Christian Church on earth as a communion of saints; resurrection; the virginity of Mary, Mother of God; the sacraments; justification by faith alone, and the role of good works in salvation. In his treatment of the sacraments, he takes great pains in showing that he does not agree with the Anabaptists and the Sacramentarians. He refers to infant baptism "as a sign of divine grace by means of which God involves himself with us and assures us that he can graciously forgive us our sins through Christ," adding that for this reason he denies "the error of the factious spirits and Anabaptists who believe that this saving sign of union and sacrament depends upon man's faith, a gift of God, and not upon God's promise, which is perpetual and unchanging."[33] "The distribution of the body and blood of Christ," he states, "is likewise the work of God by means of which such spiritual life and righteousness are fed and strengthened for the union of Christ with his followers, just as our corporal life is sustained through daily nourishment, for Christ wishes to live in us and have us live in him . . . to the end of the world."[34] He believes that one actually eats the Body and drinks the Blood of Christ that are in the Lord's Supper "under the bread and wine," for "mere bread and wine cannot cause the old man to die in us and the new man, who is one with Christ, really Christ himself, to be implanted in us." For this reason, he states, he opposes "the opinions and errors of those who take from the Lord's Supper Christ's Flesh and Blood and make of him a liar through strange, unfounded human reasoning."

Spengler also summarizes his views concerning the role of government in a Christian society and the right of armed resistance to the emperor. The prince, or government, he maintains, is "God's sword on earth," which "can be used by no person in a just and Christian manner unless he has been chosen and ordained to rule," for which reason he considers it an error that some persons conclude, contrary to God's Word, that a Christian cannot be a ruler or wield the secular sword. "Just as God rules his subjects toward righteousness through his Word and Spirit," he believes, "so he forces the godless through secular authority and the sword not to harm their neighbors," for the government must protect the innocent. If a secular government demands of a Christian an ungodly, damnable thing, he does not need to obey it, yet "he must by no means resist such a government by force or action but must passively suffer according to God's will or flee."[35]

As he had often done in the past, Spengler condemns "the terrible abomination of the Mass and its abuse under the papacy as a good work and sacrifice for the living and the dead with the invention and sanction of purgatory. . . . As no one can truthfully deny, this has been a genuine merchandizing and a fair." He again summarizes and confirms his belief "in the one sacrifice of Christ's suffering and death on the Cross for the sins of all mankind and for the eternal salvation of all who believe." He hopes that God will sustain him in this faith "until he appears with a clear and joyful conscience before Christ the just judge." He concludes with one of his favorite Bible passages, Psalm 16:1: "Preserve me, O God, for in thee I take refuge."

Martin Luther considered this confession such an excellent summary of faith that he wrote an introduction to it and had Joseph Klug publish it in Wittenberg in 1535.[36] In it he stated that next to the Bible, the "confessions of such saints as Lazarus Spengler" are the most useful guides for Christians because "one can find in them how they believed in God's Word with all their hearts, confessed God publicly, praised him with their deeds, and honored and acknowledged him in their suffering and death." "Therefore," he added, "I have published the confession of the admirable, worthy man, Lazarus Spengler, who as a true Christian devoutly accepted God's Word, believed it with all his heart, achieved many great things in its name, and finally at his departure and death confessed this faith as a comfort and strength for all weak Christians who suffer much grief and all kinds of persecution because of a faith such as that of Lazarus Spengler."

It is obvious from Spengler's confession, works of consolation, pamphlets dealing with religious subjects, and copies of sermons that he kept for frequent reference that he was a devout follower of Martin Luther. He corresponded with him ever since Luther's stop in Nuremberg on his way to and from Augsburg in 1518. Spengler frequently turned to his spiritual hero for advice on questions of doctrine, education, and politics. For example, in 1520 he wrote to Luther to seek his opinion concerning alleged doctrinal differences between Carlstadt and Melanchthon[37] and in 1525 visited Wittenberg to discuss with the reformers there details involved in setting up a new school in Nuremberg. In the same year, he requested advice from Luther concerning the correct treatment of Hans Denck and "the godless painters" of Nuremberg.[38] Three years later, he requested advice concerning Pastor Schleupner's memorandum on doing away with communion when only the celebrant was present to commune, after the city council had refused to do so.[39] In 1530, he asked Luther for his views concerning the treatment of dissidents, in 1531 on armed resistance against the emperor, and in 1533 on ways of dealing with the Zwinglians.[40] In addition to corresponding directly with Luther, Spengler maintained almost constant contact with him through common personal friends, Wenzeslas Linck, pastor of the church of the Hospital of the Holy Spirit, and Veit Dietrich, Luther's amanuensis who lived in his home and ate at his table for nearly fourteen years until he became preacher in the parish church of Saint Sebald in Nuremberg in 1535.[41]

Illustrative of Spengler's chief concerns is a letter that he wrote to Chancelor Georg Vogler on 10 October 1531. In it, a kind of a "newsletter" typical of his day, he enumerates various political and military matters of common interest, such as the rumor that Emperor Charles V planned to attend the coming Diet of Speyer. This he discounts because he has reliable information from the imperial court that Charles and Francis I of France plan to meet for important discussions at that time, that the hostile Danish king is near Amsterdam with warships, and that the emperor is still involved in his struggle with the Turks. He concludes by relating the following:

> Reliable reports of our merchants in Portugal inform us that recently a fire five miles long rained from heaven in that kingdom and, miraculously and unheard-of, the fire ignited and burned all grain, olives, and grapes in its path. We must not let this divine wonder frighten us, [although] I do not know how we can help ourselves. It seems to me that all events are forcefully hastening toward Judgment Day.[42]

Although this correspondence is concerned primarily with important religious and political matters, it also provides us with a few personal glimpses of the relations between Spengler and Luther. On 21 21 January 1534, Spengler explains in a letter to Veit Dietrich that his letter thanking him for works sent from Wittenberg had not arrived because the messenger who carried them was murdered near Coburg.[43] From 1531 to 1533, Spengler frequently expressed concern over Luther's health. In September 1532, for example, he states that he fears that the healing of the open sore on Luther's thigh might indicate serious trouble for the future and should "cause people to pray to God Almighty for this valuable man."[44] On 9 March 1534, he informs Dietrich that, among other things, "the emperor's ships" had discovered and conquered "an unbelievable land of gold," thereby indicating his interest in the explorations and discoveries in the Americas.[45] In May 1534, he wrote to his friend that he had received with great appreciation a picture of Luther, stating that he could not imagine what could have given him greater pleasure. He asked Dietrich the cost of the picture so that he could repay him for it.[46]

Everything seems to indicate that Lazarus Spengler was sincere in his expressions of Christian faith, took seriously his responsibilities for the general welfare of the citizens of Nuremberg, and led a strict, moral life. Like Luther and other reformers of his day, he was thoroughly convinced that God spoke clearly and distinctly to him through his Word and that what he learned from the Bible was unequivocally true, subject to no compromise, and unmistakably Christian. He accordingly distrusted men like Butzer who wished to solve differences between Lutherans and Zwinglians and Protestants and Catholics.[47] The Lutherans, he believed, were the only true Christians, whereas persons with differing views were tools of the devil. This was apparent in his dealings with associates, as evinced in a letter of Matthis Pfarrer, a councilman of Strassburg, to Peter Butz, secretary of that city, written on 18 September 1530. Pfarrer recommended to Butz the hiring of an able secretary who was doing excellent work in the chancellery of Nuremberg but who felt that he could not remain there because Spengler seemed to dislike him for holding somewhat different views concerning the Lord's Supper.[48]

Spengler also believed that all monasteries tended to be harmful to Christianity. Therefore he favored the dissolution of those in Nuremberg and its territory, including the monastery of Saint Clara, whose nuns, under the leadership of Caritas Pirckheimer, were certain that their faith and actions rested on the authority of the Bible. He accepted without bitterness, however, the judgment of Willibald Pirckheimer, who, in writing to a common friend, stated that, having "learned to know" Spengler's "true character . . . he gave up his friendship" with him.[49] When Melanchthon urged him to deal sympathetically with the nuns, Spengler was gracious enough to follow his advice. Likewise, he vigorously opposed Osiander on a number of occasions yet appreciated his important role in the Reformation in Nuremberg and remembered him in his will.[50] He was greatly concerned when his friend Theobald Billican, then preacher at Nördlingen, accepted the Zwinglian interpretation of the Lord's Supper in 1528 and wrote Spengler a haughty letter in response to his expression of regret over this change; yet Spengler stated that he nevertheless could "not hate Billican personally, be hostile toward him, or persecute him." Instead, he prayed to God "not to withhold his grace from him but to impart in him the luster of his divine truth."[51]

Lazarus Spengler's life and career reflected the interests and concerns of the majority of the citizens and councilmen of Nuremberg. Together with them and as one of their leaders, he accepted the basic doctrines of Luther and applied them to the urgent political, economic, social, and cultural issues of the day. There was no doubt in the minds of his contemporaries that he was a man of strong character who, for good or evil, exerted a considerable influence on the City Council of Nuremberg. Camerarius called him "the initiator and executor of all important decisions relating to the Reformation in Nuremberg."[52] As a lay leader with contacts with many important persons at home and abroad, he exerted a large influence on the Reformation throughout Germany.

NOTES

The following abbreviations have been used for frequently cited sources throughout the notes:

ARA	Ansbacher Religionsakten, in StaN
ARG	*Archiv für Reformationsgeschichte*
BB	Briefbücher, in StaN
BR	Briefe
CR	*Corpus Reformatorum: Philippi Melanchthonis Opera,* 1 (Halle, 1854)
DRA JR	*Deutsche Reichstagsakten, Jüngere Reihe*
LKAN	Landeskirchliches Archiv Nürnberg
LW	*Luther's Works,* American Edition (St. Louis and Philadelphia, 1955-)
MVGN	*Mitteilungen des Vereins für Geschichte der Stadt Nürnberg*
RB	Ratsbuch, in StaN
Ratschlb.	Ratschlagbuch, in StaN
RV	Ratsverlässe, in StaN
StadtaN	Stadtarchiv Nürnberg
StaN	Bayerisches Staatsarchiv Nürnberg
WA	Weimarer Ausgabe, *D. Martin Luthers Werks* (Weimar, 1883-)
ZbKg	*Zeitschrift für bayerische Kirchengeschichte*
ZbLg	*Zeitschrift für bayerische Landesgeschichte*
ZKG	*Zeitschrift für Kirchengeschichte*

CHAPTER ONE

1. For general accounts of Nuremberg that cover the period of the Reformation, see Emil Reicke, *Geschichte der Reichsstadt Nürnberg* (Nuremberg, 1896); Adolf Engelhardt, *Die Reformation in Nürnberg, MVGN*, 33 (1936) and 34 (1937), hereafter cited as Engelhardt, *Reformation*, 1 and 2; Friedrich Roth, *Die Einführung der Reformation in Nürnberg* (Würzburg, 1885); Gerald Strauss, *Nuremberg in the Sixteenth Century* (New York, 1966); and *Nürnberg—Geschichte einer europäischen Stadt*, ed. Gerhard Pfeiffer (Munich, 1971). *Quellen zur Nürnberger Reformationsgeschichte*, ed. Gerhard Pfeiffer (Nuremberg, 1968), contains sources for the period from June 1524 to June 1525, hereafter referred to as Pfeiffer, *Quellen*. For a detailed study of Spengler, see Hans von Schubert, *Lazarus Spengler und die Reformation in Nürnberg*, ed. Hajo Holborn, "Quellen und Forschungen zur Reformationsgeschichte," vol. 17 (Leipzig, 1934), which carries his life to 1524. See also Urbanus Gottlieb Haussdorff, *Lebens-Beschreibung eines christlichen Politici, nehmlich Lazari Spenglers, weiland vördersten Rathschreibers zu Nürnberg* (Nuremberg, 1741); Paul Kalkoff, *Die Reformation in der Reichsstadt Nürnbergs nach den Flugschriften ihres Ratsschreibers Lazarus Spenglers* (Halle, 1926); and Theodor Pressel, *Lazarus Spengler: Nach gleichzeitigen Quellen* (Elberfeld, 1862).

2. The best translation of the word *Ratsschreiber* is "council secretary," yet the English does not convey all the duties of the official or indicate the extent to which he could influence a city council.

3. See the excellent description and pictures of these two houses in Erich Mulzer, "Das Jamnitzerhaus in Nürnberg und der Goldschmid Wenzel Jamnitzer, *MVGN* 61 (1974): 48-89.

4. Karl Heinz Goldmann, *Sechshundert Jahre Stadtbibliothek Nürnberg* (Nuremberg, 1957); J. Petz, "Urkundliche Beiträge zur Geschichte der Bücherei des Nürnberger Rates, 1429-1538," *MGVN* 6 (1886): 123-74.

5. The Spengler *Geschlechtsbuch* is preserved in the Stadtbibliothek Nürnberg, Amb. 1236.8⁰.

6. Ernst Pitz, *Schrift- und Aktenwesen der städtischen Verwaltung im Spätmittelalter: Köln—Nürnberg—Lübeck* (Cologne, 1959); John P. Dawson, *The Oracles of the Law* (Ann Arbor, Mich., 1968); Rudolf Wenisch, "Aus dem Wortschatz der Nürnberger Ratsbriefbücher des 15. und 16. Jahrhunderts," *MVGN* 46 (1955): 140-261.

7. Rudolf Endres, "Zur Einwohnerzahl und Bevölkerungsstruktur Nürnbergs im 15./16. Jahrhundert," *MVGN* 57 (1970): 242-71.

8. Julia Schnelbögl, "Die Reichskleinodien in Nürnberg, 1424-1523," *MVGN* 51 (1962): 78-159.

9. Wolfgang Wüllner, *Das Landgebiet der Reichsstadt Nürnberg*, "Altnürnberger Landschaft," 19 (Nuremberg, 1970); Heinz Dannenbauer, *Die Entstehung des Territoriums der Reichsstadt Nürnberg* (Stuttgart, 1928); Gerhard Hirschmann, *Das Landgebiet der ehemaligen Reichsstadt Nürnberg* (Berchtesgaden, 1951); Fritz Schnelbögl, "Die wirtschaftliche Bedeutung ihres Landgebietes für die Reichsstadt Nürnberg," *Beiträge zur Wirtschaftsgeschichte Nürnbergs*, vol. 1, part 2 (Nuremberg, 1967), 261-317; F. L. Carsten,

Princes and Parliaments in Germany from the Fifteenth to the Eighteenth Century (Oxford, 1959), pp. 343-44, 356, contains details concerning the background of the Bavarian (or Landshut) War of Succession.

10. The letter *De . . . civitate Noribergensi commentario* is contained in German in *Die Chroniken der fränkischen Städte*, vol. 5: *Nürnberg* (Leipzig, 1874), pp. 785-804. There is an English translation in Gerald Strauss, *Nuremberg in the Sixteenth Century* (New York, 1966), pp. 58-67. The nature of the city council's authority is discussed by Gerhard Pfeiffer, "Nürnbergs Selbstverwaltung 1256-1956," *MVGN* 48 (1958): 1-25. On the role of the patricians, see Gerhard Hirschmann, "Das Nürnberger Patriziat," in *Deutsches Patriziat*, ed. Hellmuth Rössler (Limburg/Lahn, 1968), pp. 257-76, and H. H. Hofmann, "Nobiles Norimbergenses: Betrachtungen zur Struktur der reichsstädtischen Oberschicht," *ZbLg* 28 (1965): 114-50. For a discussion of the *Genannten*, see Kurt Schall, *Die Genannten in Nürnberg*, "Nürnberger Werkstücke zur Stadt- und Landesgeschichte," No. 6 (Nuremberg, 1971).

11. See Werner Schultheiss, "Albrecht Dürers Beziehungen zum Recht," in *Albrecht Dürers Umwelt*, "Nürnberger Forschungen" 15 (Nuremberg, 1971): 220-54; and "Die Einrichtung der Herrentrinkstube 1497/8 und deren Ordnung von 1561/97, *MVGN* 44 (1953): 275-85.

12. The work of the jurisconsults is discussed in Friedrich Ellinger, "Die Juristen der Reichsstadt Nürnberg vom 15. bis 17. Jahrhundert," in *Reichsstadt Nürnberg, Altdorf und Hersbruck*, ed. Fridolin Solleder and Helene Burger (Nuremberg, 1954), pp. 130-222; and Jann Whitehead Gates, "The Formulation of City Council Policy and the Introduction of the Protestant Reformation in Nuremberg 1524-1525" (Ph.D diss., Ohio State University, 1975).

13. See Kent Roberts Greenfield, *Sumptuary Law in Nürnberg: A Study of Paternal Government*, "Johns Hopkins University Studies in Historical and Political Science," vol. 36, no. 2 (Baltimore, 1918).

14. Fritz Rörig stimulated widespread interest in the role of cities in early German history with his *Die europäische Stadt und die Kultur des Bürgertums im Mittelalter* (Gottingen, 1932), translated into English and published under the title *The Medieval Town* (Berkeley, Calif., 1971). Bernd Moeller published a thought-provoking study of the imperial cities of Germany in the late Middle Ages: *Reichsstadt und Reformation*, "Schriften des Vereins für Reformationsgeschichte," vol. 69, no. 180 (Gütersloh, 1962). This was translated into French (*Villes d'Empire et reformation* [Geneva, 1966]), and this into English (*Imperial Cities and the Reformation: Three Essays* [Philadelphia, 1972]). There is an account of the spread of the Reformation in the cities primarily through lay leadership by Steven E. Ozment, *The Reformation in the Cities: The Appeal of Protestantism to Sixteenth-Century Germany and Switzerland* (New Haven and London, 1975). See also Gerald-Strauss, "Protestant Dogma and City Government in Nuremberg," *Past and Present* 37 (1967): 38-58; Harold J. Grimm, "The Reformation and the Urban Social Classes in Germany," in *Luther, Erasmus and the Reformation: A Catholic-Protestant Appraisal*, ed. John C. Olin (New York, 1969), pp. 75-86; and Ernst-Wilhelm Kohls, "Evangelische Bewegung und Kirchenordnung in oberdeutschen Reichsstädten," *Theologische Literaturzeitung* 92 (1967): 322-326.

15. Friedrich Stählin, *Humanismus und Reformation im bürgerlichen*

Raum: Eine Untersuchung der biographischen Schriften des Joachim Camerarius, "Schriften des Vereins für Reformationsgeschichte," vol. 53, no. 159 (Leipzig, 1936), p. 99.

16. See Gerald Strauss, *Nuremberg,* pp. 116-53; Leo Schuster, "Die Rolle der Nürnberger Kaufleute am Fondaco dei Tedeschi in Venedig," *Mitteilungen der Stadtbibliothek Nürnberg,* vol. 11 (1962); Fritz Schnelbögl, *Dokumente zur Nürnberger Kartographie,* "Beiträge zur Geschichte und Kultur der Stadt Nürnberg," vol. 10 (Nuremberg, 1966); Johannes Müller, "Der Umfang und die Hauptrouten des Nürnberger Handelsgebietes im Mittelalter," *Vierteljahrschrift für Sozial- und Wirtschaftsgeschichte* 6 (1908): 1-38; and Hektor Ammann, *Die wirtschaftliche Stellung der Reichsstadt Nürnberg im Spätmittelalter,* "Nürnberger Forschungen," vol. 14 (Nuremberg, 1970).

17. Endres, "Zur Einwohnerzahl," pp. 255-56; and "Sozialstruktur Nürnbergs," in *Nürnberg—Geschichte einer Europäischer Stadt,* ed. Gerhard Pfeiffer (Munich, 1971), pp. 194-99. Samuel L. Sumberg, *The Nuremberg Schembart Carnival* (New York, 1941), throws light on some aspects of the social life of the artisans and the impact of the Reformation on their popular carnival.

18. See Endres, "Zur Einwohnerzahl," p. 267; Grimm, "Urban Social Classes"; and Kurt Kaser, *Politische und soziale Bewegungen im deutschen Bürgertum zu Beginn des 16. Jahrhunderts* (Stuttgart, 1899).

CHAPTER TWO

1. See E. Bock, *Der Schwäbische Bund und seine Verfassungen (1488-1534)* (Breslau, 1927); and Johathan W. Zophy, "Lazarus Spengler, Christoph Kress, and Nuremberg's Reformation Diplomacy," *Sixteenth Century Journal* 5 (1974): 35-48. There is a chart containing diplomatic missions of Spengler in Jackson Spielvogel, "Willibald Pirckheimer and the Nürnberg City Council" (Ph.D. diss., Ohio State University, 1967), pp. 48-51.

2. StaN, Rep. 52b, no. 142, contains important documents concerning the war and the diplomacy related to it to 1507.

3. StaN, Rep. 52b, no. 142, fols. 166v-167r. The report is printed in *Willibald Pirckheimers Briefwechsel,* ed. Emil Reicke 1 (Munich, 1940): 528-29.

4. Dannenbauer, *Entstehung,* p. 183, n. 1098.

5. StaN, Rep. 52b, no. 245 (*Rechnungsvertrag*).

6. Schubert, *Spengler,* p. 99.

7. *The Writings of Albrecht Dürer,* trans. and ed. William Martin Conway (New York, 1958).

8. StadtaN, Rep. E 1, Familienpapiere Spengler, no. 46.

9. See Lewis W. Spitz, *The Religious Renaissance of the German Humanists* (Cambridge, Mass., 1963), and *Conrad Celtis, The German Arch-Humanist* (Cambridge, Mass., 1957); Irmgard Höss, "Das religiös-geistige Leben in Nürnberg am Ende des 15. und am Anfang des 16. Jahrhunderts," *Bibliothèque de la revue d'histoire ecclésiastique,* Fascicule 44, extrait des *Miscellanea historiae ecclésiasticae,* 2 (Louvain, 1967); and Gerhard Hummel, *Die humanistischen Sodalitäten und ihr Einfluss auf die Entwicklung des*

Bildungswesens der Reformationszeit (Leipzig, 1940). The humanist circle that met in Pirckheimer's home is discussed in Schubert, *Spengler*, pp. 108-47.

10. For recent studies concerning humanism and the Reformation, see Otto Herding, "Humanismus und Reformation in ihrer gegenseitigen Beziehungen," *Humanismusforschung seit 1945*, report of Deutsche Forschungsgemeinschaft (Bonn and Bad Godesberg, 1975), pp. 59-110.

11. See the helpful summary by Fritz Schnelbögl, "Stadt des Buchdrucks und Kartographie," in *Nürnberg—Geschichte einer europäischen Stadt*, ed. Gerhard Pfeiffer (Munich, 1971), pp. 215-224.

12. See *Nürnberger Ratsverlässe über Kunst und Künstler im Zeitalter der Spätgotik und Renaissance*, ed. Theodor Hampe, vol. 1 (Vienna & Leipzig, 1904), for action taken by the city council with respect to art.

13. There are selections of his notes in *The Writings of Albrecht Dürer*, pp. 207-26.

14. *Hans Sachs und Nürnberg. Bedingungen und Probleme reichsstädtischer Literatur. Hans Sachs zum 400. Todestag*, ed. Horst Brunner, Gerhard Hirschmann and Fritz Schnelbögl, "Nürnberger Forschungen," vol. 19 (Nüremberg, 1976); Josef Beifus, "Hans Sachs und die Reformation bis zum Tode Luthers," *MVGN* 19 (1911): 1-76; Waldemar Kawerau, *Hans Sachs und die Reformation*, *SVRG* vol. 7, No. 26 (1889); and Klaus Leder, *Kirche und Jugend in Nürnberg und seinem Landgebiet 1400 bis 1800* (Neustadt a.d. Aisch, 1973), pp. 111-14.

15. Ibid., pp. 15-34.

16. Paul Drews, *Willibald Pirkheimers Stellung zur Reformation* (Leipzig, 1887); Rudolph Hagen, "Willibald Pirkheimer in seinem Verhältnis zum Humanismus und zur Reformation," *MVGN* 4 (1882): 61-211; Wilhelm Eckert and Christoph von Imhof, *Willibald Pirckheimer* (Cologne, 1970); Jackson Spielvogel, "Patricians in Dissension: A Case Study from Sixteenth Century Nürnberg," in *The Social History of the Reformation*, ed. Lawrence P. Buck and Jonathan W. Zophy (Columbus, Ohio, 1972), pp. 73-90, and "Willibald Pirckheimer and the Nürnberg City Council" (Ph.D. diss., Ohio State University, 1967); and *Willibald Pirckheimers Briefwechsel*, ed. Emil Reicke, 2 vols. (Munich, 1940, 1956).

17. Hans Rupprich, "Dürer und Pirckheimer," in *Albrecht Dürers Umwelt: Festschrift zum 500. Geburtstag*, "Nürnberger Forschungen," 15 (Nuremberg, 1971), pp. 78-100. See p. 80.

18. Maria Grossmann, "Bibliographie der Werke Christoph Scheurls," *Archiv für Geschichte des Buchwesens* 70 (1968): 658-70; Phillip N. Bebb, "Christoph Scheurl's Role as Legal Adviser to the Nürnberg City Council, 1512 to 1525" (Ph.D. diss., Ohio State University, 1971).

19. Theodor Pressel, *Lazarus Spengler nach gleichzeitigen Quellen* (Elberfeld, 1862), pp. 6-7.

20. *The Writings of Albrecht Dürer*, p. 25. See Schubert, *Spengler*, pp. 121-23.

21. Gerhard Pfeiffer, "Albrecht Dürer und Lazarus Spengler," in *Festschrift für Max Spindler*, ed. Dieter Albrecht et al., (Munich, 1969), p. 380 (hereafter

cited as Pfeiffer, "Dürer und Spengler"). The drawing is reproduced in Friedrich Winkler, *Die Zeichnungen Dürers*, vol. 3 (Berlin, 1938), no. 623.

22. For a reference to Spengler's seal, see Pfeiffer, "Dürer und Spengler," p. 385. See also Heinrich Kohlhausen, *Nürnberger Goldschmiedekunst des Mittelalters und der Dürerzeit* (Berlin, 1968), p. 509.

23. *Ermanung und Undterwaysung zu einem tugendhaften Wandel* (Nuremberg, 1520). See Schubert, *Spengler*, pp. 115-18; Pressel, *Spengler*, pp. 7-8.

24. *Beschreibung des heyligen Bischoffs Eusebii: der ain junger und discipel des heyligen Sancti Hieronymi gewest ist, zu dem Bischoff Damaso und dem Römer Theodosio, von dem Leben und Sterben desselben heyligsten Hieronymi . . . durch einen sondern libhaber Sancti Hieronymi aus dem Latein in das teutsch gezogen* (Nürnberg, 1514).

25. Valentin Scherer, *Dürer, des Meisters Gemälde. Kupferstiche und Holzschnitte*, 2 ed. (Stuttgart and Leipzig, 1906), p. 273.

26. Pressel, *Spengler*, pp. 8-9.

CHAPTER THREE

1. Excellent summaries of religious conditions in Nuremberg are Irmgard Höss, "Das religiös-geistige Leben in Nürnberg am Ende des 15. und am Ausgang des 16. Jahrhunderts," *Miscellanea historiae ecclesiasticae 2* (Louvain, 1967): 17-36; and Gerhard Pfeiffer, "Das Verhältnis von politischer und kirchlicher Gemeinde in den oberdeutschen Reichsstädten," in W. P. Fuchs, Staat und Kirche im Wandel der Jahrhunderte (Stuttgart, 1966).

2. The account is given in detail in Schubert, *Spengler*, pp. 131-37.

3. See Scheurl's letter of 7 January 1518 to Staupitz in Franz v. Soden and J. K. Knaake, *Christoph Scheurls Briefbuch*, vol. 2 (repr., Aalen, 1962), no. 159; Ludwig Keller, *Johann von Staupitz und die Anfänge der Reformation* (Leipzig, 1888; repr., Nieuwkoop, 1967), pp. 22-52, 188-97; and Bernd Moeller, "The German Humanists and the Beginnings of the Reformation," in *Imperial Cities and the Reformation*, ed. and trans. H. C. Erik Middelfort and Mark U. Edwards (Philadelphia, 1972), pp. 25-26.

4. Wilhelm Reindell, *Doktor Wenzeslaus Linck aus Colditz, 1483-1547*. Part one: *Bis zur reformatorischen Thätigkeit in Altenburg*. With appendix, *Documenta Linckiana 1485-1522* (Marburg, 1892). See also Charles E. Daniel, Jr., "The Significance of the Sermons of Wenzeslaus Linck" (Ph.D. diss., Ohio State University, 1968). There are extracts of Linck's sermons made by Spengler in StadtaN, Rep. 1, Familienpapiere Spengler, no. 9: "Etlich Artickel und Christenlich leeren auss Doctor Wenzeslaus Lincken . . . predigen verzaichent Im Advent 1521. Ex Evangelio Johannis."

5. *WA* 1:689-710.

6. *WA* 1:279-314.

7. See the excellent biography by Irmgard Höss, *Georg Spalatin: Ein Leben in der Zeit des Humanismus und Reformation* (Weimar, 1956).

8. Schubert, *Spengler*, p. 174.

9. Ibid., pp. 179-81.

10. Ibid., pp. 188-89.

11. *Schutzred vnnd christenliche antwurt ains erbern liebhabers gotlicher warheyt der heyligen schrifft auff etlicher vermaint widersprechen mit anzaygung warumb Doctor Martini Luthers leer nit als unchristenlich verworffen sonder mer fur christenlich gehalten werden soll* (Nürnberg: Jobst Gutknecht, ca. 1520). There is a list of notes refuting arguments of Luther's adversaries in sixteen folios, written in Spengler's own hand in 1520 in StadtaN, Rep. 1, Familienpapiere Spengler, no. 8.

12. *WA BR* 1:609 n. 5; *LW*, 48; *Letters*, 1:148-51.

13. Printed in Rudolph Hagen, "Willibald Pirkheimer in seinem Verhältnis zum Humanismus und zur Reformation," *MVGN* 4 (1882): 61-211. For accounts of the conflict with Eck, see Engelhardt, *Reformation*, 1:33-61; Schubert, *Spengler*, pp. 201-53; Karl Schornbaum, "Nürnberg und die Bulle exsurge domine," *ZbKg* 10 (1935): 91-96; and Willehad Paul Eckert and Christoph von Imhoff, *Willibald Pirckheimer, Dürers Freund* (Cologne, 1971), pp. 269-76.

14. Pfeiffer, "Spengler und Dürer," p. 386.

15. "Widerfechtung und auflösung," StadtaN, Rep. E, Familienpapiere Spengler, no. 8. See Schubert, *Spengler*, p. 209.

16. As quoted by Engelhardt, *Reformation*, 1:46.

17. This profession (*Erbieten*) is published in modern German in Eckert and Imhoff, *Pirckheimer*, pp. 274-76. See StaN, BB 81, 274r.

18. Engelhardt, *Reformation*, 1:50-51; Haussdorff, *Spengler*, pp. 40-43.

19. *WA BR* 2:217-18.

20. Hagen, "Pirckheimer," p. 118; Schornbaum, "Nürnberg und die Bulle," p. 91-96, contains "Die Appellation der Stadt Nürnberg gegen die Bulle exsurge domine. 1520."

21. There is a copy of the city council's detailed "Instruction" to its representative Jakob Muffel in Spengler's handwriting on how to appeal to Duke William, StadtaN, Rep. E 1, Familienpapiere Spengler, no. 18.

22. Hagen, "Pirkheimer," pp. 120-23.

23. Spengler's letter of 10 January 1521 is printed in Hagen, "Pirkheimer," pp. 124-26.

24. Engelhardt, *Reformation*, 1:56-57.

25. Only Spengler's letters are extant. See Schubert, *Spengler*, p. 218.

26. Paul Kalkoff, *Pirkheimers und Spenglers Lösung vom Banne 1521* (Breslau, 1896).

CHAPTER FOUR

1. Schubert, *Spengler*, pp. 264-65. Spengler's copy of the Supplication in his own handwriting is in StandtaN, Rep. E, 1, Familienpapiere Spengler, no. 19.

2. StaN, SI L 43, no. 13.

3. Oskar Schade, *Satiren und Pasquille aus der Reformationszeit*, 3 (Hanover, 1863): 36-58; Kalkoff, *Reformation*, pp. 15-43.

4. *DRA JR*, 2, 886-892; M. M. Mayer, *Spengleriana* (Nuremberg, 1830), pp.

13-61; Pressel, *Spengler*, pp. 28-32; Schubert, *Spengler*, pp. 288-98. There is a copy of the report in Spengler's handwriting in StadtaN, Rep. E 1, Familienpapiere Spengler, no. 20.

5. Mayer, *Spengleriana*, pp. 52-59; Engelhardt, *Reformation*, 1:77.

6. Pressel, *Spengler*, pp. 28-32.

7. See, for example, StaN, RB XII, 3r, 78r, and 89r.

8. *Die tröstliche christliche Anweisung und artznei in allen widerwertigkeiten*, in Pressel, *Spengler*, pp. 32-35. See Schubert, *Spengler*, pp. 309-11.

9. Pfeiffer, "Dürer und Spengler," pp. 387-88; Friedrich Roth, *Die Einführung der Reformation in Nürnberg* (Würzburg, 1885), p. 93; Markus Zucker, *Dürers Stellung zur Reformation* (Erlangen, 1886), pp. 14-19; Heinrich Lutz, "Albrecht Dürer in der Reformationsgeschichte," *Historische Zeitschrift* 206 (1968): 32-44, who does not believe that Dürer wrote the passage in the diary and whose *psychologistische Beweisführung* is discounted by Pfeiffer; Hans Rupprich, *Willibald Pirckheimer und die erste Reise nach Italien* (Vienna, 1930); Carl C. Christensen, "The Nürenberg City Council as a Patron of the Fine Arts" (Ph.D. diss., Ohio State University, 1965); and *The Writings of Albrecht Dürer*, trans. and ed. William M. Conway (New York, 1958).

10. Schubert, *Spengler*, pp. 153, 171.

11. *The Writings of Albrecht Dürer*, p. 89.

12. StaN, RV 669, 2v (18 October 1521) shows that the city council decided to publish the Edict of Worms at the City Hall "before notaries and witnesses" to show that it was carrying out the command of the emperor.

13. Engelhardt, *Reformation*, 1: 88-92; Gerhard Pfeiffer, "Entscheidung zur Reformation," in Pfeiffer, ed., *Nürnberg—Geschichte einer europäischen Stadt* (Munich, 1971), pp. 148-49; Emil Reicke, *Nürnberg, pp. 792-94.*

14. Wilhelm Krag, *Die Paumgartner von Nürnberg und Augsburg* (Munich and Augsburg, 1919).

15. Spengler's reliance on Osiander for advice in religious matters is evident in the number of memorandums of the theologian that he bound together in a volume of documents that he used heavily. The volume is in the Landeskirchliches Archiv in Nuremberg (Fenitzerbibliothek IV, 906.2⁰). See the description of the contents of the volume by Helene Burger, "Ein reformationsgeschichtlicher Handakt Lazarus Spenglers," *ZbKg*, 31 (1962), pp. 31-39.

16. RB 12, 221v-222r; Pfeiffer, "Einführung," p. 114.

17. Ibid., p. 113.

CHAPTER FIVE

1. Willy Scheel, *Johann Freiherr von Schwarzenberg* (Berlin, 1905).

2. See Hans von der Planitz, *Berichte aus dem Reichsregiment in Nürnberg, 1521 bis 1523*, ed. Ernst Wülker and Hans Virck (Leipzig, 1898).

3. Schubert, *Spengler*, p. 323; Georg Ludewig, *Die Politik Nürnbergs im Zeitalter der Reformation* (Göttengen, 1893), p. 18; Friedrich Roth, *Die Einführung der Reformation in Nürnberg, 1517-1528* (Würzburg, 1885), pp. 104-08.

4. Schubert, *Spengler*, pp. 336-43.

5. Ibid., pp. 346-49. There is a fragmentary copy in Spengler's handwriting in StadtaN, Rep. 1, Familienpapiere Spengler, no. 10. StadtaN, Rep. 10, Nachlass Dr. Hans von Schubert, no. 2, contains Schubert's transcription of "Lazarus Spengler's Apologie Luthers" and also of Spengler's "Warumb Luthers leer not und nutz sei."

6. *Die haupt artickel durch welche gemeyne Christenheyt bysshere verfuret worden ist*, published anonymously by Nikel Schirlenz in Wittenberg in 1522. See Paul Kalkoff, *Die Reformation in der Reichsstadt Nürnberg* (Halle, 1926), pp. 43-48; Pressel, *Spengler*, pp. 46-50; and Ernst-Wilhelm Kohls, "Die Durchdringung von Humanismus und Reformation im Denken des Nürnberger Ratsschreibers Lazarus Spengler," *ZbKg* 36 (1967): 13-25. The subtitle in the original is *Grund und Anzeigen eines ganzen rechten christlichen Wesens*.

7. William R. Hitchcock, *The Background of the Knights' Revolt, 1522-1523* (Berkeley, Calif., 1958).

8. W. Bogler, *Hartmuth von Kronberg: Eine Charakterstudie aus der Reformationszeit*, "Schriften des Vereins für Reformationsgeschichte," no. 57 (Halle, 1897); Schubert, *Spengler*, pp. 362-66.

9. O. Schade, *Satiren und Pasquillen aus der Reformationszeit*, 3 vols. (Hanover, 1856, 1858), 2:60-72; Kalkoff, *Reformation*, pp. 52-60.

10. Schubert, *Spengler*, pp. 366-67; *DRA JR*, III, no. 31, pp. 160-61.

11. Planitz to Elector Frederick, 18 Nov. 1522, Planitz, *Berichte*, no. 113, pp. 248-50. For a helpful discussion of the Second Diet of Nuremberg, see Engelhardt, *Reformation*, 1:93-126.

12. Breve of Adrian VI, prepared 25 Nov. 1522, *DRA JR*, III, no. 75, 399-404.

13. Instructions of Adrian VI to Chieregati, *DRA JR*, III, no. 74, 390-99. Cf. Planitz, *Berichte*, nos. 133-34, pp. 305-11.

14. Engelhardt, *Reformation*, 1:104-14; Planitz, *Berichte*, p. 357.

15. Roth, *Reformation*, pp. 114-17; Arnd Müller, "Zensurpolitik der Reichsstadt Nürnberg," *MVGN*, 49 (1959): 66-169.

16. Engelhardt, *Reformation*, 1:109-10.

17. *DRA JR*, III, no. 117, 736-59.

18. Planitz, *Berichte*, no. 170, p. 419.

19. Waldemar Kawerau, *Hans Sachs und die Reformation*, "Schriften des Vereins für Reformationsgeschichte," no. 26, vol. 7 (1889), pp. 1-100; Josef Beifus, "Hans Sachs und die Reformation bis zum Tode Luthers," *MVGN* 19 (1911):1-76.

20. *Verantwortung und auflösung etlicher vermeinter argument und ursachen, so zu widerstand und verdruckung des wort gottes und heiligen evangelions von denen, die nit christen seien und sich doch christen rumen, täglich gepraucht werden.* O Clemen, *Flugschriften aus den ersten Jahren der Reformation*, 4 vols. (Leipzig, 1907-11), vol. 2, 44; Schubert, *Spengler*, pp. 401-6.

21. There are pictures of the two coats of arms, descriptions of them, and details of the imperial document in Haussdorff, *Spengler*, pp. 509-18. Heinrich

Kohlhaussen, *Nürnberger Goldschmiedekunst des Mittelalters und der Dürerzeit, 1240 bis 1540* (Berlin, 1968), p. 509, has a reproduction of Spengler's seal of 1518 and states that the appearance was influenced by Albrecht Dürer. He also has a reproduction of Spengler's coat of arms made by Dürer in 1516, pp. 411, 414.

22. StaN, RV, 1546, X, 9v, as printed in Hampe, *Nürnberger Ratsverlässe*, vol. 1 (Leipzig and Vienna, 1904), no. 3005, p. 416.

23. Engelhardt, *Reformation*, 1:127-44; Schubert, *Spengler*, pp. 429-34; Birgitta Mogge, "Studien zum Nürnberger Reichstag von 1524," *MVGN* 62 (1975):84-101.

24. *DRA JR*, IV, no. 28, 217-55.

25. Ibid., no. 105, 478-83.

26. See Eugen Franz, *Nürnberg, Kaiser und Reich: Studien zur reichstädtischen Aussenpolitik* (Munich, 1930), pp. 84-86.

27. *DRA JR*, IV, no. 107, 489-95; Schubert, *Spengler*, pp. 435-37. Wilhelm Borth, *Die Luthersache (causa Lutheri) 1517-1524. Die Anfänge der Reformation als Frage von Politik und Recht* (Lübeck and Hamburg, 1970), shows that Spengler connected the *gravamina* with the Lutheran cause. See also Schubert, *Spengler*, pp. 435-37.

28. Franz, *Nürnberg*, pp. 86-95; *DRA JR*, IV, no. 113, 506-8.

29. Ibid., no. 149, 590-613.

30. Ibid., no. 118, 516-24.

31. See, for example, the "Instruction der bündischen Städte an ihre Gesandten über das Verhalten hinsichtlich der evangelischen Lehre," *Urkunden zur Geschichte des Schwäbischen Bundes (1488-1533)*, ed. K. Klüpfel, part 2, *1507-1533*, "Bibliothek des Litterarischen Vereins in Stuttgart," 31 (Stuttgart, 1953): 314-16.

32. Pfeiffer, *Quellen*, Ratschlag no. 12, pp. 168-77.

33. Engelhardt, *Reformation*, 1:147.

34. Ibid., pp. 147-48.

35. Ibid., p. 149; Pfeiffer, *Quellen*, p. 186, no. 17c; Schmidt and Schornbaum, *Die fränkischen Bekenntnisse*, pp. 411-54.

CHAPTER SIX

1. See "Die teutsch mess" of Prior Volprecht, 1524, in Sehling, *Kirchenordnungen*, vol. 11: *Bayern*, part 1: *Franken* (Tübingen, 1961), pp. 39-43.

2. Engelhardt, *Reformation*, 1:153; Pressel, *Spengler*, p. 40-41.

3. Bernhard Klaus, "Die Nürnberger Deutsche Mess 1524," *Jahrbuch für Liturgik und Hymnologie*, 1 (1955): 1-46, esp. 37.

4. StaN, RV 70, 10v and 11v, as printed in Pfeiffer, *Quellen*, pp. 17-18: "Herrn Bernhart Sammat auf sein antwurt und bekandtnus, das er gesagt, er schiss in die neuen ordnung der mess, von rats wegen ain strefliche red sagen. . . ."

5. StaN, RV 704, 13v, 14r, 15r, 19r, printed in Pfeiffer, *Quellen*, pp. 5-7. The

instructions for the delegates to the bishop in Spengler's handwriting, their report to the bishop, and the bishop's answer are in S I L 30, no. 5, and are printed in ibid., pp. 271-76. See the detailed discussion of the bishop of Bamberg's case against the provosts in Gerhard Pfeiffer, "Die Einführung der Reformation in Nürnberg als kirchenrechtliches und bekenntniskundliches Problem," *Blätter für deutsche Landesgeschichte* 88 (1952): 112-33, and Engelhardt, *Reformation*, 1: 152-62. For the questions that the bishop asked the provosts and their answers, see Pfeiffer, *Quellen*, pp. 286-87.

6. "Verantwortung der beiden Pröpste Georg Pessler und Hektor Pömer, Mai, Juni, 1524," *Die Fränkischen Bekenntnisse: Eine Vorstufe zur Augsburgischen Konfession* (Munich, 1930), pp. 157-79; "Artikel, der sich die beiden pröbst, Georg Pessler zu St. Sebald und Hektor Pömer zu St. Lorenzen, verglichen haben nechst, als sie beisamen waren primo Juni 1524," Sehling, *Kirchenordnungen*, vol. 11, *Bayern*, part 1: *Franken*, pp. 44-45.

7. StaN, RV 704, 19r, printed in Pfeiffer, *Quellen*, p. 7. Scheurl's report of the mission is in ibid., pp. 264-65.

8. Engelhardt, *Reformation*, 1:156.

9. For the action of the cathedral chapter, see Pfeiffer, *Quellen*, pp. 103-4.

10. StaN, Ratschlb. 4, 150r-151v, printed in ibid., pp. 157-58, the bishop's sentence of 19 September 1524, on pp. 287-88, and the appeal of the provosts on pp. 290-91.

11. Ibid., pp. 174-77. Pfeiffer, "Einführung," pp. 121-22.

12. Pfeiffer, "Einführung," p. 133. The council's report of 7 april 1525, justifying its action to the bishop, is in Pfeiffer, *Quellen*, pp. 379-87.

13. For discussions of the religious colloquy, see Gottfried Seebass, "Der Nürnberger Rat und das Religionsgespräch vom März 1525," in *Festschrift für Gerhard Pfeiffer: Jahrbuch für fränkische Landesforschung*, 34-35 (Nuremberg, 1975): 467-99; Pfeiffer, "Warum hat Nürnberg die Reformation eingeführt?", "Evangelisches Studienzentrum Heilig Geist," Schriftenreihe Nr. 4 (Nuremberg, n.d.); Engelhardt, *Reformation*, 1:163-82; Pressel, *Spengler*, pp. 42-44. For records of the city council's action, memorandums to the council, a protocol of a Catholic, and a printed account of the colloquy, see Pfeiffer, *Quellen*, p. 37-60, 105-52, 211-58, 351-87, and 448-62. The city council's intervention in the affairs of the Carthusians is printed by Jürgen Lorz in Andreas Osiander D.Ä., *Gesamtausgabe*, vol. 1: *Schriften und Briefe 1522 bis März 1525*, ed. Gerhard Müller (Gütersloh, 1975) (hereafter cited as Müller, *Osiander Gesamtausgabe*, 1), nos. 29, 34, and 36, pp. 387-92, 425-28, 438-42. A critical edition of the unofficial, condensed report by Seebass is in ibid., no. 42, pp. 501-40.

14. StaN, RV 711, 14v, 16v, and 17r, printed in Pfeiffer, *Quellen*, pp. 33-35.

15. Ibid., pp. 39-41, 47-48, 204-7.

16. StaN, RV 713, 18v, with Spengler's comments; Pfeiffer, *Quellen*, pp. 50-51.

17. StaN, RB 12, 291r-v; Pfeiffer *Quellen*, pp. 52-53, in which Spengler shows that he did not expect good results from the colloquy. For a critical edition of the articles, see Seebass in Müller, *Osiander Gesamtausgabe*, 1, no. 39, pp. 454-63.

18. See Spengler's memorandum of 3 March 1525, in Pfeiffer, *Quellen*, Ratschlag no. 33, pp. 211-14, and his letter to Volckamer of 8 March 1525, in ibid., pp. 354-55.

19. Spengler's letter to Burgomaster Martin Geuder that accompanied the memorandum to the council is in Seebass, "Religionsgespräch," p. 499.

20. Gottfried Seebass, "Die Reformation in Nürnberg," *MVGN* 55 (1967-68): 252-69, especially 260-62: Pressel, *Spengler*, pp. 42-45.

21. Engelbrecht, *Reformation*, 1:169-70; R. Schaffer, *Andreas Stoss: Sohn des Veit Stoss und seine gegenreformatorische Tätigkeit* (Breslau, 1926), pp. 37-54.

22. Spengler to Volckamer, in Pfeiffer, *Quellen*, pp. 354-55. Scheurl's addresses in the name of the city council at the opening of each of the sessions on 3, 5, 7, and 12 March are printed in Seebass, "Religionsgespräch," appendix 2, pp. 492-97, together with a short account of the closing session of 14 March.

23. Müller, *Osiander Gesamtausgabe*, 1, no. 39, edited by Seebass.

24. Ibid., no. 43, edited by Dietrich Wünsch, pp. 541-76. Bernd Moeller, "Zwinglis Disputationen," "Studien zu den Anfängen der Kirchenbildung und des Synodalwesens im Protestantismus," part 1, *Zeitschrift der Savigny-Stiftung für Rechtsgeschichte*, Kanon. Abt., 56 (1970): 275-324, especially pp. 305-15.

25. "Handlung eines ersamen weysen Rats zu Nürnberg mit iren prädikanten MDXXV," Pfeiffer, *Quellen*, pp. 448-62, and the same, edited by Gottfried Seebass in Müller, *Osiander Gesamtausgabe*, 1:501-40.

26. The city council's explanation of its action to Michel von Kaden on 20 March is in Pfeiffer, *Quellen*, pp. 360-63.

27. "Von der evangelischen mess . . . zu Nürnberg . . . 1525," Sehling, *Kirchenordnungen*, vol. 11: *Bayern*, part 1: "Franken," pp. 51-55. It was in use only to 1526.

28. Pfeiffer, "Dürer und Spengler," p. 388.

29. Pfeiffer, *Quellen*, pp. 310-12.

30. For the memorandum of the jurisconsults and theologians of 31 May 1525 concerning the dissolution of monasteries, see ibid., pp. 243-48.

31. Josef Pfanner, ed., *Caritas Pirckheimer—Quellensammlung*, part 3: *Briefe von, an und über Caritas Pirckheimer (aus den Jahren 1498-1530)* (Landshut, 1966), pp. 172-73; Franz Machilek, "Klosterhumanismus in Nürnberg um 1500," *MVGN* 64 (1977): 10-45, esp. 38-40; Catherine Bernardi Ryan, "Charitas Pirckheimer: A Study of the Impact of the Clarine Tradition in the Process of Reformation in Nuremberg, 1525" (Ph. D. diss., Ohio State University, 1976). Highly critical of Spengler's role is Franz Binder, *Charitas Pirckheimer, Aebtissin von St. Clara zu Nürnberg* (Freiburg i. Br., 1878).

32. See Reicke, *Nürnberg*, pp. 817-22.

33. Pfanner, *Caritas Pirckheimer*, part 3, pp. 196-97. See Pfeiffer, "Dürer und Spengler," p. 390; for other changes by Spengler, see Engelhardt, *Reformation*, 1:222. There is an excellent brief sketch of the life of Caritas by Josef Pfanner in *Fränkische Lebensbilder*, ed. Gerhard Pfeiffer, vol. 2, "Veröffentlichung der Gesellschaft für Fränkische Geschichte," Reihe 7, A (Würzburg, 1968), pp. 193-216.

34. Engelhardt, *Reformation*, 1:222.

35. Pfeiffer, *Nürnberg*, p. 154.

36. For references to Melanchthon's memorandums on ceremonies and endowments late in 1525, see *Corpus Reformatorum*, vol. 1, nos. 314-15, and Pfeiffer, *Quellen*, p. 253. On poor relief, see Edward L. Rice, "The Influence of the Reformation on Nuremberg's Provisions for Social Welfare, 1521-1528" (Ph.D diss., Ohio State University, 1974).

37. "Eins Rats der Stat Nürnberg ordnung des grossen allmusens Haussarmer leut 1522," Sehling, *Kirchenordnungen*, vol. 11: *Bayern*, par. 1: "Franken," pp. 23-32. On the spread of municipal poor relief programs, see James M. Kittelson, "Humanism and the Reformation in Germany," *Central European History* 9(1976): 303-22, esp. 312-13; and Richard G. Cole, "The Dynamics of Printing in the Sixteenth Century," in *The Social History of the Reformation*, ed. Lawrence P. Buck and Jonathan W. Zophy (Columbus, Ohio, 1972), pp. 93-105, esp. 102-3.

38. *WA* 15:9-53; *LW*, vol. 45: *The Christian in Society* (Philadelphia, 1962), 2:339-78. Klaus Leder, *Kirche und Jugend in Nürnberg und seinem Landgebiet 1400 bis 1800* (Neustadt a.d. Aisch, 1973).

39. StaN, BB 91, 11; RB 13, 36v. See Clyde L. Manschreck, *Melanchthon: The Quiet Reformer* (New York and Nashville, 1958), pp. 133-34.

40. StaN, RB 13, 45r-v, 46v, 86v. Pressel, *Spengler*, p. 50. Gerhard Pfeiffer sees in Dürer's "Four Apostles" likenesses of persons who, like the artist, were much interested in Christian humanism and in the new school. See his "Albrecht Dürer's 'Four Apostles': A Memorial Picture from the Reformation Era," in *The Social History of the Reformation*, pp. 271-96. See also Carl Christensen, "Municipal Patronage and the Crisis of the Arts in Reformation Nuernberg," *Church History* 36 (1967): 140-50.

41. StaN, BB 92, 58r; *Corpur Reformatorum* 11:106.

42. *WA* 30:2, 517-88; *LW*, vol. 46: *The Christian in Society*, 3 (Philadelphia, 1967): 213-58.

43. Hermann Harrassowitz, "Geschichte der Kirchenmusik an St. Lorenz in Nürnberg," *MVGN* 60 (1973): 1-151; Pfeiffer, *Nürnberg*, pp. 217-18.

44. Translation by Matthias Loy, *Evangelical Lutheran Hymnal* (Columbus, Ohio, 1908), no. 247. See Philipp Wackernagel, *Das deutsche Kirchenlied*, 6 vols. (Leipzig, 1864-77), 3:48-49. Kyle C. Sessions kindly called my attention to a modern edition of a songbook of about 1536 that contained the song "Dieweil umbsunst ietzt alle kunst," for which Spengler provided the musical setting: *65 Deutsche Lieder für vier- bis fünfstimmigen gemischten Chor a cappella* nach dem Liederbuch von Peter Schöffer und Mathias Apiarius (Biener) (Strassburg, spätestens 1536), erste Partiturausgabe von Hans Joachim Moser (Wiesbaden, 1967) no. 45, pp. 133-35. The excellence of the setting is referred to by Robert Eitner, "Dieweil umsunst," *Monatshefte für Musikgeschichte* 26 (Leipzig, 1894): 71-74.

45. Gottfried Seebass, "Apologia Reformationis: Eine bisher unbekannte Verteidigungsschrift Nürnbergs aus dem Jahre 1528,"*ZbKg* 39 (1970): 20-74.

46. Letter of Magdeburg of 26 July 1524, in Pfeiffer, *Quellen*, pp. 277-78, and Nuremberg's answer of 9 August, ibid., pp. 280-83.

47. Seebass, "Apologia," p. 25, note 21; Pfeiffer, *Quellen*, pp. 360-63, 376.

48. The "Verzaichnus" is printed in ibid., pp. 440-47.

49. Seebass, "Apologia," pp. 27-28.

50. Printed in Erich Roth, *Die Reformation in Siebenbürgen*, 2 vols. (Cologne and Graz, 1962), 1:197-207.

51. Seebass, "Apologia," pp. 50-71.

52. Spengler's two memorandums are printed in Pfeiffer, *Quellen*, pp. 168-77 and 187-92.

53. Müller, *Osiander Gesamtschriften*, vol. 1, no. 19, pp. 165-74, ed. Hans-Ulrich Hofmann.

54. His defense of the city council's public acceptance of Lutheranism consists of a short summary of the defense he had prepared at the request of the council for the Reichsregiment in Esslingen. See Pfeiffer, *Quellen*, pp. 360-63.

CHAPTER SEVEN

1. For discussions of the Peasants' Revolt in Nuremberg, see Johann Kamann, *Nürnberg im Bauernkrieg* (Nuremberg, 1878); Engelhardt, *Reformation*, 1:183-212; and Günter Vogler, "Vorspiel des deutschen Bauernkriegs im Nürnberger Landgebiet 1524," in *Der Bauer im Klassenkampf* (Berlin, 1975). For the movement as a whole, see Günther Franz, *Der deutsche Bauernkrieg*, 8th ed. (Darmstadt, 1969).

2. Lawrence P. Buck, "Opposition to Tithes in the Peasants' Revolt: A Case Study of Nuremberg in 1524," *Sixteenth Century Journal* 4 (1973): 11-22; "Die Haltung der Nürnberger Bauernschaft im Baurenkrieg," *Altnürnberger Landschaft Mitteilungen* 19 (1970): 59-77; and "The Containment of Civil Insurrection: Nürnberg and the Peasants' Revolt, 1524-1525" (Ph.D. diss., Ohio State University, 1971).

3. Pfeiffer, *Quellen*, pp. 1-5, 153-54.

4. Kamann, pp. 14-15.

5. Ratsmandat, 21 April 1525, in Pfeiffer, *Quellen*, pp. 397-98.

6. StaN, RV, 13 May 1525, in Pfeiffer, *Quellen*, pp. 85-86.

7. Roth, *Reformation*, pp. 172-73. For Casimir's role, see Karl Schornbaum, *Die Stellung des Markgrafen Kasimir von Brandenburg zur reformatorischen Bewegung in den Jahren 1524-1527* (Nuremberg, 1900).

8. StaN, BB 90, 103r.

9. David M. Hockenbery, "The Social Background of the Radical Reformation in Nürnberg, 1524-1530" (Ph.D. diss., Ohio State University, 1972), p. 12.

10. Walter Elliger, *Thomas Müntzer: Leben und Werk* (Göttingen, 1975), pp. 536-626; Gottfried Seebass, *Müntzers Erbe. Werk, Leben und Theologie des Hans Hut* (Erlangen, 1972); Georg Baring, "Hans Denck und Thomas Müntzer in Nurnberg, 1524," *ARG* 50 (1959): 145-81; Pfeiffer, *Quellen*, pp. 6, 17, 25-32, 39-42, 415-16. The two pamphlets, *Aussgetrukte emplosung des falschen Glaubens . . .* and *Hoch verursachte Schutzrede und antwort wider das Gaistlosse Sanfft lebende fleysch zu Wittenberg . . .* are printed in *Thomas Müntzer: Schriften und Briefe*, ed. Gunther Franz, "Quellen und Forschungen

zur Reformationsgeschichte," vol. 33 (Gutersloh, 1968), pp. 265-319 and 321-43 respectively.

12. *WA BR*, 3: 432-33; *LW* 49:96-99.

13. Pfeiffer, *Quellen*, pp. 354-55.

14. Ibid., p. 32.

15. Ibid., pp. 26-27.

16. Ibid., pp. 295-99 contains Greifenberger's confession.

17. Artur Kreiner, "Die Bedeutung Hans Denks und Sebastian Franks," *MVGN* 39(1944): 155-96; Roth, *Reformation*, pp. 243-50; Gottfried Seebass, "Hans Denck," *Fränkische Lebensbilder* 6:107-29.

18. StaN RV, 21 Jan. 1525, in Pfeiffer, *Quellen*, p. 42. The opinion of the preachers concerning Denck's confession is in ibid., Ratschlag 25, pp. 200-203.

19. Ibid., p. 43.

20. "Ursachen warumb es beschwerlich sey, die drey maler hie in der Statt zu gedulden," StaN, S.I L., 78, no. 14, in Spengler's handwriting. See Hockenbery, "Social Background," pp. 67-69.

21. Pfeiffer, Ratschlag 24, 11 January 1525, *Quellen*, p. 200.

22. For a helpful summary of the influence of Erasmus on the humanists of Nuremberg with respect to the Sacramentarians, see Gottfried Krodel, "Nürnberger Humanisten am Anfang des Abendmahlsstreites," *ZbKg* 25 (1956): 40-50.

23. StaN, RB 13, 114 r. See the council letter of 11 May 1527 to Schwäbisch-Gmund, quoted at length in Hans-Dieter Schmid, *Täufertum und Obrigkeit in Nürnberg*, "Schriftenreihe des Stadtarchivs Nurnberg" (Nuremberg, 1972), p. 154 n. 54. Spengler's notes on Zwingli's doctrines are in StadtaN, Rep. 1, Familienpapiere Spengler, nos. 13-15, 30. His advice to the City Council of Memmingen concerning the Sacramentarian Controversy is in ibid., no. 28.

24. StaN, RB 13, 117r and v, 16 July 1526.

25. For the memorandum by Osiander and one by Linck and for Spengler's correspondence with Billican, see Haussdorff, *Spengler*, pp. 213-70. There is a copy of Billican's letter of 17 March 1527 in Spengler's handwriting in StadtaN, Rep. 1, Familienpapiere Spengler, no. 23.

26. Pressel, *Spengler*, pp. 80-82. Thomas A. Brady, Jr., has kindly sent me copies of correspondence between Spengler and Peter Butz, city secretary of Strassburg from 1520 to 1530, between December 1526 and December 1527, in which Spengler urges Butz to compel the preachers of his city to preach the pure Word of God with respect to the Lord's Supper as contained in Luther's writings and not the human reason applied by Zwingli. Jakob Wencker transcribed the letters, the originals of which are lost, in the seventeenth century and included them in the collection of documents called *Varia ecclesiastica*, vol. 11, no. 176, fols. 513r to 522v, in the Archives du Chapitre de St.-Thomas de Strasbourg.

27. In addition to Hans-Dieter Schmid, *Täufertum*, pp. 258-66, and "Die Haltung Nürnbergs in der Täuferfrage gegenüber dem Schwäbischen Bund und dem Schmalkaldischen Bund," *ZbKg* 40 (1971): 46-68, see Günther Bauer, *Anfänge täuferischer Gemeindebildungen in Franken*, "Einzelarbeiten aus der Kirchengeschichte Bayerns," no. 43 (Nuremberg, 1966); Claus-Peter Clasen,

"Nuernberg in the History of Anabaptism," *Mennonite Quarterly Review* 39 (1965): 25-39; and Austin P. Evans, *An Episode in the Struggle for Religious Freedom: The Sectaries of Nuremberg, 1524-1528* (New York, 1924).

28. Schmid, *Täufertum*, p. 146; George H. Williams, *The Radical Reformation* (Philadelphia, 1962), p. 177. For the questioning of Hans Hut in 1527, see Karl Schornbaum, ed., *Quellen zur Geschichte der Täufer*, vol. 2: *Markgraftum Brandenburg*, part 1: *Bayern*, "Quellen und Forschungen zur Reformationsgeschichte," vol. 16 (1934), no. 51, pp. 41-44.

29. Claus-Peter Clasen maintains that there was no connection between Anabaptism and the Peasants' Revolt in his *Anabaptism: A Social History, 1525-1619* (Ithaca, N.Y., 1972), pp. 152-72.

30. For a discussion of the city council's mandate of September 1527, concerning punishment of Anabaptists, see Schmid, *Täufertum*, pp. 157-59. Whereas Osiander favored capital punishment for those who persisted in their "heresy," Linck and Schleupner opposed it. Among the jurisconsults, Dr. Heppstein was the only one who explicitly opposed it. See Classen, *Anabaptism*, pp. 32-33.

31. *DRA JR*, 7, no. 153, 1325-27. This mandate, as well as that of Emperor Charles V of 4 January 1528, was based on the edict of 21 March 413 of Emperors Honorius and Theodosius II against the Donatists, demanding the death penalty for rebaptizing.

32. Schmid, *Täufertum*, pp. 47-71.

33. Spengler's copy is in the Landeskirchliches Archiv in Nuremberg, Fen. IV.2⁰, 248r-249r. See Schmid, *Täufertum*, p. 54 n. 245.

34. Ibid., p. 78.

35. "Wie sich gegen den Sacrament Schwurmern und irer vermainten lere zu hallten sei, zum kurtzten verzaichent," StadtaN, Rep. 1, Familienpapiere Spengler, no. 15.

36. StaN, Ansbacher Religionsakten, 38, 414r-v, in Karl Schornbaum, *Zur Politik des Markgrafen Georg von Brandenburg . . . 1528-1532* (Munich, 1906), p. 265 n. 85.

37. StaN, RB, 14, 224v-225r, summarized in Schmid, *Täufertum*, pp. 196-97; BB, 97, 55r-55v, printed in Hans-Dieter Schmid, "Die Haltung Nürnbergs," *ZbKg* 40 (1971): 46-68, especially p. 66.

38. "Ob ein weltliche oberkeyt mit gotlichem oder billichem rechten möge die widertäuffer, durch fewr oder schwert vom leben zu dem tod richten lassen." See Seebass, "An sint persequendi haeretici? Die Stellung des Johannes Brenz zur Verfolgung und Bestrafung der Täufer," *Blätter für württembergische Kirchengeschichte*, 70 (1970); Johannes Brenz, *Frühschriften*, part 2, ed. Martin Brecht et al. (Tübingen, 1974), pp. 480-98.

39. See his letter to Brenz of 26 March 1530, Brenz, *Frühschriften*, part 2, pp. 512-16.

40. Gottfried Seebass, "Apologia Reformationis: Eine bisher unbekannte Verteidigungsschrift Nürnbergs aus dem Jahre 1528," *ZbKg* 39 (1970): 20-74.

41. Mayer, *Spengleriana*, pp. 147-53.

42. This memorandum, entitled "Ob ein weltlich Oberkait Recht habe, in des Glaubens Sachen mit dem Schwert zu handeln," was published by Martin

Brecht in *ARG* 60 (1969): 65-75. James M. Estes provided an English translation and edition of the document: "Whether Secular Government Has the Right to Wield the Sword in Matters of Faith. An Anonymous Defense of Religious Toleration from Sixteenth-Century Nürnberg," *Mennonite Quarterly Review* 49 (1975): 22-37. See also Hans-Dieter Schmid, *Täufertum*, pp. 271-309; Erich Hassinger, *Religiöse Toleranz im 16. Jahrhundert. Motive-Argumente-Formen der Verwirklichung* (Basel, Stuttgart, 1966); and G. Gossert, "Johann Brenz, der Reformator Württembergs und seine Tolerationsideen," *Blätter für württembergische Kirchengeschichte* 16 (1912): 25-41.

43. Mayer, *Spengleriana*, pp. 70-73; Pressel, *Spengler*, pp. 52-53.

44. *WA* 31: 183-84; 207-13; *LW* 13: 42-72.

45. Gottfried Seebass maintains that the authors of these two memorandums were Osiander and Spengler. See his "An sint persequendi heretici?", pp. 40-99. Copies of these two documents, of the memorandum by the anonymous author and of his letter to Spengler as well as Spengler's letter to Brenz, were preserved in Schwäbisch-Hall. Only the anonymous memorandum and Spengler's letter survive elsewhere, that is, in the archives in Nuremberg. See Schmid, *Täufertum*, pp. 272 n. 5.

46. *WA* 11:262, 265-66.

47. Julius Hartmann, *Johannes Brenz: Leben und ausgewählte Schriften* (Elberfeld, 1862), pp. 105-13.

48. Seebass, "An sint persequendi haeretici?"; James M. Estes, "Church Order and the Christian Magistrate According to Johannes Brenz," *ARG* 59 (1968): 5-23; and "The Two Kingdoms and the State Church According to Johannes Brenz and an Anonymous Colleague," *ARG* 61 (1970):35-49.

49. StaN, RB, 14, 224v-225r.

CHAPTER EIGHT

1. An excellent and succinct account of the formation of the church order for Nuremberg and Brandenburg is Engelhardt, *Reformation*, 2:69-107. See also Karl Schornbaum, *Zur Politik des Markgrafen Georg von Brandenburg . . . 1528-1532* (Munich, 1906), and *Aktenstücke zur ersten Brandenburgischen Kirchenvisitation 1528* (Munich, 1928); and Hans von Schubert, *Anfänge evangelischer Bekenntnisbildung*, "Schriften des Vereins für Reformationsgeschichte," vol. 45, no. 143 (1928). Spengler's letter to Hans von Schwarzenberg, suggesting a joint visitation, is in StaN, Rep. 111, Ansbacher Religionsakten (ARA), 8, 118, and is quoted in Schornbaum, *Die erste Brandenburgische Kirchenvisitation* (Munich, 1928), pp. 3-4.

2. *LKAN*, Fen. IV, 906, 2⁰; StaN, ARA, 8, 268r-277r. For Spengler's list of conflicts between Nuremberg and Ansbach, see StadtaN, Rep. E, 1, Familienpapiere Spengler no. 25.

3. Sehling, *Kirchenordnungen*, vol. 11: *Bayern*, part 1: *Franken*, pp. 135-39. The twenty-three articles are printed in ibid., pp. 125-35, and in Schmidt-Schornbaum, *Die fränkischen Bekenntnisse*, pp. 462-73. See Konrad Kressel, "Schwabacher Konvent von 1528," *600 Jahre Stadt Schwabach 1371-1971* (Schwabach, 1971), pp. 204-216.

4. StaN, BB, 98, 156r, cited in Engelhardt, *Reformation*, 2:75.

5. Ibid., pp. 102-3.

6. The contents of the memorandum by Spengler, in StaN, ARA, 10, 103-105, are given in Engelhardt, *Reformation*, 2:103-4. See also his memorandum of the spring, 1526, answering the charges of the bishop, in StaN, S I L 30, no. 7a, printed in Pfeiffer, *Quellen*, pp. 253-58.

7. StaN, ARA, 169, cited in Engelhardt, *Reformation*, 2:106.

8. StaN, ARA, 170, cited in ibid., p. 106.

9. Ibid., 108-40; Reicke, *Nürnberg*, pp. 844-51.

10. The correspondence is given in detail in Haussdorff, *Spengler*, pp. 274-95.

11. StaN, ARA, 9, 18r, 20r; BB, 102r, 187r, cited in Engelhardt, *Reformation*, 2:113.

12. Mayer, *Spengleriana*, pp. 87-88.

13. Spengler's letter of 20 November 1531, StaN, ARA, 9, 98, quoted in Engelhardt, *Reformation*, 2:117.

14. Ibid., p. 118.

15. StaN, ARA, 9, 96, cited in ibid., p. 120.

16. StaN, ARA, 9, 313, 317, 320, 333, 336-38, 340-41, cited in ibid., pp. 122-23.

17. "Die Kirchen Ordnung, In Meiner gnedigen herrn der marggrauen zu Brandenburg Und eins Erbern Rats der Stat Nürnberg Oberkeyt und gepieten, wie man sich bayde mit der Lerr und Ceremonien halten solle. 1533," Sehling, *Kirchenordnungen*, vol. 11: *Bayern*, part 1: *Franken*, pp. 140-305.

18. The city council's role in church affairs is discussed by Gerhard Pfeiffer, "Das Verhältnis von politischer und kirchlicher Gemeinde in den deutschen Reichsstädten," in *Staat und Kirche im Wandel der Jahrhunderte*, ed. Walther Peter Fuchs (Stuttgart, 1966), pp. 79-99, and "Nürnbergs christliche Gemeinde: Geschichtliche Beobachtungen zum Verhältnis von kirchlicher und politischer Gemeinde," in *Evangelium und Geist der Zeiten: 450 Jahre Reformation in Nürnberg* (Nuremberg, 1975), pp. 45-115.

19. For council action of 20 July 1531, illustrating concern for the preaching of catechetical sermons for children, see StaN, RSB, 7, 99v-102r.

20. Mayer, *Spengleriana*, pp. 118-19.

21. Ibid., pp. 121-23. See Gottfried Seebass, *Das reformatorische Werk des Andreas Osiander* (Nuremberg, 1967), pp. 254-59, and Bernhard Klaus, *Veit Dietrich: Leben und Werk* (Nuremberg, 1958), pp. 119-20, 147-56.

CHAPTER NINE

1. Seebass, *Osiander*, p. 136.

2. Acts 5:38-39. Spengler to Peter Butz, 21 May 1526, *Politische Correspondenz der Stadt Strassburg*, vol. 1, no. 451, pp. 256-57.

3. Ekkehart Fabian, *Die Entstehung des Schmalkaldischen Bundes und seiner Verfassung 1524/29-1531/35*, "Schriften zur Kirchen- und Rechtsgeschichte," part 1 (Tübingen, 1962), pp. 24-25. Hereafter cited as Fabian, *Entstehung*.

4. Ibid., pp. 30-31. The Magdeburg Union consisted of the princes of electoral Saxony, Braunschweig-Lüneburg, Hesse, and Anhalt-Bernburg and the Counts Gebhard and Albert of Mansfeld-Hinterort.

5. StaN, BB, 91r, 68r, 92r, cited in Engelhardt, *Reformation*, 2:6.

6. On this diet see ibid. pp. 3-37; Walter Friedensburg, *Der Reichstag zu Speier 1526* (Berlin, 1887; reprinted in Nieuwkoop, 1970); Theodor Brieger, *Der Speierer Reichstag von 1526 und die religiöse Frage der Zeit* (Leipzig, 1909); and August Kluckhohn, "Der Reichstag zu Speier im Jahre 1526," *Historische Zeitschrift* 56 (1886): 193-218.

7. The Proposition is printed in Friedensburg, *Reichstag zu Speier*, Appendix 6, pp. 523-34; see also pp. 217-18.

8. Ibid., pp. 220-23.

9. Ibid., p. 241 n. 2.

10. Nuremberg to Baumgartner, 30 June 1526, StaN, BB, 93, 47r, cited in Engelhardt, *Reformation*, 2:12.

11. Friedensburg, *Reichstag zu Speier*, p. 249. See also Johathan W. Zophy, "Christoph Kress: Nürnberg's Foremost Reformation Diplomat" (Ph.D. Diss., Ohio State University, 1972). Concerning the continued cooperation of the Catholic and evangelical cities until 1529, see Hans Baron, "Religion and Politics in the German Imperial Cities During the Reformation," *English Historical Review* 52 (1937): 405-27, 614-33, especially pp. 410-11.

12. Friedensburg, *Reichstag zu Speier*, pp. 254-55.

13. Ibid., pp. 283-86.

14. Ibid., pp. 311-13.

15. For a detailed discussion of the city council's actions in justifying its religious changes, see Seebass, "Apologia," pp. 20-74.

16. Engelhardt, *Reformation*, 2:26-27.

17. Friedensburg, *Reichstag zu Speier*, appendix 7, pp. 554-57; Eugen Franz, *Nurnberg, Kaiser und Reich* (Munich, 1930), pp. 95-96.

18. Letter of the city council to its delegates, 14 August 1526, StaN, BB, 93, 120r, cited in Engelhardt, *Reformation*, 2:27.

19. StaN, BB, 93, 109v, cited in ibid., p. 28.

20. Pressel, *Spengler*, pp. 77-78; Haussdorf, *Spengler*, p. 141.

21. *LW*, 49:164-65.

22. Fabian, *Entstehung*, pp. 32-37; *DRA JR*, part 1, 265. Spengler's instructions to the delegates at the diet of cities at Ulm is discussed in Schornbaum, *Georg*, p. 295 n. 125.

23. On the Diet of Speyer of 1529, see Engelhardt, *Reformation*, 2:141-85; Johannes Kühn, *Die Geschichte des Speyerer Reichstages 1529*, "Schriften des Vereins für Reformationsgeschichte," vol. 47, part 1, No. 146 (Leipzig, 1929), and Karl Schornbaum, "Zur Politik der Reichsstadt Nürnberg vom Ende des Reichstags zu Speier 1529 bis zur Übergabe der Augsburger Konfession 1530," *MVGN* 17 (1906): 178-245.

24. Kuhn, *Speyrer Reichstag 1529*, pp. 60-61.

25. Johann Kamann, "Schreiben des Kriegshauptmanns und Diplomaten

Christoph Kress vom Speierer Reichstag 1529 an Christoph Fürer," *MVGN* 5 (1884): 226-28. Kress shows here that not all the townsmen were motivated in their politics by a strong religious faith but indicates that he would die for his.

26. Engelhardt, *Reformation*, 2:146-48; Kühn, *Speyrer Reichstag 1529*, pp. 82-85; Lazarus Spengler to Peter Butz, *Politische Correspondenz*, Vol. I, no. 451, pp. 256-57.

27. Schornbaum, *Georg*, p. 68 nn. 294-95.

28. For a discussion of Sturm's able leadership, see Thomas A. Brady, Jr., "Jacob Sturm of Strasbourg and the Lutherans at the Diet of Augsburg, 1530," *Church History* 42 (1973): 183-202. Strassburg's role in the Reformation is well covered by Miriam Usher Chrisman, *Strasbourg and the Reform: A Study in the Process of Change* (New Haven, 1967). For Spengler's advice to Michel von Kaden with respect to the protest and appeal, see *DRA JR*, 7, part 1, 632-633.

29. Kühn, *Speyrer Reichstag 1529*, pp. 179-81.

30. The text of the Protestation is in *DRA JR*, 7, part 2, no. 118, 1273-88.

31. Fabian, *Entstehung*, pp. 42-44.

32. *DRA JR*, 7, part 2, no. 167, 1345-56.

33. Hajo Holborn, *A History of Modern Germany: The Reformation* (New York, 1959), p. 208; Johann Michael Reu, *The Augsburg Confession: A Collection of Sources with an Historical Introduction* (Chicago, 1930), pp. 847-98.

34. *DRA JR*, 7, part 1, 866-67; Engelhardt, *Reformation*, 2:172; Kühn, *Speyrer Reichstag 1529*, p. 179.

35. *WA Br* 5:62-63; *LW* 49:220-21.

36. Fabian, *Entstehung*, pp. 42-44. The text of the agreement is in *DRA JR*, 7, part 2, 152, and Reu, *Augsburg Confession*, pp. 34-37.

37. *CR* 1,1069, p. 611; *LW* 49:224 n. 21.

38. *WA Br* 5:75-78; Heinz Scheible, ed., *Das Widerstandsrecht als Problem der deutschen Protestanten 1523-1546* (Gütersloh, 1969), pp. 23-24.

39. Engelhardt, *Reformation*, 2:170-71.

40. Adolf Engelhardt, "Eine missglückte Gesandtschaft unter Nürnbergs Führing," *MVGN* 32 (1934): 79-98; Franz, *Nürnberg, Kaiser und Reich*, pp. 102-3.

41. For a detailed account of the meeting at Nuremberg 23-27 May, together with the documents, see *DRA JR*, 8, part 1, ed. Wolfgang Steglich (Göttingen, 1970), pp. 3-75.

42. Ibid., pp. 25-42, 134-77. See Wolfgang Steglich, "Die Stellung der evangelischen Reichsstände und Reichsstädte . . . 1529/30, *ARG* 62 (1971): 167-70.

43. *DRA JR*, 8, part 1, 143-44.

44. Ibid., pp. 158-60.

CHAPTER TEN

1. Engelhardt, *Reformation*, 2:186-210; Wolfgang Steglich, "Die Stellung der evangelischen Reichsstände und Reichsstädte zu Karl V. zwischen

Protestation und Konfession 1529/30," *ARG* 62 (1971): 161-92, based on his edition of the *DRA JR*, 8, part 1 (1970), 76-118; Hans von Schubert, *Bündnis und Bekenntnis 1529/30*, "Schriften des Vereins für Reformationsgeschichte," 26 (1908): 1-35; and Baron, "Religion and Politics," pp. 416-17.

2. Schornbaum, *Georg*, pp. 75-76, and "Zur Politik der Reichsstadt Nürnberg vom Ende des Reichstages zu Speyer 1529 zur Uebergabe der Augsburgischen Konfession." *MVGN* 17 (1906): 178-245.

3. Ekkehart Fabian, ed., *Die Abschiede der Bündnis- und Bekenntnistage protestierender Fürsten und Städte, zwischen den Reichstagen zu Speyer und zu Augsburg, 1529-1530* (Tübingen, 1960), p. 29. Hereafter cited as Fabian, *Abschiede*.

4. *DRA JR*, 8, part 1, 97-112.

5. Spengler to Veit Dietrich, 18 Aug. 1529, in Mayer, *Spengleriana*, p. 69; Ekkehart Fabian, ed., *Die Entstehung des Schmalkaldischen Bundes und seiner Verfassung, 1524/29-1531/35: Bruck, Philipp von Hessen und Jakob Sturm. Darstellung und Quellen* (2d rev. ed., Tübingen, 1962), pp. 53-54. Hereafter cited as Fabian, *Entstehung*.

6. The recess of Rodach of 8 June 1529, in *DRA JR*, 8, part 1, 113-16; Fabian, *Abschiede*, pp. 31-33.

7. Spengler to Butz, 13 Sept. 1529, *Politische Correspondenz*, vol. 1, no. 650, pp. 392-94; see also Spengler to Butz, 21 June, no. 628, pp. 377-78, and 6 Oct., no. 660, p. 399.

8. WA 30:86-91; Fabian, *Entstehung*, p. 52, *Abschiede*, pp. 95-99. Translated into English by Henry E. Jacobs in *The Book of Concord: Or, the Symbolical Books of the Evangelical Lutheran Church*, ed. Henry E. Jacobs, 2 vols. (Philadelphia, 1908), 1:30-68.

9. Steglich, "Stellung der Reichsstände," p. 185; *DRA JR*, 8, part 1, 399-434.

10. Fabian, *Entstehung*, pp. 69-71.

11. Engelhardt, *Reformation*, 2:199-200; Schornbaum, *Georg*, p. 99.

12. StaN, ARA, 7, 218r.

13. For Chancellor Vogler's account of the meeting at Schmalkalden, see Schornbaum, *Georg*, pp. 207-11. See also *DRA JR*, 8, part 1, 529-61.

14. Ludewig, *Politik*, pp. 106-7; Schornbaum, *Georg*, pp. 96-97.

15. StaN, ARA, 7, 396r, quoted in Engelhardt, *Reformation*, 2:206-7.

16. The recess of Schmalkalden is printed in Fabian, *Abschiede*, pp. 101-4.

17. *DRA JR*, 8, part 2, 468-528. The letter of 21 December 1529 from Philip to George is printed in Scheible, *Widerstandsrecht*, pp. 43-47. For a recent account of the issue, see Cynthia Grant Schoenberger, "The Development of the Lutheran Theory of Resistance: 1523-1530," *Sixteenth Century Journal* 8 (1977): 61-76.

18. Luther to Elector John of Saxony, 22 May 1529, in *WA BR* 5, 75-78, and Scheible, *Widerstandsrecht*, pp. 23-24.

19. Ibid., pp. 29-39; *DRA JR*, part 1, 468-85, 501-9; StaN, ARA, no. 16, 198r-204v, and Suppl. 1a, 390r-395r.

20. Scheible, *Widerstandsrecht*, pp. 34-35.

21. Ibid., p. 37.

22. StaN, BB 100, 127v, cited in Engelhardt, *Reformation*, 2:209.

23. Scheible, *Widerstandsrecht*, pp. 40-42.

24. *Kurzer Auszug aus dem päpstlichen Rechte*, Kalkoff, *Reformation*, p. 103. Luther provided a forward for this work and published it in Wittenberg with the title *Ein kurczer auszuge, aus den Bebstlichen rechten der Decret und Decretalen, Ynn den artickeln, die ungeferlich Gottes Wort und dem Evangelio gemes sind, oder wenigsten nicht widderstreben, Mit einer schönen Vorrhede*. Mart. Luth. Wittenberg: Joseph Clugk, 1530. *WA*, 30: 215-19. See Ernst-Wilhelm Kohls, "Die Durchdringung von Humanismus und Reformation im Denken des Nürnberger Ratsschreibers Lazarus Spengler," *ZbKg* 36 (1967): 13-25. Kohls emphasizes the combination of humanism and Reformation in Spengler's thought.

25. Kalkoff, *Reformation*, pp. 105-18. Cochlaeus, who had written a sharp attack on the *Kurzer Auszug*, later summarized his attitude toward Spengler in his letter of 18 Oct. 1530 to Pirckheimer, in which he stated that he feared that "Lazarus, who has been buried in sin so many years and himself smells bad, will putrify the reputation of the fair city, the emperor, and almost the entire world. You will see what happens if you continue to trust the city to the Jewish crowd (*Zippschaft*)." See *Caritas Pirckheimer: Quellensammlung*, part 3, *Briefe*, p. 273.

26. Fabian, *Abschiede*, pp. 118-19.

27. No definitive history of the Diet of Augsburg of 1530 can be written until after the publication of volume 9 of the *DRA JR*. Helpful studies that include Nuremberg's role are those by Engelhardt, *Reformation*, 2:211-67, and *Der Reichstag zu Augsburg 1530 und die Reichsstadt Nürnberg* (Nuremberg, 1929); Hans von Schubert, *Der Reichstag von Augsburg im Zusammenhang der Reformationsgeschichte*, "Schriften des Vereins für Reformationsgeschichte, no. 150, vol. 48 (Leipzig, 1930), and "Bekenntnisbildung und Religionspolitik," *ZKG* 29 (1908) and 30 (1909); Johannes von Walther, "Der Reichstag von Augsburg 1530," *Luther-Jahrbuck* 12 (1930): 1-90; Gerhard Müller, "Augsburg und Nürnberg im Urteil päpstlicher Nuntien 1530-1532," *ZbKg* 39 (1970): 75-82; and Gerhard Pfeiffer, "Nürnbergs kirchenpolitische Haltung im Frühjahr 1530," *ZbLg* 33 (1970): 183-200. For sources see *DRA JR*, 8, parts 1-2; Karl Eduard Förstemann, ed., *Urkundenbuch zu der Geschichte des Reichstages zu Augsburg im Jahre 1530*, 2 vols. (Osnabrück, 1966, reprint of 1833 edition); *The Book of Concord*, ed. Henry E. Jacobs, vol. 2; and Johann Michael Reu, *The Augsburg Confession: A Collection of Sources with an Historical Introduction*, two parts (Chicago, 1930). For reports of Nuremberg's representatives to the city council, see *CR*, 2, and Wilhelm Vogt, ed., "Die Korrespondenz des Nürnberger Rates mit seinen zum Augsburger Reichstag von 1530 abgeordneten Gesandten," *MVGN* 4 (1882): 1-60.

28. Engelhardt, *Reformation*, 2:211-12.

29. For the opinion of Nuremberg's jurisconsults of 7 May 1530, concerning preparations for the diet, see Schornbaum, "Zur Politik," pp. 211-14; for that of the theologians, pp. 215-41.

30. The politico-religious alternatives facing Charles at Innsbruck are

indicated in Karl Brandi, *The Emperor Charles V*, trans. C. V. Wedgwood (New York, 1939), pp. 303-6. The reports of Campeggio are given in *Nuntiaturberichte aus Deutschland*, 1. Abteilung 1533-59, 1. Ergänzungsband 1530-31, ed. Gerhard Müller (Tübingen, 1963), pp. 75-82, and by Gerhard Müller, *Die römische Kurie und die Reformation 1523-1534*, "Quellen und Forschungen zur Reformationsgeschichte," 38 (Gütersloh, 1969). Campeggio's opposition to leniency with respect to the Protestants is discussed by Eduard Wilhelm Mayer, "Forschungen zur Politik Karls V. während des Augsburger Reichsstags," *ARG* 13(1916): 40-73, 124-46.

31. Vogt, ed., "Korrespondenz," *MVGN* 4 (1882): 1-8; Ludewig, *Politik*, p. 111.

32. Schornbaum, "Zur Politik," *MVGN* 17 (1906): 199; Engelhardt, *Augsburg*, p. 17; *DRA JR*, 8, part 1, 601, 602, 615, 617.

33. Spengler's memorandum is cited in Engelhardt, *Reformation*, 2: 218-19.

34. StaN, Ratschl.b, 6, 280v-283r, printed in Schornbaum, "Zur Politik," *MVGN* 17 (1906): 211-14.

35. StaN, S.IL., 68, no. 6, printed in Schornbaum, "Zur Politik," *MVGN* 17 (1906): 215-41.

36. The Augsburg Confession is printed in *CR*, 2, no. 739, 130-39; Förstemann, *Urkundenbuch*, vol. 1, 310-559; Reu, *The Augsburg Confession*, part 2, pp. 167-303; and translated into English by Charles P. Krauth in *The Book of Concord*, 1:30-68.

37. *CR*, 2, no. 712, 83-85. Advice of the theologians and jurisconsults of 10 June 1530, in Schornbaum, "Zur Politik," *MVGN* 17 (1906): 214-44.

38. StaN, RV of 14 June 1530, H. 2, folio 26, quoted in Engelhardt, *Reformation*, 2, 225.

39. *Reformed Confessions of the 16th Century*, ed. Arthur C. Cochrane (Philadelphia, ca. 1966), pp. 51-88.

40. Ludewig, *Politik*, p. 112.

41. *CR*, 2, no. 743, 142-44.

42. Ibid., no. 821, 249-52; Förstemann, *Urkundenbuch*, 2:133-76; Reu, *Augsburg Confession*, part 2, pp. 326-43.

43. Engelhardt, *Reformation*, 2:235-36.

44. *CR*, 2, no. 779, 189-92; Engelhardt, *Augsburg*, pp. 47-48.

45. Haussdorff, *Spengler*, pp. 81-95; Pressel, *Spengler*, pp. 70-74.

46. Vogt, ed., "Korrespondenz," *MVGN*, 4 (1882): 25-27.

47. Ibid., pp. 31-32.

48. *CR*, 2, no. 842, 278-80.

49. Ibid., no. 846, 286-288; no. 848, 289-291.

50. Quoted in Engelhardt, *Reformation*, 2:242-43. See Engelhardt, *Augsburg*, pp. 71-72; Vogt, ed., "Korrespondenz," *MVGN* 4 (1882): 36-37.

51. Haussdorff, *Spengler*, pp. 58-70.

52. *WA Br* 5, 572-74; *LW* 49, 406-12.

53. Förstemann, *Urkundenbuch*, vol. 2, no. 168, 306-10.

54. *CR*, 2, no. 899, 363-65; no. 902, 372-73; Mayer, *Spengleriana*, pp. 76-77.

55. Haussdorff, *Spengler*, pp. 77-78.

56. Förstemann, *Urkundenbuch*, vol. 2, 474-78.

57. The *Apologia* is printed in Latin in ibid., 483-529, and in German, 530-98. It is printed in English in Reu, *Augsburg Confession*, part 2, pp. 392-98, and *The Book of Concord*, 1:69-302.

58. Melanchthon revised the *Apologia* for publication in April 1531.

59. Vogt, ed., "Korrespondenz," pp. 44-45.

60. Ibid., 45-47; *CR*, 2, no. 917, 392-93; Engelhardt, *Reformation*, 2:254-55.

61. *WA Br* 5, 634-35.

62. Förstemann, *Urkundenbuch*, vol. 2, no. 249, 715-20; no. 305, 839-41; no. 308, 845-46. The final answer of the Protestants to Elector Joachim of Brandenburg on 22 Oct. is in ibid., no. 263, 759-61.

63. *WA Br* 5, 444-45, 608-9; *LW, Letters,* 49:356-59, 415-19.

CHAPTER ELEVEN

1. For general accounts and sources of the Schmalkaldic League, see Otto Winckelmann, *Der Schmalkaldischer Bund 1530-1532 und der Nürnberger Religionsfriede* (Strassburg, 1892); Ekkehard Fabian, *Entstehung*; Hans Baron, "Religion and Politics"; and Franz, *Nürnberg, Kaiser und Reich*.

2. Engelhardt, *Reformation*, 2:267-92. Elector John, Landgrave Philip of Hesse, Duke Ernest of Braunschweig-Lüneburg, Prince Wolfgang of Anhalt-Bernburg, and Counts Gebhard and Albert of Mansfeld attended in person. Count Albert also represented Philip of Braunschweig-Grubenhagen and served as an adviser to Elector John. Georg Vogler and Kaspar von Seckendorf were sent by Margrave George. Christoph Kress and Leo Schürstab represented Nuremberg and also Heilbronn, Reutlingen, Windsheim, and Weissenburg. Jakob Sturm, accompanied by councilman Jakob Meyer, represented Strassburg and spoke also for Constance, Zurich, and Basel. Present also were representatives from Bremen, Magdeburg, and Ulm. Georg Besserer of Ulm spoke also for Biberach, Isny, Lindau, Kempten, and Memmingen.

3. Spengler to Veit Dietrich, 3 February 1531, Mayer, *Spengleriana*, p. 79; Fabian, *Entstehung*, p. 154.

4. Memorandum of Luther, Bugenhagen, Jonas, and Melanchthon to Elector John, 6 March 1530, printed in Scheible, *Widerstandsrecht*, pp. 60-63.

5. For the memorandum of the electoral jurists, see Scheible, *Wilderstandsrecht*, pp. 63-66.

6. The memorandums of Luther, Melanchthon, Spalatin, and Jonas of 26-28 October 1530, and of Luther, Jonas, Butzer, and Melanchthon for Elector John Frederick and Landgrave Philip of 13-14 November 1538 are printed in Scheible, *Widerstandsrecht*, pp. 67-68, 92-94.

7. Spengler to Veit Dietrich, 3 February 1531, Mayer, *Spengleriana*, pp. 78-79.

8. *Politische Correspondenz*, 1:568, cited in Engelhardt, *Reformation*, 2:277.

9. The recess is printed in Winckelmann, *Der Schmalkaldische Bund*, pp. 291-96; Fabian, *Die Schmalkaldischen Bundesabschiede* (Tübingen, 1958), pp. 11-17.

10. See Fabian, *Entstehung*, pp. 162-64 and 170, for comments on main provisions.

11. StaN, ARA, Suppl. Ia, Nos. 61-87, cited in Engelhardt, *Reformation*, 2:278.

12. StaN, Ratschlb., 24, 394-99, 428, cited in Seebass, *Osiander*, pp. 160-61.

13. StaN, BB, 102, 106r, cited in Engelhardt, *Reformation*, 2:284-85.

14. Ludewig, *Politik*, pp. 136-37; Engelhardt, *Reformation*, 2:284-85; Fabian, *Entstehung*, p. 172.

15. Spengler to Veit Dietrich, 3 February 1531, Mayer, *Spengleriana*, pp. 78-79.

16. Haussdorff, *Spengler*, p. 174.

17. Spengler to Veit Dietrich, 22 April 1531, Mayer, *Spengleriana*, pp. 82-86.

18. Spengler to Veit Dietrich, 20 February 1531, Mayer, *Spengleriana*, pp. 81-82.

19. Fabian, *SBA*, pp. 24-38.

20. Printed in Fabian, *Entstehung*, pp. 357-76.

21. Winckelmann, *Der Schmalkaldische Bund*, pp. 175-264.

22. Engelhardt, *Reformation*, 2:299-301, and "Der Nürnberger Religionsfriede von 1532," *MVGN* (1933) 31:17-123.

23. Ludewig, *Politik*, pp. 142-44; Engelhardt, *Reformation*, 2:307-8. For a discussion of the importance of the Turkish threat in Protestant negotiations with the emperor, see Stephan A. Fischer-Galati, *Ottoman Imperialism and German Protestantism 1521-1525* (New York, 1972), especially pp. 38-56.

24. *Politische Correspondenz*, vol. 2, no. 159, cited in Engelhardt, *Reformation*, 2:333-34.

25. Luther to Elector John, *WA BR* 6:325-26; *LW* 50:56-60; Spengler to Veit Dietrich, 4 July 1532, Mayer, *Spengleriana*, pp. 94-97.

26. Ludewig, *Politik*, p. 147.

27. Spengler to Veit Dietrich, 29 July 1532, Mayer, *Spengleriana*, p. 98.

28. Letters of Spengler to Veit Dietrich in Mayer, *Spengleriana*, of 21 January 1534, pp. 139-40; of 9 March, p. 145; and of 13 April, pp. 149-51.

29. Letters of Spengler to Veit Dietrich, in ibid., of 24 May 1534, pp. 157-58; and of 12 June 1534, pp. 160-61.

30. Ludewig, *Politik*, p. 151.

31. Spengler to Veit Dietrich, 7 August 1545, Mayer, *Spengleriana*, pp. 162-63.

CHAPTER TWELVE

1. StaN, RB, 119r; Pressel, *Spengler*, p. 91.

2. StaN, RB, 15, 81r-v.

3. Mayer, *Spengleriana*, pp. 88-90.

4. Ibid., p. 105.

5. Ibid., p. 99.

6. Ibid., pp. 128, 130, 134. For more of Spengler's comments on the plague,

see his letters of 7 and 25 September and 17 October 1533, to his sister-in-law Juliana in Jurgen U. Ohlau, "Neue Quellen zur Familiengeschichte der Spengler: Lazarus Spengler und seine Söhne," *MVGN* 52 (1963-64): 232-55, specifically pp. 241-44.

7. Mayer, *Spengleriana*, p. 143.

8. Ibid., pp. 154-57, 162.

9. Ibid., pp. 164-68.

10. Pressel, *Spengler*, p. 40.

11. Georg Freiherr Kress von Kressenstein, "Ein markgräflicher Kanzleirath über Lazarus Spengler," *MVGN* 1 (1879): 94-95.

12. Peutinger, *Briefwechsel*, no. 240, pp. 382-84; no. 278, pp. 443-44; *DRA JR*, 4, no. 107, pp. 382-84.

13. Hermann Heimpel, "Nürnberg und das Reich des Mittelalters," *ZbLg* 16 (1951): 231-64, especially pp. 262-63; Franz, *Nürnberg, Kaiser und Reich*, pp. 131-35; Baron, "Religion and Politics," pp. 614-20.

14. *Von den französischen Krankheit oder von den Imposturen*, in Paracelsus (Theophrastus von Hohenheim), *Sämtliche Werke in zeitgemässer kurzer Auswahl*, ed. J. Strebel, 8 vols. (St. Gall, 1944-49), 7:275.

15. "Mein Lazarus Spenglers Glaubens bekanntnus," "Ratio fidei mei, 1527," and "Testamentum unnd Glaubens bekanndtnus Lazarus Spenglers Ratschreiber, 1534" are preserved in StadtaN, Rep. 1, Familienpapiere Spengler, no. 4.

16. Haussdorff, *Spengler*, pp. 469-70.

17. Ibid., pp. 24, 473.

18. Ibid., pp. 474-75.

19. They stood north of the house of Wenzel Jamnitzer (1508-58), the goldsmith. See Erich Mulzer, "Das Jamnitzerhaus in Nürnberg und der Goldschmied Wenzel Jamnitzer," *MVGN* 61 (1974): 48-89, and Haussdorff, *Spengler*, pp. 480-81.

20. Pressel, *Spengler*, p. 83.

21. Bayerisches Staatshauptarchiv München, RKG, 12024, nos. 15 and 21; also StaN, IBN, 4bl., 166a, cited in Mulzer, "Jamnitzerhaus," p. 234.

22. Ibid., p. 235; Haussdorff, *Spengler*, pp. 484-85.

23. Ohlau, "Neue Quellen," pp. 232-55; Hans von Schubert, *Spengler*, p. 176; and Haussdorff, *Spengler*, pp. 476-77.

24. StaN, ARA, 9, fasc. 101, 632.

25. "Bedenck Zettel fur Lazarum Spengler Mein Sone, den ich Ime In seinem abschaiden In das Niderland mit getailt hab, davon er mir auch ein copy seiner Handschrifft uberantword hatt." The copy is preserved in StadtaN, Rep E 1, Familienpapiere Spengler, no. 2.

26. "Bedenkzettle fur Franntzen Spengler meinen Vettern den Ich Ime In seinem abschaiden gein Augspurg mitgetailt hab." The manuscript is in StadtaN, Rep. E 1, Familienpapiere Spengler, no. 3. It is through Franz that Hans von Schubert, author of the detailed biography of Lazarus Spengler to the year 1525, descended.

27. For the first account of young Lazarus Spengler's experiences as a

merchant, see Ohlau, "Neue Quellen," pp. 232-55. See also Enrique Otte, "Jacob und Hans Cromberger und Lazarus Nürnberger, die Begründer des Deutschen Amerikahandels," *MVGN* 52 (1963-64): 129-62. For an account of the business interests of the Tucher family in the Netherlands, see Kurt Pilz, "Nürnberg und die Niederlande," *MVGN* 43 (1952): 1-153.

28. Pressel, *Spengler*, pp. 83-84; Haussdorff, *Spengler*, p. 23.

29. *Ein trostliche Christenliche Anweisung und Artzney in allen Widerwertikaiten*, printed in Nuremberg by Fridrich Peypus in 1521. See Pressel, *Spengler*, pp. 32-35.

30. *Ein kurzer begriff, wie sich ein warhaffter Christ in allem seinen wesen und wandel gegen Got und seinem nechsten halten sol*, printed in Erfurt by Melchior Sachs in 1526. Pressel, *Spengler*, pp. 86-87; Haussdorff, *Spengler*, p. 560.

31. *Wie sich eyn Christen mensch inn trübsal vnd widerwertigkayt trösten, vnd wo er die rechten hilff vnd Ertznay derhalben suchen soll*, printed in Nuremberg by Jobst Gutknecht in 1529. Pressel, *Spengler*, pp. 83-86; Haussdorff, *Spengler*, p. 560.

32. The final version (1533) of the *Ratio fidei mei* is printed in Haussdorff, *Spengler*, pp. 485-503, and Pressel, *Spengler*, pp. 93-99.

33. Haussdorff, *Spengler*, pp. 497-98.

34. Ibid., p. 198.

35. Ibid., pp. 499-500.

36. *Bekendnis Lazari Spengler weiland Syndici der Stadt Nurmberg. Mit Vorrhede Dr. Mart. Luth. Wittemberg*, printed in Wittenberg 1535 by Joseph Klug, and in Nuremberg that same year by Jobst Gutknecht. See Pressel, *Spengler*, p. 100.

37. *WA BR*, 2, 217-218; *LW*, 48:184-85.

38. *WA BR*, 3, 432-433; *LW*, 49:97-99.

39. *WA BR*, 4, 534-536; *LW*, 49:205-10; Haussdorff, *Spengler*, pp. 154-62.

40. For Luther's response to questions concerning armed resistance to the emperor, see Scheible, *Widerstandsrecht*, pp. 60-69; and for Spengler's position, ibid., pp. 29-39, 50-56.

41. Thirty-four letters of Spengler to Veit Dietrich are printed in Mayer, *Spengleriana*, pp. 62-168. They cover the years 1529 to 1534.

42. There is a copy of this letter in the archives of the Germanisches Nationalmuseum in Nuremberg in the Sammlung Böttiger.

43. Mayer, *Spengleriana*, p. 137.

44. Ibid., p. 146.

45. Ibid.

46. Ibid., p. 158.

47. Ibid., p. 55.

48. Mathis Pfarrer to Peter Butz, 18 September 1530, *Politische Correspondenz*, vol. 1, no. 792, 498-99.

49. Eckert and Imhoff, *Pirckheimer*, p. 367.

50. Mayer, *Spengleriana*, p. 121.

51. Pressel, *Spengler*, pp. 80-82; Haussdorff, *Spengler*, p. 82. There is a copy of this letter from Billican in Spengler's handwriting in StadtaN, Rep. 1, Fàmilienpapiere Spengler, no. 23.

52. This tribute to Spengler by Joachim Camerarius in the latter's *Vita Melanchthonis* is quoted in Haussdorff, *Spengler*, p. 44: "Norimbergae tum Principes Senatus erant Casper Nucelius & Hieronymus Ebnerus, & Lazarus Spenglerus, nomine quidem scriba Senatus, sed revera consiliorum omnium fere autor ac gubernator etc. excellebat explorata & perspecta multis difficilibus & arduis negotiis fide atque industria."

BIBLIOGRAPHY

I. UNPUBLISHED PRIMARY SOURCES

Bayerisches Staatsarchiv Nürnberg
Repertorium 15 a

A-Laden, Akten
S I L 30, No. 7 a
S I L 43, No. 13
S I L 68, No. 6
S I L 68, No. 11

Repertorium 51   Ratschlagbücher
Repertorium 60 a   Verlässe des innern Rates
Repertorium 60 b   Ratsbücher
Reportorium 61 a   Briefbücher des innern Rates
Repertorium 111   Ansbacher Religionsakten

Stadtarchiv Nürnberg
Repertorium E 1, Familienarchive   Familienpapiere Spengler
Repertorium E 10, Nachlässe   Nachlass Dr. Hans von Schubert

Landeskirchliches Archiv
Fenitzerbibliothek IV, No. 906.2⁰   Spengler Handschrift

Germanisches Nationalmuseum Nürnberg
Archiv   Sammlung Böttiger

II. PUBLISHED PRIMARY SOURCES

Aurifaber, Johann. *Briefe und Acten zu der Geschichte des Religionsgespräches zu Marburg 1529 und des Reichstages zu Augsburg 1530.* Ed. Friedrich Wilhelm Schirrmacher. Gotha, 1876. Reprint. Amsterdam, 1968.

Die Bekenntnisschriften der evangelisch-lutherischen Kirche. 5th ed. Göttingen, 1963.

Brecht, Martin. "Ob ein weltlich Oberkait Recht habe, in des Glaubens Sachen mit dem Schwert zu handeln: Ein unbekanntes Nürnberger Gutachten zur Frage der Toleranz aus dem Jahre 1530." *Archiv für Reformationsgeschichte* 60 (1969): 65-75.

Brenz, Johannes. *Frühschriften.* Part 2. Ed. Martin Brecht et al. Tübingen, 1974.

Burger, Helene. "Ein reformationsgeschichtlicher Handakt Lazarus Spenglers." *Zeitschrift für bayerische Kirchengeschichte* 31 (1962): 30-39.

Clemen, Otto, ed. *Flugschriften aus den ersten Jahren der Reformation.* 4 vols. Leipzig, 1907-11.

Deutsche Reichstagsakten, Jüngere Reihe (Deutsche Reichstagsakten unter Karl V.). 2d ed., reprint. Göttingen, 1962.

Dürer, Albrecht. *The Writings of Albrecht Dürer.* Trans. and ed. William Martin Conway. New York, 1958.

Estes, James M. "Whether Secular Government Has the Right to Wield the Sword in Matters of Faith: An Anonymous Defense of Religious Toleration from Sixteenth-Century Nürnberg." *Mennonite Quarterly Review* 49 (1975): 22-37.

Fabian, Ekkehart, ed. *Die Abschiede der Bündnis- und Bekenntnistage protestierender Fürsten und Städte, zwischen den Reichstagen zu Speyer und zu Augsburg, 1529-1530.* Tübingen, 1960.

———, ed. *Die Beschlüsse der oberdeutschen Schmalkaldischen Städtetage.* Part 1: *1530/31*; part 2: *1531/32*. Tübingen, 1959.

———, ed. *Die schmalkaldischen Bundesabschiede.* "Schriften zur Kirchen- und Rechtsgeschichte," parts 7 and 8. Tübingen, 1958.

Förstemann, Karl Eduard, ed. *Urkundenbuch zu der Geschichte des Reichstages zu Augsburg im Jahre 1530.* 1833-35. Reprint. 2 vols. Osnabrück, 1966.

Die fränkischen Bekenntnisse. Eine Vorstufe der Augsburgischen Konfession. Ed. Wilhelm Ferdinand Schmidt and Karl Schornbaum. 2 parts. Munich, 1930.

Franz, Günther, ed. *Quellen zur Geschichte des Bauernkrieges.* "Ausgewählte Quellen zur deutschen Geschichte der Neuzeit," No. 2. Munich, 1965.

Gussmann, Wilhelm, ed. *Quellen und Forschungen zur Geschichte des Augsburgischen Glaubensbekenntnisses.* 2 vols. Leipzig, 1911.

Hampe, Theodor, ed. *Nürnberger Ratsverlässe über Kunst und Künstler im Zeitalter der Spätgotik und Renaissance.* "Quellengeschichte für Kunstgeschichte und Kunsttechnik," N.S., 11 vols. Vol. 1. Vienna, 1904.

Jacobs, Henry, E., ed. *The Book of Concord: Or, the Symbolical Books of the Evangelical Lutheran Church.* 2 vols. Philadelphia, 1908.

Kamann, Johann. "Schreiben des Nürnberger Kriegshauptmanns und Diplomaten Christoph Kress vom Speierer Reichstag 1529 an Christoph Fürer." *Mitteilungen des Vereins für Geschichte der Stadt Nürnberg* 5 (1884): 226-28.

Kidd, B. J. *Documents Illustrative of the Continental Reformation.* Oxford, 1911.

Klaus, Bernhard. "Die Nürnberger Deutsche Mess 1524." *Jahrbuch für Liturgik und Hymnologie* 1 (1955): 1-46.

Klüpfel, Karl August. *Urkunden zur Geschichte des Schwäbischen Bundes (1488-1533)*. In two parts. *Bibliothek des Literarischen Vereins in Stuttgart*, 14 (1846) and 31 (1853).

Kress von Kressenstein, Georg Freiherr von. "Acht Briefe Wilibald Pirkheimers." *Mitteilungen des Vereins für Geschichte der Stadt Nürnberg* 1 (1879): 67-90.

———. "Ein markgräflicher Kanzleirath über Lazarus Spengler." *Mitteilungen des Vereins für Geschichte der Stadt Nürnberg* 1 (1879): 94-95.

Luther, Martin. *Luther's Works*. To be complete in 55 vols. St. Louis, Mo., 1955--, and Philadelphia, 1957--.

———. *D. Martin Luthers Werke*. 58 vols. to date. *Briefwechsel*, 14 vols.; *Tischreden*, 6 vols.; and *Deutsche Bibel*, 12 vols. Weimar, 1883--.

Mayer, Moritz Maximilian, ed. *Spengleriana*. Nuremberg, 1830.

Melanchthon, Philip. *Corpus Reformatorum, Philippi Melanthonis opera quae supersunt omnia*, Ed. K. G. Bretschneider and H. E. Bindseil. Vols. 1-28. Halle, 1834-60.

———. *Melanchthons Briefwechsel*. Ed. Heinz Scheible. Vol. 1: *Regesten 1-1109 (1514-1530)*. Stuttgart-Bad Cannstatt, 1977.

Müntzer, Thomas. *Thomas Müntzer: Schriften und Briefe*, Ed. Günther Franz. "Quellen und Forschungen zur Reformationsgeschichte," Vol. 33. Gütersloh, 1968.

Nuntiaturberichte aus Deutschland. 1. Abteilung 1533-59. 2 supplementary vols. Ed. Gerhard Müller. Tübingen, 1963, 1969.

Osiander, Andreas. *Andreas Osiander d.Ä. Gesamtausgabe*. Vol. 1: *Schriften und Briefe 1522 bis März 1525*. Ed. Gerhard Müller and Gottfried Seebass. Gütersloh, 1975.

Paracelsus (Theophrastus von Hohenheim). *Sämtliche Werke in zeitgemässer Kürzung*. Ed. J. Strebel. 8 vols. St. Gall, 1944-49.

Peutinger, Conrad. *Briefwechsel*. Ed. E. König. Munich, 1923.

Pfeiffer, Gerhard, ed. *Quellen zur Nürnberger Reformationsgeschichte . . . (Juni 1524-Juni 1525)*. "Einzelarbeiten aus der Kirchengeschichte Bayerns," Vol. 45. Nuremberg, 1968.

Pirckheimer, Charitas. *Caritas Pirckheimer: Quellensammlung*. In 3 parts. Ed. Josef Pfanner. Part 1: *Das Gebetbuch der Caritas Pirckheimer*. Landshut, 1961. Part 2: *Die "Denkwürdigkeiten" der Caritas Pirckheimer aus den Jahren 1524-1528*. Landshut, 1962. Part 3: *Briefe von an und über Caritas Pirckheimer aus den Jahren 1498-1530*. Landshut, 1966.

Pirckheimer, Willibald. *Dokumente, Studien, Perspektive*. Nuremberg, 1970.

———. *Willibald Pirckheimers Briefwechsel*. Ed. Emil Reicke and Arnold Reimann. 2 vols. Munich, 1940, 1956.

Planitz, Hans von der. *Bericht aus dem Reichsregiment in Nürnberg, 1521 bis 1523*. Ed. Ernst Wülker and Hans Virck. Leipzig, 1898.

Politische Correspondenz der Stadt Strassburg im Zeitalter der Reformation. Ed. Hans Virck and Otto Winkelmann. 3 vols. Strassburg, 1882-98.

Quellen zur Geschichte der Wiedertäufer (Täufer). Ed. Karl Schornbaum. Vol. 2: *Markgrafentum Brandenburg*. Vol. 5: *Bayern*, part 2: *Reichsstädte:*

Regensburg, Kaufbeuren, Rothenburg, Nördlingen, Schweinfurt, Weissenburg. "Quellen und Forschungen zur Reformationsgeschichte," Vol. 16 (Leipzig, 1934), and Vol. 23 (Gütersloh, 1951).

Reformed Confessions of the Sixteenth Century. Ed. Arthur C. Cochrane. Philadelphia, 1966.

Reu, Johann Michael. *The Augsburg Confession: A Collection of Sources with an Historical Introduction.* Chicago, 1930.

Schade, Oskar, ed. *Satiren und Pasquille aus der Reformationszeit.* 3 vols. Hanover, 1856-58.

Scheible, Heinz, ed. *Das Widerstandsrecht als Problem der deutschen Protestanten 1523-1546.* Gütersloh, 1969.

Scheurl, Christoph. *Briefbuch: Ein Beitrag zur Geschichte der Reformation und ihrer Zeit.* Ed. Franz Freiherr von Soden and J. K. F. Knaake. 2 vols. Potsdam, 1867. Reprint, Aalen, 1962.

——. "Epistola ad Staupizium," letter of 15 December 1516 to Staupitz concerning the polity and government of Nuremberg. In *Die Chroniken der fränkischen Städte.* Vol. 5: *Nürnberg.* Leipzig, 1874.

Schornbaum, Karl. *Aktenstücke zur ersten Brandenburgischen Kirchenvisitation 1528.* "Einzelarbeiten aus der Kirchengeschichte Bayerns," Vol. 10. Munich, 1928.

Sehling, Emil, ed. *Die evangelischen Kirchenordnungen des XVI. Jahrhunderts.* Vol. 11: *Bayern,* part 1: *Franken.* Tübingen, 1961.

Siebenkees, Johann Christian, ed. *Materialien zur Nürnbergischen Geschichte.* 4 vols. Nuremberg, 1792-95.

Simon, Matthias. *Ansbachisches Pfarrerbuch. Die Evangelische-Lutherische Geistlichkeit des Fürstentums Brandenburg-Ansbach, 1528-1806.* Nuremberg, 1955-57.

——. *Nürnbergisches Pfarrerbuch. Die Evangelische-Lutherische Geistlichkeit der Reichsstadt Nürnberg und ihres Gebietes 1524-1806.* Nuremberg, 1965.

Spengler, Lazarus. *Antwort auff das unwarhafft gedicht; so Johan Cocleus, der sich Doctor nennet, Widder den Gedruckten auszug Bebstlicher rechten: newlich hat ausgehen lassen.* D. Hieronymus von Bernishausen [Lazarus Spengler]. N. p. 1530.

——. *Bekenntnis Lazari Spengler weiland Syndici der Stadt Nurmberg.* Mit Vorrhede D. Mart. Luth (eri). [Wittenberg: Joseph Klug, 1535.]

——. *Beschreibung des heyligen Bischoffs Eusebij . . . von dem Leben und Sterben desselben heyligsten Hieronymi . . . durch einen sondern libhaber Sancti Hieronymi aus dem Latein in das teutsch gezogen.* Nuremberg: Hieronymus Höltzel, 1514. Woodcut by Albrecht Dürer.

——. *Ermanung vnd Vndterweisung zu einem tugendhaften Wandel.* [Nuremberg: Friedrich Peypus, 1520.]

—— *Die haubt artickel durch welche gemeyne Christenheyt bysshere Verfuret worden ist. Daneben auch grund vnnd antzeygen eyns gantzen rechten Christenlichen wessens,* [ed.] Nicolaus von Amsdorf. Wittemberg, [Nickel Schirlentz, 1522.]

——. *Ein kurczer Auszuge, aus den bebstlichen Rechten der Decret und*

Decretalen, Jnn den artickeln, die ungeferlich Gottes Wort und dem Evangelio gemes sind, oder zum wenigsten nicht widderstreben, Mit einer schönen Vorrhede Mart. Luth. Wittembergk: Joseph Clugk, 1530.

———. *Ain kurtzer begriff, wie sich ain warhaffter Christ in allem seinen wesen und wandel gegen Gott und seinem nechsten halten sol.* Erfurt: Melchior Sachs, 1526.

———. *Schutzred unnd christenliche antwurt ains erbern liebhabers götlicher worheit der hailigen geschrifft, auff etlicher widersprechen mit antzeigunge warumb Doctor Martini Luthers leer nitt samm vnchristenlich verworffen sonder mer als Christenlich gehalten werden soll. . . . Apologia.* [Augsburg: Silvan Otmar,] 1519.

———. *Ein trostliche Christenliche Anweisung und Artzney in allen Widerwertikaiten.* [Nuremberg: Fridrich Peypus, 1521.]

———. *Verantwortung und auflösung etlicher vermeinter argument und ursachen, so zu widerstand und verdruckung des wort gottes und heiligen evangelions von denen, die nit christen seien und sich doch christen rumen, täglich gepraucht werden.* In Otto Clemen, ed. *Flugschriften aus den ersten Jahren der Reformation.* 2:44.

———. *Wie sich eyn Christen mensch inn trübsal vnd widerwertikayt trösten, vnd wo er die rechten hilff vnd Ertznay derhalben suchen soll.* [Nuremberg: Jobst Gutknecht,] 1529.

Tetleben, Valentin von. *Protokol des Augsburger Reichstages 1530 (von) Valentin von Tetleben.* Ed. Herbert Grundmann. Gütersloh, 1958.

Vogt, Wilhelm, ed. "Die Korrespondenz des Nürnberger Rates mit seinen zum Augsburger Reichstag von 1530 abgeordneten Gesandten." *Mitteilungen des Vereins für Geschichte der Stadt Nürnberg,* 4 (1882): 1-60.

Westermayer, Hans, ed. *Die Brandenburgisch-Nürnbergische Kirchenvisitation und Kirchenordnung 1528-1533.* Erlangen, 1894.

III. SECONDARY ACCOUNTS

Albrecht Dürers Umwelt: Festschrift zum 500. Geburtstag Albrecht Dürers am 21. Mai 1971. "Nürnberger Forschungen," Vol. 15. Nuremberg, 1971.

Ammann, Hektor. *Die wirtschaftliche Stellung der Reichsstadt Nürnberg im Spätmittelalter.* "Nürnberger Forschungen," Vol. 13. Nuremberg, 1970.

Baring, Georg. "Hans Denck und Thomas Müntzer in Nürnberg, 1524." *Archiv für Reformationsgeschichte* 50 (1959): 145-81.

Baron, Hans. "Religion and Politics in the German Imperial Cities during the Reformation." *English Historical Review* 52 (1937): 405-27, 614-33.

Bauer, Günther. *Anfänge täuferischer Gemeindebildungen in Franken.* Einzelarbeiten aus der Kirchengeschichte Bayerns," No. 43. Nuremberg, 1966.

Bebb, Phillip N. "The Lawyers, Dr. Christoph Scheurl, and the Reformation in Nürnberg." In *The Social History of the Reformation,* ed. Lawrence P. Buck and Jonathan W. Zophy, pp. 52-72. Columbus, Ohio, 1972.

Beifus, Joseph. "Hans Sachs und die Reformation bis zum Tode Luthers." *Mitteilungen des Vereins für Geschichte der Stadt Nürnberg,* 19 (1911): 1-76.

Benzing, Josef. *Die Buchdrucker des 16. und 17. Jahrhunderts im deutschen Sprachgebiet.* Wiesbaden, 1963.

———. "Humanismus in Nürnberg 1500-1540." In *Albrecht Dürers Umwelt,* pp. 255-96. Nuremberg, 1971.

Berger, Arnold Erich, ed. *Reformation.* Vol. 4: *Lied-, Spruch- und Fabeldichtungen im Dienste der Reformation.* Leipzig, 1935-36.

Binder, Franz. *Charitas Pirkheimer Aebtissin von St. Clara zu Nürnberg: Ein Lebensbild des 16. Jahrhunderts.* 2d ed. Freiburg i. Br., 1878.

Bock, Ernst. *Der Schwäbische Bund und seine Verfassungen. 1488-1534.* Breslau, 1927.

Bogler, W. *Hartmuth von Kronberg: Eine Charakterstudie aus der Reformationszeit.* "Schriften des Vereins fur Reformationsgeschichte," No. 57 (Halle, 1897).

Borth, Wilhelm. *Die Luthersache (causa Lutheri) 1517-1524. Die Anfänge der Reformation als Frage von Politik und Recht.* "Historische Studien," No. 414. Lübeck, 1970.

Brady, Thomas A., Jr. "Jacob Sturm of Strasbourg and the Lutherans at the Diet of Augsburg, 1530." *Church History* 42 (1973):183-202.

Brandi, Karl. *The Emperor Charles V.* Trans. C. V. Wedgwood. New York, 1939.

Brecht, Martin. *Die frühe Theologie des Johannes Brenz.* Tübingen, 1946.

Brieger, Theodor. *Der Speierer Reichstag von 1526 und die religiöse Frage der Zeit.* Leipzig, 1909.

Buck, Hermann. *Die Anfänge der Konstanzer Reformationsprozesse, Österreich, Eidgenossenschaft und Schmalkaldischer Bund 1510/22-1531.* "Schriften zur Kirchen- und Rechtsgeschichte," 29/31. Tübingen, 1964.

Buck, Lawrence P. "The Containment of Civil Insurrection. Nürnberg and the Peasants' Revolt, 1524-1525." Ph.D. dissertation, Ohio State University, 1971.

———. "Die Haltung der Nürnberger Bauernschaft im Bauernkrieg," *Altnürnberger Landschaft Mitteilungen* 19 (1970): 59-77.

———. "Opposition to Tithes in the Peasants' Revolt: A Case Study of Nuremberg in 1524." *Sixteenth Century Journal* 4 (1973): 11-22.

Burger, Helene. "Ein reformationsgeschichtlicher Handakt Lazarus Spenglers." *Zeitschrift für bayerische Kirchengeschichte* 31 (1962): 31-39.

———. *Nürnberger Totengeläutbücher II: St. Lorenz 1454-1517.* Neustadt/ Aisch, 1967.

Cardauns, Ludwig. *Die Lehre vom Widerstandsrecht des Volkes gegen die rechtmässige Obrigkeit im Luthertum und im Calvinismus des 16. Jahrhunderts.* Bonn, 1903.

Carsten, F. L. *Princes and Parliaments in Germany: From the Fifteenth to the Eighteenth Century.* Oxford, 1959.

Chrisman, Miriam Usher. *Strasbourg and the Reform: A Study in the Process of Change.* New Haven, Conn., 1967.

Christensen, Carl C. "Dürer's 'Four Apostles' and the Dedication as a Form of Renaissance Art Patronage." *Renaissance Quarterly* 20 (1967): 325-34.

———. "Iconoclasm and the Preservation of Ecclesiastical Art in Nürnberg," *Archiv für Reformationsgeschichte* 61 (1970): 205-21.

———. "Municipal Patronage and the Crisis of the Arts in Reformation Nuernberg." *Church History* 36 (1967): 140-50.

Clasen, Claus-Peter. *Anabaptism: A Social History, 1525-1619.* Ithaca, N.Y., 1972.

———. "Nürnberg in the History of Anabaptism." *Mennonite Quarterly Review* 39 (1965): 25-39.

Cole, Richard G. "The Dynamics of Printing in the Sixteenth Century." In *The Social History of the Reformation,* ed. Lawrence P. Buck and Jonathan W. Zophy, pp. 93-105. Columbus, Ohio, 1972.

———. "Propaganda as a Source of Reformation History." *Lutheran Quarterly* 22 (1970): 166-71.

Daniel, Charles E. Jr. "Hard Work, Good Work, and School Work: An Analysis of Wenzeslaus Linck's Conception of Civic Responsibility." In *The Social History of the Reformation,* ed. Lawrence P. Buck and Jonathan W. Zophy, pp. 44-51. Columbus, Ohio, 1972.

———. "Wenzeslaus Linck as Preacher." Ph.D. dissertation, Ohio State University, 1968.

Dannenbauer, Heinz. *Die Entstehung des Territoriums der Reichsstadt Nürnberg.* Stuttgart, 1928.

Dawson, John P. *The Oracles of the Law.* Ann Arbor, Mich., 1968.

Drews, Paul. *Wilibald Pirckheimer: Stellung zur Reformation. Ein Beitrag zur Beurteilung des Verhältnisses zu Humanismus und Reformation.* Leipzig, 1887.

Eckert, Willehad Paul, and Christoph von Imhoff. *Willibald Pirckheimer: Dürers Freund im Spiegel seines Lebens, seiner Werke und seiner Umwelt.* Cologne, 1971.

Eitner, Robert, "Dieweil umsunst." *Monatshefte für Musikgeschichte,* 26 (1894): 71-74.

Elliger, Walter. *Thomas Müntzer: Leben und Werk.* Göttingen, 1975.

Ellinger, Friedrich. "Die Juristen der Reichsstadt Nürnberg vom 15. bis 17. Jahrhundert." In *Reichsstadt Nürnberg, Altdorf und Hersbruck,* ed. Fridolin Soleder and Helene Burger, pp. 130-222. Nuremberg, 1954.

Endres, Rudolf. "Zur Einwohnerzahl und Bevölkerungsstruktur Nürnbergs im 15./16. Jahrhundert." *Mitteilungen des Vereins für Geschichte der Stadt Nürnberg* 57 (1970): 242-71.

———. "Sozialstruktur Nürnbergs." In *Nürnberg—Geschichte einer europäischer Stadt,* ed. Gerhard Pfeiffer, pp. 194-99. Munich, 1971.

Engelhardt, Adolf. "Eine missglückte Gesandschaft unter Nürnbergs Führung." *Mitteilungen des Vereins für Geschichte der Stadt Nürnberg* 32 (1934): 79-98.

———. "Der Nürnberger Religionsfriede von 1532," *Mitteilungen des Vereins für Geschichte der Stadt Nürnberg* 31 (1933): 17-123.

———. *Die Reformation in Nürnberg.* In *Mitteilungen des Vereins für Geschichte der Stadt Nürnberg,* Vols. 33 (1936) and 34 (1937).

——. *Der Reichstag zu Augsburg 1530 und die Reichsstadt Nürnberg.* Nuremberg, 1929.

Estes, James M. "Church Order and the Christian Magistrate According to Johannes Brenz." *Archiv für Reformationsgeschichte* 59 (1968): 5-23.

——. "Johannes Brenz and the Problem of Church Order in the German Reformation." Ph.D. dissertation, Ohio State University, 1964.

Evangelical Lutheran Hymnal. Columbus, Ohio, 1908.

Evangelium und Geist der Zeiten: 450 Jahre Reformation in Nürnberg. Nuremberg, 1975.

Evans, Austin Patterson. *An Episode in the Struggle for Religious Freedom: The Sectaries of Nuremberg, 1524-1528.* New York, 1924.

Fabian, Ekkehart, ed. *Die Entstehung des Schmalkaldischen Bundes und seiner Verfassung, 1524/29-1531/35: Brück, Philipp von Hessen und Jakob Sturm. Darstellung und Quellen mit einer Brück-Bibliographie.* "Schriften zur Kirchen- und Rechtsgeschichte, Darstellung und Quellen," part 1. 2d rev. ed. Tübingen, 1962.

Fischer-Galati, Stephen. *Ottoman Imperialism and German Protestantism, 1521-1555.* New York, 1972.

Franz, Eugen. *Nürnberg, Kaiser und Reich.* "Studien zur reichsstädtischen Aussenpolitik." Munich, 1930.

Franz, Günther. *Der deutsche Bauernkrieg.* 8th ed. Darmstadt, 1969.

Friedensburg, Walter. "Die Reformation und der Speierer Reichstag von 1526." *Luther Jahrbuch* 8 (1926): 120-95.

——. *Der Reichstag zu Speier 1526.* Nieuwkopp, 1970; reprint of edition of Berlin, 1887.

Gates, Jann Whitehead. "The Formulation of City Council Policy and the Introduction of the Protestant Reformation in Nuremberg 1524-1525." Ph.D. dissertation, Ohio State University, 1975.

Genee, Rudolph. *Hans Sachs und seine Zeit: Ein Lebens- und Kulturbild in der Zeit der Reformation.* 2d ed. Leipzig, 1902.

Goldmann, Karl Heinz. *Sechshundert Jahre Stadtbibliothek Nürnberg.* Nuremberg, 1957.

Gossert, G. "Johann Brenz, der Reformator Württembergs und seine Tolerationsideen." *Blätter für württembergische Kirchengeschichte,* 16 (1912): 25-41.

Grabner, Adolph. *Zur Geschichte des zweiten Nürnberger Reichsregiments 1521-23.* "Historische Studien," no. 41. Berlin, 1903.

Greenfield, Kent Roberts. *Sumptuary Law in Nürnberg: A Study in Paternal Government.* "Johns Hopkins Studies in Historical and Political Science," Vol. 36, No. 2. Baltimore, 1918.

Grimm, Harold J. "The Reformation and the Urban Social Classes in Germany." In *Luther, Erasmus, and the Reformation: A Catholic-Protestant Appraisal,* ed. John C. Olin, pp. 75-86. New York, 1969.

Grossmann, Maria. "Bibliographie der Werke Christoph Scheurls." *Archiv für Geschichte des Buchwesens* 70 (1968): 658-70.

Grundmann, Herbert. "Landgraf Philipp von Hessen auf dem Augsburger

Reichstag 1530." *Schriftenreihe der Historischen Kommission*, 5 (1958): 341-423.

Habich, Georg. *Die deutschen Schaumünzen des XVI. Jahrhunderts.* Vol. 1, part 2. Munich, 1931.

Hagen, Rudolph. "Willibald Pirkheimer in seinem Verhältnis zum Humanismus und zur Reformation." *Mitteilungen des Vereins für Geschichte der Stadt Nürnberg.* 4 (1882): 61-211.

Hampe, Theodor. *Crime and Punishment in Germany as Illustrated by the Nuremberg Malefactors' Books.* Trans. Malcolm Letts. London, 1929.

Hans Sachs und Nürnberg. Bedingungen und Probleme reichsstädtischer Literatur. Hans Sachs zum 400. Todestag am 19. Januar 1976, ed. Horst Brunner et al. "Nürnberger Forschungen," Vol. 19. Nuremberg, 1976.

Harrassowitz, Hermann. "Geschichte der Kirchenmusik an St. Lorenz in Nürnberg." *Mitteilungen des Vereins für Geschichte der Stadt Nürnberg,* 60 (1973): 1-151.

Hartfelder, Karl. *Philipp Melanchthon als Praeceptor Germaniae.* Berlin, 1889.

Hartmann, Julius. *Johannes Brenz: Leben und ausgewählte Schriften.* Elberfeld, 1862.

Harvey, Judith Walters. "The Influence of the Reformation on Nürnberg Marriage Laws, 1520-1535." Ph.D. dissertation, Ohio State University, 1972.

Hassinger, Erich. *Religiöse Toleranz im 16. Jahrhundert. Motive-Argumente-Formen der Verwirklichung.* Basel and Stuttgart, 1966.

Haussdorff, Urbanus Gottlieb. *Lebens-Beschreibung eines christlichen Politici, nehmlich Lazari Spenglers, weiland vördersten Rathschreibers zu Nürnberg.* Nuremberg, 1741.

Heerwagen, Heinrich. "Die Kartause in Nürnberg 1380-1525." *Mitteilungen des Vereins fur Geschichte der Stadt Nurnberg,* 15 (1902): 88-132.

Heerwagen, Heinrich Wilhelm. *Zur Geschichte der Nürnberger Gelehrtenschulen in dem Zeitraum von 1485-1526.* Nuremberg, 1860.

Heimpel, Hermann. "Nürnberg und das Reich des Mittelalters." *Zeitschrift für bayerische Landesgeschichte* 16 (1951): 231-64.

Herding, Otto. *Humanismusforschung seit 1945.* Report of the Deutsche Forschungsgemeinschaft. Bonn and Bad Godesberg, 1975.

Hillerbrand, Hans J. "The Reformation and the German Peasants' War." In *The Social History of the Reformation,* ed. Lawrence P. Buck and Jonathan W. Zophy, pp. 106-36. Columbus, Ohio, 1972.

Hirsch, Emanuel. *Die Theologie des Andreas Osiander und ihre geschichtlichen Voraussetzungen.* Göttingen, 1919.

Hirschmann, Gerhard. *Das Landgebiet der ehemaligen Reichsstadt Nürnberg.* Berchtesgaden, 1951.

———. "Das Nürnberger Patriziat." In *Deutsches Patriziat,* ed. Hellmuth Rössler, pp. 257-76. Limburg/Lahn, 1968.

Hitchcock, William R. *The Background of the Knights' Revolt, 1522-1523.* Berkeley, Calif. 1958.

Hockenbery, David. M. "The Social Background of the Radical Reformation in Nürnberg, 1524-1530." Ph.D. dissertation, Ohio State University, 1972.

Höss, Irmgard. *Georg Spalatin 1484-1545. Ein Leben in der Zeit des Humanismus und der Reformation.* Weimar, 1956.

——. "Das religiös-geistige Leben in Nürnberg am Ende des 15. und am Anfang des 16. Jahrhunderts." *Bibliothèque de la revue d'histoire ecclésiastique,* Fascicule 44, extrait des *Miscellanea historiae ecclésiastique,* II (Louvain, 1967).

——, and Thomas Klein, eds. *Das Zeitalter des Humanismus und der Reformation.* Vol. 3: *Geschichte Thüringens,* ed. Hans Patze and Walter Schlesinger. Cologne and Graz, 1967.

Hofmann, Hanns Hubert. "Nobiles Norimbergenses: Betrachtungen zur Struktur der reichsstädtischen Oberschicht." *Zeitschrift fur bayerische Landesgeschichte* 28 (1965): 114-150.

Holborn, Hajo. *A History of Modern Germany: The Reformation.* New York, 1959.

Hummel, Gerhard. *Die humanistischen Sodalitäten und ihr Einfluss auf die Entwicklung des Bildungswesens der Reformationszeit.* Leipzig, 1940.

Kalkoff, Paul. "Luthers Verhältnis zur Reichsverfassung und die Rezeption des Wormser Edikts." *Historische Vierteljahrschrift,* 16 (1916-18): 265-89.

——. *Pirkheimers und Spenglers Lösung vom Banne 1521.* Breslau, 1898.

——. *Die Reformation in der Reichsstadt Nürnberg nach den Flugschriften ihres Ratsschreibers Lazarus Spengler.* Halle/Saale, 1926.

Kamann, Johann. *Nürnberg im Bauernkrieg.* Nuremberg, 1878.

Kaser, Kurt. *Politische und soziale Bewegungen im deutschen Bürgertum zu Beginn des 16. Jahrhunderts.* Stuttgart, 1899.

Kawerau, Waldemar. *Hans Sachs und die Reformation.* "Schriften des Vereins für Reformationsgeschichte," Vol. 7, No. 26 (1889), pp. 1-100.

Kellenbenz, Hermann. "Wirtschaftsleben im Zeitalter der Reformation." In *Nürnberg—Geschichte einer europäischen Stadt,* ed. Gerhard Pfeiffer, pp. 186-93. Munich, 1971.

Keller, Ludwig. *Johann von Staupitz und die Anfänge der Reformation.* 1888. Reprint, Nieuwkoop, 1967.

Kircher, Albrecht. *Deutsche Kaiser in Nürnberg. Eine Studie zur Geschichte des öffentlichen Lebens der Reichsstadt Nürnberg von 1500-1612.* Nuremberg, 1955.

Kist, Johannes. *Charitas Pirckheimer, ein Frauenleben im Zeitalter des Humanismus und der Reformation.* Bamberg, 1948.

——. *Das Klarissenkloster in Nürnberg bis zum Begin des 16. Jahrhunderts.* Nuremberg, 1929.

Kittelson, James M. "Humanism and the Reformation in Germany." *Central European History* 9 (1976): 303-22.

Klassen, Herbert. "The Life and Teachings of Hans Hut." *Mennonite Quarterly Review* 33 (1959): 171-205, 267-304.

Klaus, Bernhard. "Die Nürnberger Deutsche Mess 1524." *Jahrbuch für Liturgik und Hymnologie* 1 (1955); 1-46.

———. *Veit Dietrich: Leben und Werk.* "Einzelarbeiten aus der Kirchengeschichte Bayerns," Vol. 32. Nuremberg, 1958.

Kluckhohn, August. "Der Reichstag zu Speier im Jahre 1526." *Historische Zeitschrift* 56 (1886); 193-218.

Kohlhaussen, Heinrich. *Nürnberger Goldschmiedekunst des Mittelalters und der Dürerzeit 1240 bis 1540.* Berlin, 1968.

Kohls, Ernst-Wilhelm. "Die Durchdringung von Humanismus und Reformation im Denken des Nürnberger Ratsschreibers Lazarus Spengler." *Zeitschrift für bayerische Kirchengeschichte* 36 (1967): 13-25.

———. "Evangelische Bewegung und Kirchenordnung in oberdeutschen Reichsstädten." *Theologische Literaturzeitung* 92 (1967), 322-26.

Krabbel, Gerta. *Caritas Pirckheimer. Ein Lebensbild aus der Zeit der Reformation.* Münster, 1940.

Krag, Wilhelm. *Die Paumgartner von Nürnberg und Augsburg.* Munich and Augsburg, 1919.

Kreiner, Artur. "Die Bedeutung Hans Denks und Sebastian Franks." *Mitteilungen des Vereins für Geschichte der Stadt Nürnberg* 39 (1944): 155-96.

Kressel, Konrad. "Schwabacher Konvent von 1528." In *600 Jahre Stadt Schwabach 1371-1971,* pp. 204-16. Schwabach, 1971.

Krodel, Gottfried. "Nürnberger Humanisten am Anfang des Abendmahlsstreites." *Zeitschrift für bayerische Kirchengeschichte* 25 (1956): 40-50.

———. "State and Church in Brandenburg-Ansbach-Kulmbach, 1524-1526." *Studies in Medieval and Renaissance History* 5 (1968): 141-213.

Kuczynski, Arnold, ed. *Thesaurus libellorum historiam Reformationis illustrantium. Verzeichniss einer Sammlung von nahezu 3000 Flugschriften Luthers und seiner Zeitgenossen.* 1870-74. Reprint, Nieuwkoop, 1960.

Kühn, Johannes. *Die Geschichte des Speyerer Reichstages 1529.* "Schriften des Vereins für Reformationgeschichte," Vol. 17, Part 1, No. 146. Leipzig, 1929.

Kuspit, Donald B. "Dürer and the Lutheran Image." *Art in Ameria* 63 (1974): 56-61.

Lecler, Joseph, S. J. *Toleration and the Reformation.* Trans. T. L. Weslow. 2 vols. New York, 1960.

Leder, Klaus. *Kirche und Jugend in Nürnberg und seinem Landgebiet 1400 bis 1800.* Neustadt/Aisch, 1973.

Leiser, Wolfgang. "Nürnbergs Rechtsleben." In *Nürnberg—Geschichte einer europäischen Stadt,* ed. Gerhard Pfeiffer, pp. 171-76. Munich, 1971.

Liermann, Hans W. L. "Protestant Endowment Law in the Franconian Church Ordinances." In *The Social History of the Reformation,* ed. Lawrence P. Buck and Jonathan W. Zophy, pp. 340-54. Columbus, Ohio, 1972.

Looshorn, Johann. *Die Geschichte des Bisthums Bamberg.* Vol. 4. *Das Bisthum Bamberg von 1400-1556.* Bamberg, 1900.

———. *Weigand von Redwitz: Fürstbischof von Bamberg 1522-1556.* Bamberg, 1900.

Ludewig, Georg. *Die Politik Nürnbergs im Zeitalter der Reformation.* Göttingen, 1893.

Lutz, Heinrich. "Albrecht Dürer in der Reformationsgeschichte." *Historische Zeitschrift* 206 (1968): 32-44.

Machilek, Franz. "Klosterhumanismus in Nurnberg um 1500." *Mitteilungen des Vereins fur Geschichte der Stadt Nurnberg* 64 (1977): 10-45.

Manschreck, Clyde L. *Melanchthon: The Quiet Reformer.* New York, 1958.

Maurer, Wilhelm. "Humanismus und Reformation im Nürnberg Pirckheimers und Dürers." *Jahrbuch für fränkische Landeskunde* 31 (1971): 19-34.

――. *Der junge Melanchton..* 2 vols. Göttingen, 1967-68.

Mayer, Eduard Wilhelm. "Forschungen zur Politik Karls V. während des Augsburger Reichstags." *Archiv für Reformationsgeschichte* 13 (1916): 40-73, 124-46.

Meyer, Christian. *Geschichte der Burggrafschaft Nürnberg und der späteren Markgrafschaften Ansbach und Bayreuth.* Tübingen, 1908.

Moeller, Bernd. "Augustana-Studien." *Archiv für Reformationsgeschichte* 57 (1966); 76-95.

――. *Reichsstadt und Reformation.* "Schriften des Vereins für Reformationsgeschichte," Vol. 69, No. 180. Gütersloh, 1962. English edition: *Imperial Cities and the Reformation: Three Essays.* Ed. and trans. from the French by H. C. Erik Middelfort and Mark U. Edwards. Philadelphia, 1972.

――. "Zwinglis Disputationen. Studien zu den Anfängen der Kirchenbildung und des Synodalwesens im Protestantismus," Part 1. *Zeitschrift der Savigny-Stiftung für Rechtsgeschichte, Kanonische Abteilung* 56 (1970): 275-324.

Mogge, Birgitta. "Studien zum Nürnberger Reichstag von 1524." *Mitteilungen des Vereins für Geschichte der Stadt Nürnberg* 62 (1975): 84-101.

Moser, Hans Joachim. ed. *65 Deutsche Lieder für vier- bis fünfstimmigen gemischten Chor a cappella* nach dem Liederbuch von Peter Schöffer und Mathias Apiarius (Biener). . . . Wiesbaden, 1967.

Müller, Arnd. "Zensurpolitik der Reichsstadt Nürnberg." *Mitteilungen des Vereins für Geschichte der Stadt Nürnberg* 49 (1959): 66-169.

Müller, Gerhard. "Augsburg und Nürnberg im Urteil päpstlicher Nuntien 1530-1532." *Zeitschrift für bayerische Kirchengeschichte* 39 (1970): 75-82.

――. "Die drei Nuntiaturen Aleanders in Deutschland 1520/21, 1531/32, 1538/39." *Quellen und Forschungen aus Italienischen Archiven und Bibliotheken* 39 (Tübingen, 1959): 222-76.

――. *Die römische Kurie und die Reformation 1523-1534.* "Quellen und Forschungen zur Reformationsgeschichte," Vol. 38. Gütersloh, 1969.

Müller, Johannes. "Der Umfang und die Hauptrouten des Nürnberger Handelsgebietes im Mittelalter." *Vierteljahrschrift fur Sozial- und Wirtschaftsgeschichte* 6 (1908): 1-38.

Müllner, Johann. *Kurzgefasste Reformations-Geschichte der freyen Reichs-Stadt Nürnberg.* Nuremberg, 1770.

Mulzer, Erich. "Das Jamnitzerhaus in Nürnberg und der Goldschmied Wenzel Jamnitzer." *Mitteilungen des Vereins für Geschichte der Stadt Nürnberg* 61 (1974): 48-89.

Nürnberg, Stadtarchiv. *Beiträge zur Wirtschaftsgeschichte Nürnbergs.* Vol. 1. Nuremberg, 1967.

Oberman, Heiko A. *Forerunners of the Reformation: The Shape of Late Medieval Thought.* New York, 1966.

Ohlau, Jürgen U. "Neue Quellen zur Familiengeschichte der Spengler. Lazarus Spengler und seine Söhne." *Mitteilungen des Vereins für Geschichte der Stadt Nürnberg* 52 (1963-64): 232-55.

Otte, Enrique. "Jacob und Hans Cromberger und Lazarus Nürnberger, die Begründer des Deutschen Amerikahandels." *Mitteilungen des Vereins für Geschichte der Stadt Nürnberg* 52 (1963-64): 129-62.

Ozment, Steven E. *The Reformation in the Cities: The Appeal of Protestantism to Sixteenth-Century Germany and Switzerland.* New Haven, Conn., 1975.

Panovsky, Erwin. *Albrecht Dürer.* 2 vols. Princeton, N.J., 1943.

Petz, J. "Urkundliche Beiträge zur Geschichte der Bücherei des Nürnberger Rates, 1429-1538." *Mitteilungen des Vereins für Geschichte der Stadt Nürnberg* 6 (1886): 123-74.

Pfanner, Josef. "Caritas Pirckheimer." In *Fränkische Lebensbilder,* comp. Gerhard Pfeiffer. "Veröffentlichungen der Gesellschaft für Fränkische Geschichte," Reihe 7, A, Vol. 2 (Würzburg, 1968), pp. 193-216.

Pfeiffer, Gerhard, "Albrecht Dürer und Lazarus Spengler." In *Festschrift für Max Spindler,* ed. Dieter Albrecht et al. Munich, 1969.

———. "Albrecht Dürer's 'Four Apostles': A Memorial Picture from the Reformation Era." In *The Social History of the Reformation,* ed. Lawrence P. Buck and Jonathan W. Zophy, pp. 271-96. Columbus, Ohio, 1972.

———. "Die Einführung der Reformation in Nürnberg als kirchenrechtliches und bekenntniskundliches Problem." *Blätter für deutsche Landesgeschichte* 98 (1952): 112-33.

———. "Entscheidung zur Reformation." In Gerhard Pfeiffer, ed., *Nürnberg— Geschichte einer Europäischen Stadt,* pp. 146-54. Munich, 1971.

———. *Festschrift für Gerhard Pfeiffer. Jahrbuch für fränkische Landesforschung,* Vols. 34-35. Neustadt/Aisch, 1975.

———. comp. *Fränkische Lebensbilder.* "Veröffentlichungen der Gesellschaft für Fränkische Geschichte," Reihe 7, A. Würzburg, 1967--.

———, ed. *Nürnberg—Geschichte einer europäischen Stadt.* Munich, 1971.

———. "Nürnbergs christliche Gemeinde: Geschichtliche Beobachten zum Verhältnis von kirchlicher und politischer Gemeinde." In *Evangelium und Geist der Zeiten: 450 Jahre Reformation in Nürnberg,* pp. 45-115. Nuremberg, 1975.

———. "Nürnbergs kirchenpolitische Haltung im Frühjahr 1530." *Zeitschrift für bayerische Landesgeschichte* 33 (1970): 183-99.

———. "Nürnbergs Selbstverwaltung 1256-1956." *Mitteilungen des Vereins für Geschichte der Stadt Nürnberg* 48 (1958): 1-25.

———. "Das Verhältnis von politischer und kirchlicher Gemeinde in den deutschen Reichsstädten." In *Staat und Kirche im Wandel der Jahrhunderte,* ed. Walther Peter Fuchs, pp. 79-99. Stuttgart, 1966.

———. "Warum hat Nürnberg die Reformation eingeführt?" "Evangelisches Studienzentrum Heilig Geist," No. 4 (Nuremberg, n.d.).

Pflug-Hartung, Julius Albert Georg von, ed. *Im Morgenrot der Reformation*. Stuttgart, 1924.

Pilz, Kurt. "Nürnberg und die Niederlande." *Mitteilungen des Vereins für Geschichte der Stadt Nürnberg* 43 (1952): 1-153.

Pitz, Ernst. *Schrift- und Aktenwesen der städtischen Verwaltung im Spätmittelalter: Köln—Nürnberg—Lübeck*. Cologne, 1959.

Pressel, Theodor. *Lazarus Spengler: Nach gleichzeitigen Quellen*. Elberfeld, 1862.

Puchner, Otto. "Hieronymus Baumgartner." *Neue Deutsche Biographie*, 1: 664.

Reicke, Emil. "Albrecht Dürers Gedächtnis im Briefwechsel Willibald Pirckheimers." *Mitteilungen des Vereins für Geschichte der Stadt Nürnberg* 28 (1928): 363-406.

———. *Geschichte der Reichsstadt Nürnberg*. Nüremberg, 1896.

Reimann, Arnold. *Die älteren Pirckheimer. Geschichte eines Nürnberger Patriziergeschlechtes im Zeitalter des Frühhumanismus bis 1501*. Leipzig, 1944.

Reindell, Wilhelm. *Doktor Wenzeslaus Linck aus Colditz, 1483-1547*. Part One: *Bis zur reformatorischen Thätigkeit in Altenburg*. Marburg, 1892.

Rice, Edward Lloyd. "The Influence of the Reformation on Nuremberg's Provisions for Social Welfare, 1521-1528." Ph.D. dissertation, Ohio State University, 1974.

Richter, Ernst Arnold. *Der Reichstag zu Nürnberg 1524*. Leipzig, 1888.

Rörig, Fritz. *Die europäische Stadt und die Kultur des Bürgertums im Mittelalter*. Göttingen, 1932.

Roller, Hans-Ulrich. *Der Nürnberger Schembartlauf. Studien zum Fest- und Maskenwesen des späten Mittelalters*. Tübingen, 1965.

Roth, Erich. *Die Reformation in Siebenbürgen*. 2 vols. Cologne, 1962.

Roth, Friedrich. *Die Einführung der Reformation in Nürnberg, 1517-1528*. Würzburg, 1885.

Rupprich, Hans, ed. *Dürer. Schriftlicher Nachlass*. Berlin, 1966.

———. "Dürer und Pirckheimer." In *Albrecht Dürers Umwelt. Festschrift zum 500. Geburtstag*. "Nürnberger Forschungen," Vol. 15 (Nuremberg, 1971), pp. 78-100.

———. "Willibald Pirckheimer. Beiträge zu einer Wesenserfassung," *Schweizer Beiträge zur allgemeinen Geschichte* 15 (1957): 64-100.

———. *Willibald Pirckheimer und die erste Reise nach Italien*. Veinna, 1930.

Ryan, Catherine Bernardi. "Charitas Pirckheimer: A Study of the Impact of the Clarine Tradition in the Process of Reformation in Nuremberg, 1525." Ph.D. dissertation, Ohio State University, 1976.

Schaffer, Reinhold. *Andreas Stoss, Sohn des Veit Stoss und seine gegenreformatorische Tätigkeit*. "Breslauer Studien zur historischen Theologie," No. 5. Breslau, 1926.

———. "Die Entstehung des Territoriums der Reichsstadt Nürnberg," *Mitteilungen des Vereins für Geschichte der Stadt Nürnberg* 30 (1931): 363-73.

Schall, Kurt. *Die Genannten.* "Nürnberger Werkstücke zur Stadt- und Landesgeschichte," No. 6. Nuremberg, 1971.

Scheel, Willy. *Johann Freiherr von Schwarzenberg.* Berlin. 1905.

Scherer, Valentin. *Dürer, des Meisters Gemälde, Kupferstiche und Holzschnitte.* 2d ed. Stuttgart, 1906.

Schmid, Hans-Dieter. "Die Haltung Nürnbergs in der Täuferfrage gegenüber dem Schwäbischen Bund und dem Schmalkaldischen Bund." *Zeitschrift für bayerische Kirchengeschichte* 40 (1971): 41-68.

———. *Täufertum und Obrigkeit in Nürnberg.* "Schriftenreihe des Stadtarchivs Nürnberg," No. 10. Nuremberg, 1972.

Schnelbögl, Fritz. *Dokumente zur Nürnberger Kartographie.* "Beiträge zur Geschichte und Kultur der Stadt Nürnberg," Vol. 10. Nuremberg, 1966.

———. "Die fränkischen Reichsstädte." *Zeitschrift für bayerische Landesgeschichte* 31 (1968): 421-74.

———. "Ein Nachtmal mit Dürer 1527." *Mitteilungen des Vereins für Geschichte der Stadt Nürnberg* 47 (1956): 446-51.

———. "Stadt des Buchdrucks und Kartographie." In *Nürnberg—Geschichte einer europäischer Stadt,* ed. Gerhard Pfeiffer, pp. 215-24. Munich, 1971.

———. "Die wirtschaftliche Bedeutung ihres Landgebietes für die Reichsstadt Nürnberg." In *Beiträge zur Wirtschaftgeschichte Nürnbergs,* Vol. 1, Part 2 (Nuremberg, 1967), pp. 261-317.

Schnelbögl, Julia. "Die Reichskleinodien in Nürnberg, 1424-1523." *Mitteilungen des Vereins fur Geschichte der Stadt Nürnberg* 51 (1962): 78-159.

Schoenberger, Cynthia Grant. "The Development of the Lutheran Theory of Resistance: 1523-1530." *Sixteenth Century Journal* 8 (1977): 61-76.

Schornbaum, Karl. *Die erste Brandenburgische Kirchenvisitation.* "Einzelarbeiten aus der Kirchengeschichte Bayerns," Vol. 10. Munich, 1928.

———. "Nürnberg und die Bulle *exsurge Domine.*" *Zeitschrift für bayerische Kirchengeschichte* 10 (1935): 91-96.

———. *Zur Politik des Markgrafen Georg von Brandenburg . . . 1528-1532.* Munich, 1906.

———. "Zur Politik der Reichsstadt Nürnberg vom Ende des Reichstages zu Speyer 1529 bis zur Übergabe der Augsburgischen Konfession 1530." *Mitteilungen des Vereins fur Geschichte der Stadt Nürnberg* 17 (1906): 178-245.

———. *Die Stellung des Markgrafen Kasimir von Brandenburg zur reformatorischen Bewegung in den Jahren 1524-1527.* Nuremberg, 1900.

Schraepler, Horst W. *Die rechtliche Behandlung der Täufer in der deutschen Schweiz, Südwestdeutschland und Hessen.* "Schriften zur Kirchen- und Rechtsgeschichte," Part 4. Tübingen, 1957.

Schubert, Friedrich Hermann. *Die deutschen Reichstage in der Staatslehre der frühen Neuzeit.* Göttingen, 1966.

Schubert, Hans von. *Anfänge evangelischer Bekenntnisbildung.* "Schriften des Vereins für Reformationsgeschichte," Vol. 45, No. 143 (1928).

———. *Bekenntnisbildung und Religionspolitik (1524-1534).* *Untersuchungen und Texte.* Gotha, 1910.

———. *Bündnis und Bekenntnis 1529-1530.* "Schriften des Vereins für Reformationsgeschichte," Vol. 26, No. 98 (1908), pp. 1-35.

———. *Lazarus Spengler und die Reformation,* publ. and ed. Hajo Holborn. "Quellen und Forschungen zur Reformationsgeschichte," Vol. 17. Leipzig, 1934.

———. *Der Reichstag von Augsburg im Zusammenhang der Reformationsgeschichte.* "Schriften des Vereins für Reformationsgeschichte," Vol. 48, No. 150 (1930).

Schultheiss, Werner. "Albrecht Dürers Beziehung zum Recht." In *Albrecht Dürers Umwelt.* "Nürnberger Forschungen," 15 (Nuremberg, 1971): 220-54.

———. "Die Einrichtung der Herrentrinkstube 1497/8 und deren Ordnung von 1561/97." *Mitteilungen des Vereins für Geschichte der Stadt Nürnberg* 44 (1953): 275-85.

Schuster, Leo. *Die Rolle der Nürnberger Kaufleute am Fondaco dei Tedeschi in Venedig.* "Mitteilungen der Stadtbibliothek Nürnberg," Vol. 11. Nuremberg, 1962.

Seebass, Gottfried. "Apologia Reformationis: Eine bisher unbekannte Verteidigungsschrift Nürnbergs aus dem Jahre 1528." *Zeitschrift für bayerische Kirchengeschichte* 39 (1970): 20-74.

———. "An sint persequendi haeretici? Die Stellung des Johannes Brenz zur Verfolgung und Bestrafung der Täufer." *Blätter für württembergische Kirchengeschichte* 70 (1970): 40-99.

———. "Bauernkrieg und Täufertum in Franken." *Zeitschrift für Kirchengeschichte* 85 (1974): 140-56.

———. "Hans Denck." In *Fränkische Lebensbilder,* comp. Gerhard Pfeiffer, pp. 107-29. "Veröffentlichungen der Gesellschaft für Fränkische Geschichte," Reihe 7, A, Vol. 6 (Würzburg, 1975).

———. *Müntzers Erbe. Werk, Leben und Theologie des Hans Hut.* Erlangen, 1972.

———. "Der Nürnberger Rat und das Religionsgespräch vom März 1525." In *Festschrift für Gerhard Pfeiffer.* "Jahrbuch für fränkische Landesforschung," Vols. 34-35. Nuremberg, 1975.

——— "The Reformation in Nürnberg." In *The Social History of the Reformation,* ed. Lawrence P. Buck and Jonathan W. Zophy, pp. 17-40. Columbus, Ohio, 1972.

———. *Das reformatorische Werk des Andreas Osiander.* Nuremberg, 1967.

Sessions, Kyle C. "Christian Humanism and the Freedom of a Christian: Johann Eberlin von Günsberg to the Peasants." In *The Social History of the Reformation,* ed. Lawrence P. Buck and Jonathan W. Zophy, pp. 137-55. Columbus, Ohio, 1972.

———, ed. *Reformation and Authority: The Meaning of the Peasants' Revolt.* New York, 1968.

Simon, Matthias. "Wann fand die erste evangelische Abendmahlsfeier in den Pfarrkirchen zu Nürnberg statt?" *Mitteilungen des Vereins für Geschichte der Stadt Nürnberg* 45 (1954): 361-71.

Simonsfeld, Henry. *Der Fondaco dei Tedeschi in Venedig und die deutsch-venetianischen Handelsbeziehungen.* 2 vols. Stuttgart, 1887.

Spielvogel, Jackson. "Patricians in Dissension: A Case Study from Sixteenth Century Nürnberg." In *The Social History of the Reformation,* ed. Lawrence P. Buck and Jonathan W. Zophy, pp. 73-90. Columbus, Ohio, 1972.

———. "Willibald Pirckheimer and the Nürnberg City Council." Ph.D. dissertation, Ohio State University, 1967.

———. "Willibald Pirckheimer's Domestic Activity for Nürnberg." *Moreana* 25 (1970): 17-29.

Spitz, Lewis W. *Conrad Celtis, The German Arch-Humanist.* Cambridge, Mass., 1957.

———. *The Religious Renaissance of the German Humanists.* Cambridge, Mass., 1963.

Stählin. Friedrich. *Humanismus und Reformation im bürgerlichen Raum: Eine Untersuchung der biographischen Schriften des Joachim Camerarius.* "Schriften des Vereins für Reformationsgeschichte," Vol. 53, No. 159 (1936).

Steglich, Wolfgang. "Die Stellung der evangelischen Reichsstände und Reichsstädte zu Karl V. zwischen Protestation und Konfession 1529/30." *Archiv für Reformationsgeschichte* 62 (1971): 161-92.

Steiger, Hugo. *Das Melanchthongymnasium in Nürnberg, 1526-1926. Ein Beitrag zur Geschichte des Humanismus.* Munich, 1926.

Steinmetz, David Curtis. *Misericordia Dei: The Theology of Johannes von Staupitz in its Late Medieval Setting.* "Studies in Medieval and Reformation Thought," Vol. 4 Leiden, 1968.

Strauss, Gerald. *Nuremberg in the Sixteenth Century.* New York, 1966.

———. "Protestant Dogma and City Government in Nuremberg." *Past and Present* 37 (1967): 38-58.

Tschackert, Paul. "Lazarus Spengler als Verfasser des von Luther 1530 herausgegebenen 'Kurzen Auszügen aus den päpstlichen Rechten.'" *Zeitschrift für Kirchenrecht* 22 (1889): 435-38.

Veit, Ludwig. *Handel und Wandel mit aller Welt. Aus Nürnbergs grosser Zeit.* Nuremberg, 1960.

Vogler, Günter. "Vorspiel des deutschen Bauernkriegs im Nürnberger Landgebiet 1524." In *Der Bauer im Klassenkampf.* Berlin, 1975.

Wackernagel, Philipp. *Das deutsche Kirchenlied.* 6 vols. Leipzig, 1864-77.

Walther, Johannes von. "Der Reichstag von Augsburg 1530." *Luther-Jahrbuch,* 12 (1930).

Wenisch, Rudolf. "Aus dem Wortschatz der Nürnberger Ratsbücher des 15. und 16. Jahrhunderts." *Mitteilungen des Vereins für Geschichte der Stadt Nürnberg* 46 (1955): 140-261.

Werminghoff, Albert. *Konrad Celtis und sein Buch über Nürnberg.* Freiburg i. Br., 1921.

Werner, Theodor Gustav. "Nürnbergs Erzeugung und Ausfuhr wissenschaftlicher Geräte im Zeitalter der Entdeckungen." *Mitteilungen des Vereins für Geschichte der Stadt Nürnberg* 53 (1965): 69-149.

Westermann, Hugo August. *Die Türkenhilfe und die politisch-kirchlichen Parteien auf dem Reichstag zu Regensburg, 1532.* Heidelberg, 1910.

Westermayer, Hans. *Die Brandenburgisch-Nürnbergische Kirchenvisitation und Kirchenordnung 1528-1533.* Erlangen, 1894.

Will, Georg Andreas. *Nürnbergisches Gelehrten-Lexicon.* Continued by Christian Conrad Nopitsch. 8 vols. Altdorf and Nuremberg. 1755-1808.

Williams, Georg H. *The Radical Reformation.* Philadelphia, 1962.

Winckelmann, Otto. "Die Armenordnungen von Nürnberg (1522), Kitzingen (1523), Regensburg (1523) und Ypern (1925)." *Archiv für Reformationsgeschichte* 10 (1912-13): 242-80.

――――. *Der Schmalkaldischer Bund 1530-1532 und der Nürnberger Religionsfriede.* Strasbourg, 1892.

Winkler, Friedrich. *Die Zeichnungen Dürers.* Vol. 3. Berlin, 1938.

Wüllner, Wolfgang. *Das Landgebiet der Reichsstadt Nürnberg.* "Altnürnberger Landschaft," Vol. 19. Nuremberg, 1970.

Zophy, Jonathan W. "Christoph Kress: Nürnberg's Foremost Reformation Diplomat." Ph.D. dissertation, Ohio State University, 1972.

――――. "Lazarus Spengler, Christoph Kress, and Nuremberg's Reformation Diplomacy." *Sixteenth Century Journal* 5 (1974): 35-48.

Zucker, Markus. *Dürers Stellung zur Reformation.* Erlangen, 1886.

INDEX

Aachen, 8

Adelmann von Adelmannsfelden, Bernhard (1459-1523), 34, 35, 38-42, 48

Adrian VI, pope (1522-23), 62, 134

Albert, archbishop of Mainz (1514-15), 122, 150, 163-64

Albert, grandmaster of Teutonic Knights and duke of Prussia (1525-68), 58, 65, 166

Albert IV, the Wise, duke of Bavaria-Munich (1465-1508), 8, 25

Albert Achilles, margrave of Brandenburg (1440-86), 4

Aleander, Jerome, cardinal (1480-1542), 43, 48, 49

Alms, 85

Alt, Georg, 24

Altdorf, 8, 86

Altenburg, 33, 52

Althammer, Andreas, 110

America, 21, 181

Amsdorf, Nikolaus von, 59

Amsterdam, 13

Anabaptists, 80, 88, 100-107, 140, 146, 154, 159, 162, 188

Anhalt, 159

Ansbach, 7, 71, 115, 117

Antwerp, 13, 174

Apology, Augsburg Confession, 153-54, 163, 164

Appellation after Diet of Speyer, 1529, 134-35, 164

Aquinas, St. Thomas (1225-1274), 36

Art, 22

Artisans, 9, 13-14

Arzt, Ulrich, 50

Astronomy, 21

Augsburg, 13, 20, 98, 133, 168, 180; Diet of (1518), 20, 105; (1530), 115, 144-53, 163, 164

Augsburg Confession (Confessio Augustana, 1530), 115, 147, 152, 153, 163

Augustine, St. (A.D. 354-430), 29, 32, 62

Augustinians, 32, 33, 52, 53, 63, 78, 82

Bamberg, 8, 36, 40, 51, 95, 129; bishop of, 38, 40, 50, 52, 58, 74-77, 80, 81, 111, 113, 121

Barcelona, 129

Basel, 13

Baumgartner, Bernhard (d. 1549), 51, 129, 147, 163

Baumgartner, Hieronymus (1498-1565), 51, 60, 86, 110, 124, 147, 152

Bavaria, 8, 39, 71, 121

Bavarian (Landshut) War of Succession, 8, 18, 32

Bayer, Stefan, 140, 148, 173, 174

Behaim, Martin (1459-1507), 5

Behaim, Sebald and Barthel, 97-98
Beheim, Georg (1448-1521), 33, 51
Benedictines, 53, 82
Beringer, Diepold. *See* Schuster, Diepold
Bernhardi, Bartholomäus von Feldkirchen, 38
Besler, Nikolaus, 32
Besserer, Bernhard, 139
Biberach, 159
Bible, 22, 36, 54, 64, 67, 74, 75, 76, 78, 139, 151; Luther's translation of, 22, 171
Billican, Theobald, 99, 100, 182
Boleyn, Ann, 166
Bologna, 23, 27, 33, 144
Bonaventura, St., 36
Bora, Katharina von, 51, 155
Boschenstein, Johann, 86
Brandenburg, 38, 46
Brandenburg-Ansbach, 134, 138, 143, 165
Brandenburg-Nuremberg Church Order, 110, 114-18, 172
Brant, Sebastian, 22
Braunschweig-Grubenhagen, 159
Braunschweig-Lüneburg, 159
Breitengraser, Wilhelm, 87
Bremen, 159
Brenz, Johannes (1499-1570), 103, 105, 115, 117, 142, 152
Breslau, 128
Brück, Gregor (1483-1557), 151, 153
Buda, 13
Bugenhagen, Johann (1485-1558), 117, 146
Buhler, Sebald, 5
Burgos, Mandate of, 70, 73, 81
Burgrave, 7
Burkhard, Georg aus Spalt (Spalatin, 1484-1545), 35, 58
Butz, Peter, 129, 138, 181
Butzer, Martin (1491-1551), 58, 100, 147, 161, 181

Cajetan, Tommaso de Vio, cardinal (1469-1534), 20, 35, 38
Cambrai, Peace of, 138, 144
Camerarius, Joachim (1500-1574), 86, 148, 171, 182
Campeggio, Lorenzo, cardinal (1474-1539), 66, 67, 69, 70, 71, 144

Canon law, 143
Capito, Wolfgang, 147
Carinthia, 177
Carlstadt, Andreas (ca. 1480-1541), 38, 93, 96-97, 100, 180
Carmelites, 35, 53, 78, 82
Cartagena, 177
Carthusians, 53, 77-78, 82
Cartography, 21
Casimir, Margrave, of Brandenburg-Ansbach (1515-1527), 18, 19, 65, 94, 124
Cassiodorus, 59
Catherine, queen of England, 166
Catholics, 80, 81, 127, 150, 151, 165
Celtis, Conrad (1459-1508), 5, 21, 24-25
Censorship of books, 50, 62, 67, 75, 97, 99
Charles IV, emperor (1346-78), 9
Charles V, emperor (1519-56; d. 1558), 45, 47, 57, 61, 70, 73, 95, 115, 122, 126, 129, 132, 135, 157, 166, 180
Chieregati, Francesco (1478-1539), 61-62, 63, 64
Christian II, king of Denmark and Norway (1513-23; d. 1559), 74
Christian humanism, 13, 28-29
Christian mysticism, 13, 97
Church ceremonies, 74, 88
Church council, 41, 59, 61, 63, 65, 66, 69, 75, 76, 86, 90, 123, 125, 126, 130, 132, 150, 151, 154, 159, 163, 165
Church liturgy, 116
Church Order, Brandenburg-Nuremberg, 110, 114-18, 169
Cities, 12, 61, 66, 68, 121-22, 125, 132, 170
Citizens' oath, 9
Classes, social, 13-14, 31, 63
Clement VII, pope (1523-34), 65, 122, 129, 144, 149, 151, 163
Clergy, 12, 20, 31-32, 45, 47-48, 84, 85, 113; appointment of, 51-52, 85
Coburg, 146, 155, 161
Cochläus, Johannes (1479-1552), 24, 143
Cognac, League of, 122
Colloquy, Marburg, 140
Colloquy, Nuremberg, 78-82, 88, 90
Cologne, 26
Colon (Columbus), Fernando, 22
Columbus, Christopher, 22

Commerce, 13
Common chest, 82, 172
Common man, 13-14, 63
Confessio tetrapolitana, 147
Confutation at Diet of Augsburg (1530), 148, 152
Constance, 132, 147, 159
Copernicus, Nicholas (1473-1548), 21, 52
Corpus Christianum, 11-12
Cracow, 13
Craftsmen. *See* Artisans
Creuszner, Friedrich, 22
Cuba, 176
Culture, 21-27

D'Ailly, Pierre, 59
Damascus, 176
Dance Statute, 14
Danhauser, Peter, 24
Decet pontificum romanum, 26, 43, 45
Denck, Johann or Hans (1495-1527), 96-97, 100, 180
Dessau, League of, 122
Dietrich, Veit (1506-49), 87, 104, 115, 118, 166, 167, 169, 180
Dinkelsbühl, 95
Döber, Andreas, 82
Dolman, Jakob, 80
Dominicans, 26, 31, 53, 77, 78, 82
Donauwörth, 4
Dürer, Albrecht (1471-1528), 22, 23, 25, 28, 29, 33, 34, 50, 83, 97, 172, 173
Duns, Scotus, 36

Ebner, Hieronymus (1477-1532), 19, 25, 27, 29, 32-34, 50, 58, 60, 82, 83, 86, 134, 167, 170, 173
Ebner, Lienhard, 80, 81
Eck, Johann (1486-1543), 27, 34, 35-36, 38-43, 147, 150, 151
Eck, Leonhard von, 71, 112
Education, 24, 60, 85-87, 180
Ehinger, Johann, 134-35
Eichstätt, bishopric of, 25, 84, 112, 121
Ellinger, 84
Eltersdorf, 100
Empire. *See* Holy Roman Empire
Endowments, religious, 31, 85

Engelthal, convent, 32
England, 166
Epidemics, 170
Erasmus, Desiderius (1466-1536), 26, 60, 143
Erber, Georg, 80
Erlangen, 7
Erich, duke of Braunschweig-Lüneburg, 122
Ernest, duke of Braunschweig-Lüneburg, 122
Esslingen, 70, 76
Eternal Peace (*Ewiger Landfrieden*), 46
Ethics, 12, 28, 31
Etzlaub, Erhard, 22
Eusebius, 59
Evangelicals, 71, 100, 127, 129, 132
Exsurge domine, 26, 38, 39, 43

Feilitsch, Philip von, 58
Feldkirchen. *See* Bernhardi, Bartholomaus
Ferdinand, archduke, king of Bohemia and Hungary (1526-64), Roman king (1531), emperor (1556-64), 60, 65, 66, 68, 69, 71, 74, 95, 115, 129, 133, 157, 158, 165-66
Fondaco dei Tedeschi, 5, 13, 38, 177
France, 17, 166
Francis I, king of France (1515-47), 45, 122, 129, 144, 180
Francis, duke of Lüneburg, 139, 148, 151
Franciscans, 53, 77, 78, 83
Franconia, 7, 94
Franconian Knights, 19
Frankfurt a.M., 8, 66, 162
Frankfurt Fair, 46
Frauentraut, Alexius, 134-35
Frederick II, emperor (1212-50), 7
Frederic (III) the Wise, elector of Saxony (1486-1525), 20, 27, 35, 38, 58, 60, 64-65
Frederick I, margrave of Brandenburg (1415-40) (Frederick VI, burgrave of Nuremberg), 7
Frederick, Count Palatine, 58, 131, 152
Fries, Michael, 80
Frosch, Johann, 35, 161-62
Fürer, Christoph (1479-1537), 25, 29, 33
Fürer, Sigmund (d. 1547), 25, 29, 33, 62

Fürnschild, Sebastian, 80
Fugger family, 174

Gebel, Mathes, 22
General welfare, 9, 12, 14, 31, 51, 59, 93, 132, 171
Genoa, 13, 134
George, margrave of Brandenburg-Ansbach (1527-43), 90, 101, 102, 109, 112, 117, 130, 132, 137, 139, 143, 145, 147-51, 153, 158, 159, 172
George, duke of Bavaria-Landshut (1479-1503), 8
George, duke of Saxony (1500-1539), 58, 122, 128, 157
George III, bishop of Bamberg, 40
Germanic Museum, 53
Germany. See Holy Roman Empire
Geuder, Martin, 39, 82
Goethe, Johann Wolfgang von (1749-1832), 24
Goslar, 87
Gospel, 59, 62, 64, 66, 67, 68, 75, 79, 88, 90, 132, 142, 152
Gotha-Torgau, League of, 123
Gräfenberg, 8
Gratian, 143
Graumann, Johann. See Poliander
Gravamina, 20, 35
Gregory VII, pope (1073-85), 53
Greifenberger, Hans, 97
Grieninger, Heinrich, 24
Groland, Leonhard, 19, 20, 43
Gründlach, convent, 82
Gutknecht, Jobst, 34, 117

Hamburg, 13
Hänlein, Johannes, 32
Haller, Sebald, 145
Hedio, Caspar, 147
Heidelberg, University of, 27, 34, 81
Heidelberg Disputation, 34
Heilbronn, 132, 151, 159, 163
Heller, Sebastian, 152, 166, 171
Henry IV, emperor (1056-1106), 59
Henry VII, emperor (1308-13), 7
Henry VIII, king of England (1509-47), 166

Heresy, 103, 104, 143
Heppstein, Johann, 75, 116, 147
Hersbruck, 8
Hesse, 134, 143, 159
Hessus, Eobanus (Eoban Elius), 86, 171
Heyden, Sebald, 87
Hiltpoltstein, 49
Hirnkofen, Georg von (Rennward), 5, 177
Hirsvogel, Ludwig, 80
Höpel, Jorg, 124, 125, 170, 173
Hohenzollern, burgraves of Nuremberg, 7
Holy Roman Empire, 3, 46, 57, 122; imperial forest of, 7; loyalty to, 67, 68, 73, 159, 171-72
Holzschuher, Georg (d. 1526), 18
Holzschuher, Hieronymus (d. 1529), 25, 28, 33, 36, 60, 82
Hospital of the Holy Spirit, 12, 24, 33, 53, 63, 85, 87, 96
Hospital of St. Elisabeth, 53
Hubmaier, Balthasar (1480-1528), 100
Humanism, 21, 24, 32
Hut, Hans (d. 1527), 96, 100, 104
Hutten, Ulrich von (1488-1523), 43, 64
Hymns, 64, 87

Imperial Chamber Court (Reichskammergericht), 11, 46, 57, 61, 70, 123, 129, 157, 163, 165, 174
Imperial Council of Regency (Reichsregiment), 46, 51, 61, 63, 70, 74, 76, 82, 87, 123, 127, 129
Imperial regalia, 7, 158
Indulgence, 37, 45
Ingolstadt, 4, 52, 81
Innsbruck, 22, 144
Intellectual circle, 20-27, 86-87
Isabella, queen of Denmark, 74
Isny, 132, 159

Jaeger, Thomas. See Venatorius
Jerome, St. (A.D. ca. 340-420), 29, 62
John, elector of Saxony (1525-32), 123, 125, 127, 130, 132, 133, 134, 138, 139, 143, 144, 145, 147, 150, 151, 158, 159
John Frederick, elector of Saxony (1532-47), 139, 148
Jonas, Justus, 117, 146, 152
Jurisconsults, 9, 11, 146

Kaden, Michael von, 82, 129, 130, 133-35, 145
Kaufmann, Cyrus, 155
Kempten, 132, 151, 159
Kirnhofen, Jörgen von, 49
Klug, Joseph, 179
Knights' Revolt, 46, 61
Koberer, Georg, 114, 174
Koberger, Anton (1445-1513), 21, 22
Kolditz, 33
Koler, Christoph, 74, 110, 147, 158
Kraft, Adam (d. 1507), 5, 22
Kress, Christoph (1484-1535), 74, 110, 124, 126, 129, 138, 139, 145, 147, 148, 150, 161, 171
Kress, George, 98
Kronberg, Hartmuth von, 61
Kulmbach, 96

Landshut, 177
Landshut War of Succession. See Bavarian War of Succession
Lauf, 8
Lauffen, 166
Leipzig, University of, 5, 21, 33
Leipzig Debate, 35-36
Lichtenstein, Nikolaus, 80
Linck, Wenceslas (1483-1547), 13, 33-34, 35, 53, 85, 86, 103, 105, 114, 133, 174, 180
Lindau, 132, 147, 159
Lisbon, 5, 13
Lochinger, Hans, 173
Lord's Supper, 52, 53, 73, 74, 82, 88, 98-100, 116, 118, 139, 146, 147, 179, 182
Lotther, M., 36
Louis II, king of Hungary and Bohemia (1516-26), 122
Louis V, Count Palatine (1508-44), 163-64
Low Countries, 45, 162, 174
Loyosa, Cardinal, 151
Lübeck, 13
Lucian, Marcus Annaeus (A.D. 39-65), 26
Luther, Katharina von Bora, 51, 155
Luther, Martin (1483-1546), 12, 20, 26, 27, 33-38, 41, 47, 48, 50, 59, 85, 86, 96, 104, 117, 128, 133, 143, 144, 146, 151, 152, 154, 170, 171, 179, 181; and armed resistance to emperor, 161; coat of arms of, 155; Commentary on Galatians, 39;

Commentary on Psalm 110, 34; Freedom of a Christian Man, 60; Ninety-five Theses, 34; On Keeping Children in School, 86; Sermon on Good Works, 39; Sermon on Indulgences, 34; To the Councilmen . . . that They Establish . . . Christian Schools, 85
Lutheran books, 67
Lutheranism, 63, 67, 68, 71, 73, 80, 122
Lyons, 13, 134, 176

Madrid, Treaty of, 122
Magdeburg, 87, 159
Magdeburg, League of, 123, 125
Magellan, Ferdinand (ca. 1480-1521), 21
Mansfeld, 159
Marburg, Colloquy of, 139
Margaret of Austria (1482-1530), regent of the Low Countries, 162
Marsiglio of Padua (d. 1343), 59
Marsilius. See Prenninger, Marsilius
Marstaller, Michael, 75
Martin, Brother, 77
Martinian sodality, 34-35
Mary, queen of Hungary and Bohemia (1505-58), 162
Mass, Catholic, 53, 73, 74, 82, 116, 117, 146, 150, 151, 179
Maximilian I, emperor (1493-1519), 8, 17, 18, 20, 22
Meissen, 38
Meistersingers, 23-24, 64-65, 87
Melanchthon, Philip (1497-1560), 5, 34, 53, 59, 83, 84-86, 117, 133, 137, 146, 150, 152, 153, 172, 180, 182; Common Points of Proof, 60
Memmingen, 178, 132, 147, 159, 171
Merchants, 13
Merseburg, 38
Milan, 13
Miltitz, Karl von, 38
Minkwitz, Hans von, 138
Mohács, Battle of, 123
Monasteries, dissolution of, 52-54, 67, 82-85, 127
Monasticism, 151, 182
Mühlhausen, 98
Müller, Johann, 124
Müntzer, Thomas

Muffel, Jakob, 41, 82
Munich, 25; State Archive of, 174
Music, 22
Mysticism, 18

Nadler, Ulrich, 18
Neoplatonism, 52
Netherlands, 45, 162, 175
Neunhof, 39
Neustadt an der Aisch, 94
Ninety-five Theses. See Luther, Martin
Nördlingen, 5, 99, 132, 182
Nöttelein, Georg, 22
Nützel, Kaspar (1471-1529), 18, 19, 20, 25, 28, 29, 32, 34, 43, 50, 58, 62, 83, 85, 110
Nuremberg, 7-12, 124, 125, 131, 132, 133, 140, 143, 144, 151, 159, 163, 165; archives of, 6; and armed resistance to emperor, 133, 137, 138, 141-44, 158-59, 179; castle of, 7, 74; chancellery of, 6; City Hall of, 14, 23; ethics in, 12-13; forests of, 7-8; jurisconsults of, 9, 11; law courts of, 10-11; laws in, 21; library of, 4, 20; loyalty of, to empire, 12, 122, 123, 137, 138, 162; Lugisland Tower, 42; population of, 32; sumptuary laws in, 10; territory of, 8
Nuremberg, Diet of (1522), 58-59; (1522-23), 60-65; (1524), 65-71, 124, 151
Nuremberg, Religious Peace of (1532), 114, 157-66

Oecolampadius, Johannes (1482-1531), 26, 38, 99
Oelhaven, Sixt, 48
Opel, 160
Osiander, Andreas (1498-1552), 21, 52, 58, 71, 74, 80, 81, 93, 97, 102, 105, 110, 114, 117, 118, 147, 160, 174, 182
Ottmar, Silvan, 36
Our Lady, Church of, 52

Pack Affair, 128-29, 133
Padua, 25
Palatinate, 46, 49
Pamphlets, 94
Papacy, 36, 43, 47, 60, 66, 73, 143
Paracelsus (Theophrastus Bombastus von Hohenheim [1493?-1541]), 172
Patricians, 9-10

Paumgartner. *See* Baumgartner
Pavia, 25, 122
Peasants' Revolt, 46, 84, 93-95, 100
Pegnitz River, 53
Pentz, Georg (ca. 1500-1550), 97-98
Pesler, Georg (ca. 1470-1536), 33, 51, 74-77, 80
Petreius, Johann, 21
Petri, Adam, 36
Peutinger, Konrad (1467-1547), 35, 171
Peypus, Friedrich, 22, 53
Pfarrer, Matthis, 139, 181
Pfinzing, Melchior (1481-1535), 51
Pfinzing, Sebald (1487-1537), 62, 74
Pflüger, Konrad, 80
Phillip, landgrave of Hesse (1500-1567), 123, 125, 127, 128, 132, 133, 143, 145, 148, 151, 159, 165-66
Piacenza, 135, 139, 142, 145
Pillenreuth, convent, 83
Pirckheimer, Caritas (1467-1532), 54, 83, 182
Pirckheimer, Clara (1480-1533), 54, 192
Pirckheimer, Johann (1440-1501), 24, 25
Pirckheimer, Katharina, 54, 83
Pirckheimer, Willibald (1470-1530), 18, 21, 23, 25-26, 38-43, 53, 58, 171, 182
Pistorius, Friedrich (1486-1553), 53, 80
Planitz, Hans von der (d. 1535), 58, 62, 161
Platonic Academy, 26
Pleydenwurff, Wilhelm, 21
Pomer, Hector (1495-1541), 51, 52, 74-77, 80
Poliander (Graumann, Johann), 80
Polo, Marco, 22
Poor relief, 84-85
Portugal, 5, 176
Prague, 13
Preaching, 46-47
Pregler, Jobst, 80
Prenninger, Marsilius, 75
Printing, 21, 67
Protestants, 132, 150, 151, 152, 153, 154; alliance of, 133, 137-55; and armed resistance against emperor, 133, 136, 138, 141-44
Protestation of 1529, 132-35, 136, 163, 164
Ptolemy, 26

Rab, Hermann, 36
Ratibor, 160
Reformation, 162, 182; in Germany, 3, 23; in Nuremberg, 49-54, 73-75, 87, 90, 182
Regensburg, 74
Regensburg, Diet of (1531), 71, 163, 164, 165
Regensburg Union, 71, 122
Rehlinger, Ulrich, 66
Reicheneck, 8
Reichskammergericht. See Imperial Chamber Court
Reichsregiment. See Imperial Council of Regency
Reuchlin, Johannes (1455-1522), 26, 53
Reutlingen, 132, 148, 151, 159
Rio de la Plata, 176
Rodach, 133, 137-38
Rorer, Jakob, 42
Rothenburg ob der Tauber, 94
Rurer, Johann, 72, 112

Sachs, Hans (1494-1576), 23-24, 63-64, 93; The Wittenberg Nightingale, 63-64
Sacramentarians, 96, 98-100, 133, 140, 146, 154, 178
Saint Clara Convent, 53, 78, 83, 182
Saint Egidien (St. Giles) Monastery, 24, 35, 53, 77, 78, 85, 86
Saint Gall, 98, 132
Saint Jakob Church, 53, 80, 84
Saint John Cemetery, 172
Saint Katherine Convent, 53, 54, 78, 83
Saint Lorenz Church, 24, 51, 78
Saint Mary Church, 52, 85
Saint Sebald Church, 22, 24, 51, 78, 173
Saint Vitus Church, 53
Salzburg, archbishop of, 58, 71
Satler, Adam, 98
Saxony, Electoral, 39, 117, 134, 159
Schedel, Hartmann (1440-1514), 5, 21, 23, 59
Scheurl, Christoph (1481-1542), 9, 25, 26-27, 43, 66, 74, 75, 78, 80, 81, 116
Schirlenz, Nikel, 59
Schleicher, Daniel, 139
Schleiffer, Barbara, 31

Schleupner, Dominicus (d. 1547), 52, 71, 77, 80, 110, 114, 162, 175, 180
Schmalkalden, 135, 139, 141, 154
Schmalkaldic League, 144, 158-62, 165, 169, 171
Schmid, Katharina, 177
Schmutterherr, Kaspar, 6
Schöner, Johann (1477-1547), 21, 86
Scholasticism, 31, 38, 60
Schools, 24, 60, 85-87, 180
Schreyer, Sebald, 24
Schürstab, Leo, 163
Schuster, Diepold, 67, 95-96
Schwabach, 7, 109-10, 138, 141
Schwabach Articles, 106, 139, 145
Schwabach visitation articles, 110
Schwäbisch-Hall, 105, 115, 163
Schwarzenberg, Hans (Johann), von (1463-1528), 19, 58, 109
Schweinfurt, 163, 164
Science, 21-22
Seville, 13, 176, 177
Sickingen, Franz von (1481-1523), 61
Sigismund, emperor (1410-37), 7
Sigismund I, king of Poland (1506-48), 166
Sigismund, archduke of Tyrol, 25
Silesia, 52, 149, 160
Sitzinger, Lukas, 110
Sixtus IV, pope (1471-84), 51
Social groups, 13-14, 31, 63
Sodalitas celtica, 24, 25
Sodalitas staupitziana, 33
Sommer, Wolfgang, 42
Spalatin, Georg. See Burkhard, Georg
Spanish Inquisition, 145
Spengler, Franz, 176
Spengler, Georg (1424-96), 4
Spengler, Juliana Tucher, 5, 6, 172, 173, 174, 175, 176, 177
Spengler, Lazarus (1479-1534)
  —and censorship of books, 62, 97; character of, 3-4, 171-72, 178-82; coat of arms of, 28, 65; diplomatic service of, 7, 8, 17-20, 46-47; and excommunication, 38-43, 48-49; functions as secretary, 3; home of, 4, 173; on infant baptism, 184; loyalty of, to empire, 65, 66, 122, 123, 138, 141-42, 158-59, 160, 165, 171-72, 179; will and testament of, 170-71, 172-75

—family of: brother Georg, 5, 33, 65, 172, 173, 177-78; brother Paulus, 5; parents, 4; sister Felicitas, 5; sister Magdalena, 5; sister Martha, 5, 36, 175, 177, 178; sister Margaretha, 5, 49, 175, 177, 178; sister Ursula, 5, 82, 173, 175; son Christoph, 170, 172-73; son Georg, 177; son Hieronymus, 172, 177; son Lazarus, 6, 172, 175-77; son Sebald, 6, 172, 175, 177

—*Admonition and Instruction* (1520), 26; "Apology" (1527), 87-89, 103-4, 125; "Changes in Ceremonies" (1528), 89-90; "Counterattack" (1520), 39; *Defense [of] . . . Luther's Teaching* (1519), 36-38, 39; *Excerpts from Papal Laws* (1529), 89, 143; letter of consolation to Georg Spengler (1525), 177-78; letter of consolation to Margaretha (1521), 49-50, 177; letter of consolation to Martha (1529), 178; memorandums, 41, 46, 63, 66, 67-69, 71-72, 76, 78, 84, 87-90, 119, 112-13, 138, 141, 146; poems to Dürer (1509), 28; report on Diet of Worms (1521), 47-49; *Responsibility for and Analysis of Some Alleged Arguments* (1523), 64; *St. Jerome* (1514), 29; *The Main Articles* (1522), 59-60; *Through Adam's Fall* (1524), 87; "Why Luther's Teaching is a necessity" (1521), 59

Spengler, Paulus, 173

Speyer, Diet of (1526), 111, 123-28, 137, 151; (1529), 101, 113, 128-35

Staupitz, Johann von (ca. 1468-1524), 9, 13, 27, 32-33, 35

Stierberg, 8

Stoss, Andreas (ca. 1477-1540), 80, 82

Stoss, Veit (ca. 1447-1533), 5, 22, 80

Stockheimer, Leonhard, 145

Stöckl, Blasius, 77-78

Strassburg, 66, 87, 88, 124, 125, 132, 138, 139-40, 144, 145, 147, 159

Stromer, Ulman, 18

Sturm, Jakob (1498-1553), 126, 130, 131, 132, 139

Sulmeister, Hans, 6

Sulmeister, Margaretha, 174

Swabia, 26

Swabian League, 17, 18, 46, 50, 61, 85, 94, 101, 102, 106, 119, 111, 113, 121, 128, 129, 133, 138

Tetzel, Anton, 18, 19, 32

Tetzel, Christoph, 127, 129, 130, 138, 158

Tetzel, Friedrich, 83

Tetzel, Johann

Teutonic Knights, 53, 58, 78, 84, 118

Thun, Friedrich von, 58

Toleration, 103, 104-6

Torgau, 146

Torgau Articles, 146

Transylvania, 88

Trier, 61, 69

Trivium, 24

Tucher, Anton (1458-1524), 19, 25, 27, 32, 58

Tucher, Bernhard, 110

Tucher, Endres, 25, 33, 62

Tucher, Felicitas, 54

Tucher, Hans, 103, 176

Tucher, Helene, 27

Tucher, Juliana. *See* Spengler, Juliana Tucher

Tucher, Martin, 25, 27, 33, 74, 110

Tucher, Sixtus, 24

Tübingen, 34, 81

Turks, 20, 59, 61, 65, 122, 123, 126, 144, 151, 163, 165

Ulm, 66, 70, 88, 124, 125, 132, 138, 139-40, 144, 145, 159

Ulmer, Daniel, 4

Ulrich, duke of Württemberg, 165-66

Ulsenius, Dietrich, 24

Upper Palatinate, 18

Vadian, Joachim, 25

Velden, 8

Venatorius (Jager), Thomas (d. 1551), 53, 71, 80, 86

Venice, 5, 9, 13, 23

Vienna, 144

Vischer, Peter, Jr. (1460-1529), 5, 22

Visitation of churches, 88, 109-14

Vogel, Wolfgang, 100

Vogler, Georg (d. 1550), 19, 65, 71, 109, 113, 116, 117, 132, 139, 142, 160, 166, 171, 175, 180

Volckamer, Clemens (d. 1541), 74, 79, 95, 102, 139, 145, 147, 161

Volprecht, Wolfgang (d. 1528), 32, 34, 53, 75-77, 80
Voyt, Heinrich, 42

Wagner, Richard (1813-83), 24
Waldenstein, Werner von, 161
Weigand von Redwitz, bishop of Bamberg (1522-56), 75-77
Weiss, Adam, 110
Weissenburg, 132, 151, 159, 163
Welfare Ordinance, 85
Welser family, 174
Welser, Jakob, 25, 33
Wiesenthau, Wolf Chr. von. 110, 139
William, duke of Bavaria, 40, 41
Wittenberg, University of, 6, 27, 33, 38, 53, 180

Wöhrd, 65, 67 ("Peasant from." See Schuster, Diepold)
Wolfgang, duke of Bavaria (d. 1514), 5
Wolgemut, Michael (1434-1519), 5
Word of God, 59, 62, 66, 68, 71, 74, 78, 79, 80, 88, 95, 97, 100, 105, 152, 161
Worms, Diet of, 43-49
Worms, Edict of, 49, 50, 61, 63, 65, 66, 70, 71, 121, 123, 124, 130, 133, 142, 144, 154, 180
Wurttemberg, 165-66
Wurzburg, 19, 94, 95; bishop of, 40, 112, 121

Zisselgasse, 4, 173
Zwingli, Ulrich (1484-1531), 25, 94, 95
Zwinglianism, 80, 88, 137, 138, 145, 161

DATE DUE

SEP 26 1990			
GAYLORD			PRINTED IN U.S.A.